P9-DTV-181

Diversity and Complexity in Feminist Therapy

458-4574

Diversity
and Complexity
in Feminist Therapy

Laura S. Brown, PhD, ABPP
Maria P. P. Root, PhD
Editors

Diversity and Complexity in Feminist Therapy, edited by Laura S. Brown and Maria P. P. Root, was simultaneously issued by The Haworth Press, Inc., under the same title, as special issues of the journal *Women & Therapy*, Volume 9, Numbers 1/2 and 3, 1990, Ellen Cole and Esther D. Rothblum, Editors.

Harrington Park Press
New York • London

ISBN 0-918393-74-4

Published by

Harrington Park Press, 10 Alice Street, Binghamton, NY 13904-1580
EUROSPAN/Harrington, 3 Henrietta Street, London WC2E 8LU England

Harrington Park Press, is a subsidiary of The Haworth Press, Inc., 10 Alice Street, Binghamton, NY 13904-1580.

Cover design by Marshall Andrews.

Library of Congress Cataloging-in-Publication Data

Diversity and complexity in feminist therapy / Laura S. Brown, Maria P. P. Root, editors.
 "Simultaneously issued by The Haworth Press, Inc. . . . as a special issue of the journal Women & therapy, volume 9, numbers 1/2 and 3, 1990."
 Includes bibliographical references.
 ISBN 0-918393-74-4
 1. Feminist therapy. I. Brown, Laura S. II. Root, Maria P. P.
RC489.F45D58   1990b
616.89'14 — dc20   90-31689
                                                                        CIP

CONTENTS

ABOUT THE EDITORS

Laura S. Brown, PhD, ABPP, is a clinical psychologist in private practice and Clinical Associate Professor of psychology at the University of Washington. She has written and presented internationally on issues of feminist therapy theory development and has been active in work to bring anti-racist and multicultural perspectives to the practice of feminist therapy. Her paper on feminist therapy with post-traumatic stress disorder won the 1987 Distinguished Publication Award of the Association for Women in Psychology. Dr. Brown is a Diplomate in Clinical Psychology of the American Board of Professional Psychology, and was recently appointed Book Review Editor of the journal *Women & Therapy.*

Maria P. P. Root, PhD, is a clinical psychologist in private practice and a visiting faculty member, for the 1989-1990 academic year, at the Department of Psychology at the University of Hawaii. She has written extensively in the area of trauma and disordered eating, in addition to her publications on and practice with Asian-American and biracial clients. She is currently newsletter editor of the *Society for the Psychological Study of Ethnic Minority Issues,* Division 45 of the American Psychological Association.

EDITORIAL INTRODUCTION

In 1982, the Feminist Therapy Institute (FTI) was established by a group of advanced feminist therapists who began meeting together to share our work and offer each other the collegial consultation and support that we often found lacking in our home communities where we were teachers, therapists, and leaders. At the time of our first conference, held in Vail, Colorado in May of that year, we commented on something missing among us. Although we had young women and old, lesbian and heterosexual women, therapists from all the helping professions and various class backgrounds, we were all white. We noted it, regretted it, and even felt guilty about it. And for five years, as we held the annual Advanced Feminist Therapy Institute conference (AFTI), we institutionalized it. Despite lamenting the absence of women of color among our ranks, and the lack of presentations with a multicultural perspective *every year*, we took few steps to remedy this deficit. While we claimed to be against racism, we failed to act anti-racist; our multiculturality was limited by the similarity among our members.

At our 1986 AFTI, held in Minneapolis, Minnesota, two women of color, brave and angry, called FTI on its racism and said, "Enough!" Although the ensuing process was painful for many of those present, it became the catalyst for serious change in FTI in our movement to becoming an actively anti-racist and multicultural organization. This volume is one product of that action.

In 1988, FTI held its annual AFTI meeting in Seattle, Washington. The conference committee, co-chaired by Laura Brown and Anne Ganley, came to its task dedicated to make this conference one in which issues of racism and multiculturalism were more than a token effort. The conference committee made several decisions about participants and format that were necessary to aggressively move towards a multicultural vision that can start to speak to all women, not just white women. The first decision was to insist that the presentations conform to the theme, *Diversity in Feminist Therapy*; the committee only accepted proposals that attempted to advance the multicultural development of feminist therapy. Three other unprecedented exceptions to a six year format were approved by the steering committee of FTI. First, it was decided that one-fourth of the conference slots (15) be reserved for women of color. Since FTI does not have this number of women of color as members, these slots were open for non-member women of color who might be potential members. Further, it was decided that if these spots were not filled by women of color, they would not be filled by white women. All spots were filled. Second, an anti-racism workshop, led by P. Catlin Fullwood from Seattle, Washington, was presented and attended by all conference participants (as is the format of AFTI conferences). Lastly, we invited a Filipina psychologist from the University of the Philippines and the Children's Rehabilitation Center, Elizabeth Protacio Marcelino, to join us. She broadened our conceptualization past a Western, White perspective of theory and therapy.

The result of these efforts was three intense, exhausting and exhilarating days of exchange of ideas among women who had taken up our challenge to confront racism, again, but at a personal level in a group which had previously institutionalized it. The experience was not the same for all women; particularly for women of color, it was a reminder of how alive racism is even in an organization dedicated to educating itself and acting in non-oppressive ways. It was both intellectually and emotionally stimulating in ways that many had not felt for years. For all women, it was an attempt to believe that despite the current national racist political climate, there is still hope.

This collection of papers represents a sampling of those presented at the Seattle AFTI. In and of itself, this collection is unprecedented in two significant ways. First, the white women in this volume have made it incumbent upon themselves to educate themselves and their colleagues to be anti-racist and multicultural in theory and practice. Secondly, almost one-half of the authors are women of color. In the anti-racism workshop, Catlin Fullwood observed that this seems to be a critical ratio which moves interactions beyond tokenism and tolerance. This level of representation has enabled women of color to speak up and speak the truth, even when it may be perceived by some as a betrayal of an ethnic community and by others a threat to institutionalized truths.

This collective work is exceptionally creative, diverse, and joined together by what we see as an extraordinarily high level of conceptualization. It is a commitment to explore what is meant by diversity and complexity in women's lives. Some of the authors are well-known in the field of feminist therapy; others are publishing professionally for the first time. Of note is that almost all of the women of color in this volume have published previously.

We are excited about this special collection and hope that you will read each and every article. This work collectively and separately breaks new ground in the development of theory in feminist therapy. It clarifies that anti-racist and multicultural efforts are not "special interests" for a few, but essential for all in our personal and professional, and thus, political lives. The articles in this volume run the gamut from the highly theoretical work of Mary Ballou, Susan Barrett, Laura Brown, Marcia Hill, and Elizabeth Protacio Marcelino, who challenge us to examine the paradigms by which we know and collect evidence of "truth" to the very personal story of Rachel Josefowitz Siegel's struggle with oppression and her respect for the differences between her experiences of oppression and other women's experiences. In between these pages are many pieces that blend theory and application to comprehend the ambivalence, conflict, and specialness of women's relationships with women such as the articles by Sandra Coffman, Dorsey Green,

Beverly Greene, Diane Palladino, and Yanela Stephenson; women's development in a multicultural context is addressed in the articles by Julia Boyd, Carla Bradshaw, Joan Hertzberg, Elizabeth Protacio Marcelino, and Maria Root. Christine Ho, Valli Kanuha, and Beverly Greene provide applied pieces that are ground breaking respect to the ethnic groups they represent. Elizabeth Rave and Lynne Bravo Rosewater challenge white women to examine what they are doing that is anti-racist. In this collection, we also begin to open feminist therapy theorizing to perspectives drawn from non-Western cultures, and to see how our visions of female development may be limited by viewing them within a Western cultural framework (as in Carla Bradshaw's and Elizabeth Protacio Marcelino's work). We are especially pleased to publish the work of Elizabeth Protacio Marcelino, who is among the pioneers of those developing an indigenous psychology for the Philippines.

Clearly, this introduction has attempted to provide you a context within which to read this collection. We believe that in order to fully appreciate each of the articles in this volume, our readers must be able to place the authors in their own ethnic contexts. Working together as a white, Jewish woman (L. B.) and Eurasian woman (M. R.), we have become more aware of how the personal is political and how our own personal experiences as members of our ethnic groups have shaped and formed our perceptions of what we do, as well as the feminist therapy theory that we develop. The diversity among the women represented in this volume is Black, White, Asian American, Filipina, Jewish, Hispanic, Italian American, immigrant, exiled, and native born from early thirties to late sixties.

We are proud, as editors, to present a volume that is multicultural in content and authorship. This volume allows us more power to realize our visions. We see this as a first step in moving feminist therapy to a more inclusive, global perspective, and back into a more political and activist stance on the oppression that we want to defeat. We thank all of the authors for their contributions to this collection.

The first section of this collection, *Diversity and Complexity in Feminist Therapy*, deals with expanding theory toward looking at specific applications or populations for which current feminist therapy theory has not proved adequate. The second section moves away from these specifics toward broader conceptualizations of the meaning of diversity in feminist therapy. We would like to thank Ellen Cole for midwifing the final stages of this volume.

Laura S. Brown
Maria P. P. Root
November 1988

The Meaning
of a Multicultural Perspective
for Theory-Building in Feminist Therapy

Laura S. Brown, PhD, ABPP

SUMMARY. This article critically examines the development of theory in feminist therapy and raises the question of whether feminist therapy is currently a therapy reflecting the lives and realities of all women. Internal and external barriers to the inclusion of women of color, poor women, and other non-white or middle class groups in the process of feminist therapy theory-building are examined. A specific topic within feminist therapy theory, that of women and eating, is analyzed as an example of how a Eurocentric bias comes to pervade feminist therapy theorizing. Finally, some suggestions are made regarding directions that must be taken in theory development for feminist therapy to become genuinely multicultural and representative of the variety and diversity of women's lives.

Theories in psychotherapy are powerful tools for the creation of shared realities. The theory to which a therapist adheres prescribes

---

Laura S. Brown is a clinical psychologist in private practice in Seattle, WA, and Clinical Associate Professor of Psychology at the University of Washington. She is in the second generation born in America; her grandparents were Jews from Russian Poland. She has written many articles on feminist therapy theory.

Author note: "I would like to take this opportunity to thank Anne Ganley for having inspired me to write this paper on this topic; her willingness to raise these issues and her clarity of vision about them has been an essential part of the development of my thinking over the years. I would also like to thank Miriam Vogel, Maria Root, Francesca Profiri and Hannah Lerman for their comments on earlier drafts of this paper, all of which have become a part of my ongoing thought process."

Correspondence may be addressed to the author at: 4527 First Ave NE, Seattle, WA 98105.

1

not only the technique and approach used to make interventions, but also describes the nature of reality, normalcy and psychopathology. Different schools of psychotherapy vary in the degree to which an underlying and coherent theory is essential to their practice. Psychoanalysis, for instance, is heavily theoretically based, with theory pervading all aspects of practice from assessment onward. Ericksonian hypnotherapy can be said to be almost atheoretical, with the emphasis being on the development of intervention tools and symptomatic relief rather than on an understanding of etiological factors.

Feminist therapy has in the past lacked a theory that was specifically related to the practice of psychotherapy. This is not to say that feminist therapy has been atheoretical. Rather, its theories have been political and sociological, derived from feminist political analysis of the place of women and other oppressed groups in society. This analysis has leaned heavily on the critique of sexism in extant theories of personality and psychotherapy, generating powerful awareness regarding the differential treatment of women in the practice of assessment and psychotherapy. These political and critical analyses have for the most part been overlaid onto or woven into the psychotherapeutic theories ascribed to by a particular feminist therapist. The result has been a myriad of feminist therapies that share certain core precepts but vary widely in their descriptions of normative human growth and development, pathology, and appropriate psychotherapeutic intervention strategies.

In the past decade, some feminist therapists have begun to attempt development of a unified theory of feminist therapy that would allow us to expand our applications of practice by making our work more theoretically coherent. Without such a theory feminist therapy has risked becoming simply a collection of women therapists working with women in certain identified areas such as violence, lesbianism, eating disorders, or women in transition. Without theory, it becomes difficult if not impossible to create feminist therapy applications and preventative interventions with men, children, families, and larger social systems. Lerman (1987) has described the criteria that such a theory must meet in order to be a *feminist* theory of personality, psychopathology and psychotherapy. The criterion that I would like to address here is one which has proved to be the most problematic for the majority of theory-builders in feminist therapy and yet will be essential if we are to create a therapy theory that is consistent with the stated goals of political feminism. This criterion is that a feminist theory "encompasses the diversity and complexity of women and their lives" (p.173).

Feminist therapy and feminist therapy theory have been developed by and with white women. Currently, feminist therapy theory is neither diverse nor complex in the reality it reflects. It has been deficient from the start in its inclusiveness of the lives and realities of women of color, poor or working class women, non-North American women, women over sixty-five, or women with disabilities. Commonly cited landmark volumes in feminist therapy such as Miller (1976), Sturdivant (1980) or Greenspan (1983) appear to describe the realities of white women only, with occasional passing references to the fact that women of color, women with disabilities, poor women, and so on may bear even heavier burdens of oppression than do their white, able-bodied and financially more secure sisters. The *Handbook of Feminist Therapy* which arose from the first Advanced Feminist Therapy Institute acknowledges the absence of women of color as authors or subjects of discussion, although lesbians and (more superficially) women in poverty are addressed in that volume (Rosewater and Walker, 1985). These books focus on applications of feminist therapy rather than theory. However, they accurately reflect the zeitgeist in which theory is being developed.

Authors who have made explicit attempts to create feminist theories of female development such as Eichenbaum and Orbach (1983), Chodorow (1979), Gilligan (1982) or Dinnerstein (1976) have similarly positioned the women that they are describing squarely in the family and social structures of white, Northern European and North American society. This is also the case for the Stone Center group of authors (e.g., Jordan, Surrey & Kaplan, 1983, Wolfman, 1984; Miller, 1982) who have built their theoretical constructions around Miller's (1976) original work and their own clinical observations of a primarily white client group. As Lorde (1980) cogently puts it, "As white women ignore their built-in privilege of whiteness and define *woman* in terms of their own experience alone, then women of Color become 'other,' the outsider whose experience and tradition is too alien to comprehend" (p.117). It seems as if the lives of women of color have been too alien to comprehend, and too far from sight to be included in the theories of feminist therapists.

To a large degree, this failure of feminist therapy theorists to address the lives of all women, and its consequent difficulties with the "diversity and complexity" criterion can be traced to the training of feminist therapists in traditional systems and theories of personality and psychotherapy. Such systems are themselves highly culture-bound. In consequence, even the feminist therapist who enters into her professional training determined to take a feminist perspective will be confronting a base of data and theory that are white, Western, heterosexual and male. Most feminist therapists have been quick to identify the masculinist biases inherent in other theories and the practices that are associated with them. Many have also been able to cull out the heterosexist and homophobic biases. But the subtle aspects of racist and classist assumptions have been less visible and less salient to many white feminist therapists, who have benefited from privilege of race and (in many instances) class, as they are invisible to many white women (Greene, 1986).

In the social and behavioral sciences, the form taken by racism and classism is to make people invisible. The three Black subjects whose responses are thrown out of the data pool because they disturb the symmetry of the statistics, or the questions about class never asked because of the non-conscious assumption that we live in a classless society typify the ways in which people who are non-white or non-middle class disappear or become invisible to the science of psychology.

Specific coursework on people of color is scarce. Wyatt and Parham (1985), reporting on a survey of American Psychological Association approved graduate programs and internships in clinical and counseling psychology found that of those small number of programs bothering to respond to their questionnaire, only 7% indicated that their students had any courses available in "culturally sensitive training." Most of what was available occurred at the internship level, e.g., far into the training process and was optional rather than required coursework. Although programs accredited by both psychology and social work require "diversity" to be represented in the training of practitioners, this requirement is broadly interpreted and often operationalized as one lecture on working with minorities in a psychotherapy or assessment course.

Aside from its collusion with racism in white trainees, this particular version of racism and classism also often has profound limiting impacts on the vision of women of color or poor women who enter professional training. The risks to self, safety, and pursuit of the advanced degree or tenure that may develop when attempting to make visible such subtle, "civilized" racist or classist tactics are often too great for a graduate student or newly degreed faculty woman to tolerate. In learning not to comment, it also becomes possible to join with white culture in learning not to see these forms of oppression (Brown, 1987a; Evans, 1985; Tyler, Sussewell and Williams-McCoy, 1985).

The process of professional socialization which is seen as central to many graduate training programs in the helping professions and the behavioral sciences (*Accreditation Handbook of the American Psychological Association*, 1987) is also a socialization into this narrow, all-white and middle class reality. In an academic culture where it is still considered too risky to raise feminist questions, anti-racist or class-conscious feminism has even less room. As Jones (1985), paraphrasing Sue (1983) puts it,

> These conflicts (between the traditional values of the professions and new concerns regarding people of color) make it easier to confront the problems by recruiting and admitting increasing numbers of ethnic minority persons to the guild than to pitch battle on core values. (p.454)

Implied, but not stated, is that once people of color are recruited to the guild, a process of internal colonization will take place with resulting allegiance to the white, Western values of the guild in question, psychotherapy and behavioral sciences.

Evans (1985), commenting on the training of graduate students in psychology to deliver services to people of color, notes that psychologists are often trained to have "a lack of hope and lack of optimism about Black people" which constitutes "the greatest impediments to the proper utilization of psychotherapy with them" (p.459). She theorizes that this lack of hope comes from "lack of 'the stuff' out of which conviction and hope are born, i.e., broad knowledge and appreciation of different cultures . . . and the histories of people showing their travail and their indomitability" (p.459). In other words, lack of data and lack of awareness go hand in hand to create trained-in insensitivity to and ignorance of the broad spectrum of realities for people of color and other oppressed groups.

This almost hypnotic induction of therapists in training into a white, Western, and subtly racist worldview seems to act as the filter on the sensitivities of feminist therapists who are attempting to generate our own non-sexist, non-masculinist data sources. My sense is that feminist therapy theory has always been one part sociology, e.g., description of the external reality and social context, and one part phenomenology, e.g., description of lived and felt internal reality as experienced from within the social context. The special contribution of feminist therapy has been to attempt to describe the interactive relationships of internal and external realities. But through the filters of our original trainings, we have developed a social context of white women, and a phenomenology of white female experiences. In addition, we have tended to approach our understanding of behavior via linear models of causality which limit our understandings of the variety of contextual factors that can influence the development of personality (Lerner, 1988).

For example, if we review research in feminist psychology, which has largely provided the base of empirical data from which we have constructed our visions of the external context and reality, we find that such research has been conducted almost overwhelmingly by and with white women. The cliched "white-male-middle-class-college-sophomore" research subject has often been replaced by his sister. When we speak, for instance, of female socialization, a term used constantly in the feminist therapy literature as an explanation for a myriad of observed phenomena, we are describing information on that process that has been gathered almost entirely from a white subject pool. We insist on the importance of context (Parlee, 1979) and then seem to forget that there are many contexts. Socialization to be a white, middle-class Jewish woman is not socialization to be a Black, middle-class Southern Baptist woman. Socialization into one age cohort's female gender role will be different from that experienced by another cohort, even holding all other demographic variables constant (see Brown, 1986a for an analysis of how such contextual variations can affect the assessment process). Whose socialization are we referring to when we cite "female socialization" as the source of X or Y problems described in our samples of women? This tendency to ignore the variable of race, in particular, when making attempts to understand female behavior has become strikingly evident to me in the six years that I have served as an editorial reviewer for one of the primary outlets for such research, *Psychology of Women Quarterly*.

During that time, it has been unusual to find an article either among those I review or those published in the journal that has specifically addressed the lives and realities of women of color in North America, women living outside of white, Western culture, women living in poverty, and so on. Such articles seem to appear primarily in special issues, word-ghettoes in which the articles are invited and strenuously sought out as relevant to the "special" group in this particular issue (e.g., a special issue on Black women published in 1982 and more recently, a special issue on Hispanic women, published in late 1987).

One of the strengths of feminist psychology research is that it often uses as a heuristic the issues that arise from the life of the researcher herself. Thus questions are asked about menstruation and mothering and the experience of being sexually harassed or acquaintance rape or working in non-traditional careers or surviving an abusive relationship. However, this particular means of making the personal political has been a deficit in regards to developing a more multicultural base, given that most of those conducting the research continue to be white women, and are often women raised in the middle class. "Personal" has encompassed a narrow range of experiences. The lack of diversity among those currently in the field of feminist psychology has functioned to limit the scope of the questions asked.

Likewise, we find this tendency to overgeneralize from white women's experience in the literature that is more phenomenological. It is within this literature that the recent development of a rapprochement with psychodynamic theories such as Jungian analysis, object relations, and self psychology has occurred. While such a marriage would have been seen as anathema early in the development of feminist therapy practice, and is still looked at askance by many feminist therapists, it has become increasingly clear that such theories exert a strong pull for many feminist therapists, myself included. My sense, based solely on my own reading of these materials and my conversations with other feminist therapists who find them useful is that this attraction is due to the highly phenomenological and clinical aspects of these theories. Without being as overtly sexist and thus offensive as orthodox psychoanalysis, the psychodynamic, intrapsychic theories offer intriguing hypotheses about the experience of internal reality, glimpses that have appeared useful to feminist theoreticians of personality such as Chodorow (1979) and Gilligan (1982).

Such a focus on internal experience was mostly absent from early writings in feminist therapy; in scanning Sturdivant's (1980) review of the feminist therapy literature predating her book I was struck by the de-emphasis on the intrapsychic and the insistence on a view of female psychology that is no longer considered core to the thinking of many feminist therapists. For instance, Sturdivant (1980) writes about the importance of seeing women as not-in-relationship, even though her work post-dates Miller's (1976) original formulation of the concept of woman-in-relationship. Eight years later Miller's paradigm seems to be central to the formulation of many feminist therapy personality theorists. What seems to have happened is that as feminist therapists grew more secure in our critiques of the sexism that imbued traditional (e.g., psychodynamic) therapies, we became more comfortable in retaking possession of intrapsychic phenomena and attempting to describe them from a more female-centered perspective.

Yet here, too, the cradle and context of internal, phenomenological reality are white and Western. In reading many of the interpretations of Winnicott's (1953) descriptions of the "good enough mother" as the organizing principle of an infant's developing emotional life, a construct on which object relations theory and the feminist psychodynamicists build heavily, I have been impressed with the taken for granted notions about the social structures for childrearing that are inherent in the work that has built upon his descriptions. While Winnicott himself was attempting to describe the phenomenological experience of being well cared-for from the vantage point of an infant (saying that mothers do not exist without infants) his use of the gendered and particularistic term "mother" has led most of object relations theory very far afield from his apparent original intent. The issue of infant phenomenology has been lost in the prescription of maternal behaviors for mothers who are always women. I often joke that if you look carefully enough you can discover that this "mother" was actually a nanny. Winnicott's description of the internal life of the infant had become that of a child born into material comfort and cared for by one whose sole work in life is childcare. Aside from the class-bound assumptions of the external context that informs this internal reality, it accounts little if at all for social systems in which child-raising does not take place within a nuclear, heterosexual, two-parent, father-as-sole-breadwinner style family system.

Since such a model represents the reality for less than half of North American families, one must either infer pathology to large numbers of persons, or expand, if not abandon, those theories of development that insist on such a model as the only healthy and normal one. How do such theories make sense of cultures in which the grandmother raises the children, ones in which the father is absent or lacking sanctioned cultural meaning for the child, or where child-raising is shared by several adults of various genders and biological relationships to the child? How can one account for the internal reality of the person developing her personality within such social contexts? The psychodynamic theories give us ways to investigate those questions, but as currently stated, give us answers that are severely limited in their generalizability because they are culture-bound.

Also problematic in these theories are assumptions regarding the causes of intrapsychic phenomena. Lerner (1988), critiquing the feminist psychoanalytic theorists, points out that when they adopt the assumptions of psychodynamic theories regarding the centrality of *mother*-child relations; even when that relationship has been reframed into a properly feminist positive perspective, the feminist psychoanalytic writers have neglected to attend to the influence or presence of the father. Such models also tend to ignore the family and the cultural system in which a child develops, as well as the interplay of relationships between these factors. While Lerner acknowledges the importance that these writers have had in bringing certain aspects of phenomenology to light, she points out that since psychodynamic thinking emphasizes the primacy of the mother as the shaper of personality, such theories subtly convey a meta-message of mother blaming even when the overt content is to value the mother-child relationship and honor the mother's role in the face of sexist reality. In other words, by re-entering reality as mapped by psychodynamic thought, we inevitably encounter sexism. What Lerner does not say is that by defining "mother" in racially and culturally particularistic manners, we also weave racism into our models.

The embrace of a psychodynamic framework of phenomenology based primarily in the available theoretical systems moves feminist therapy theory development even further away from a multicultural perspective and places it more firmly in a white, Western mode. For feminist therapy theorists wishing to describe the diversity and complexity of women's lives, and to do so in a manner that avoids inadvertent recreation of woman-blaming methodologies these questions and critiques are central and cannot be ignored. These theoretical systems are phenomenological, and thus descriptive of powerful yet non-quantifiable and experiential data. They are consequently more seductive and difficult to challenge as regards their racism or ethnocentrism than might be a system which is more oriented towards observable external phenomena. And in that they are phenomenological, they are also clinically powerful explanatory fictions for many of the experiences of the white women writing these theories. This lends such theories a spurious but strongly felt validity that embeds them in the thinking of many feminist therapists.

I would like to very briefly examine one aspect of the recent work done by feminist object relations theorists as they attempt to build feminist therapy theory. I will use this to illustrate how the over-immersion in traditional systems of personality and psychotherapy obscures the issue of culture. One area in which this group of authors has been particularly prolific has been that of women's relationship to food and their bodies (Orbach, 1978, 1982, 1986; Chernin, 1985; Surrey, 1984) a topic that I am intimately familiar with due to my own attempts at theory development (Brown, 1985, 1986b, 1987b). Since all women eat and have female bodies, regardless of culture, it provides us with an example of female experience that occurs for all women in every social context, and thus could be a starting-point for multicultural theory development. Instead, this topic serves as an excellent example of how the experiences of non-white, non-Western women disappear in what are otherwise striking studies of women's phenomenology. Food, weight, and the struggle with each are described and defined as universal experiences for women; only occasionally do these authors point out how this universe is bounded by both class and culture. The relationship between mothers and daughters is conceptualized as primary to the development of this struggle; the roles of fathers, families, and cultures disappear.

Orbach, Surrey and Chernin all attend very closely to "the mother-daughter relationship" as a source of the very common difficulties that "women" experience regarding their body size and food intake. I place quotes around these words because of how strongly culture-bound these descriptions of mothers, daughters, and women are. An apt quote comes from Chernin: "We are a unique generation of women — the first in history to have the social and psychological opportunity to surpass with ease the life choices our mothers have made" (p.12). At this point one begins to nod in agreement — and yet must stop and ask, "Whose history? The history of which women, what mothers?" Such a statement may be true as regards white, middle class, educationally privileged women. How true is it for an American Indian woman living in a reservation community, the middle-class Black woman encountering barriers that while subtle are still obstacles to the full use of her education and professional development or a poor white woman from the depressed Rust Belt who has been pushed out of a decently-paid factory job like the one her mother held into minimum wage service work in a fast-food outlet?

This sort of careful challenging of statements that appear on the surface to be intuitively correct becomes important when we reflect that it is from such assumptions about female existence and experience that much respected and widely-read theoretical work in feminist therapy has been developed. I do not wish to discount the importance of the work being done by these theorists; rather, I wish to call attention to what is missing and what will continue to be absent without conscious attention to its absence.

Sayers (1988) in a review of two books that have evolved from the British school of feminist object relations theory (founded by Orbach and Eichenbaum and their colleagues) points out that by attempting to cut a feminist analysis to fit this theoretical perspective, the British feminist therapists represented in these books come close to losing entirely that which is feminist in their theory. Political analysis, which predominated feminist therapy writing in its first decade, seems to be in danger of being replaced by an almost entirely intrapsychic approach with occasional bows to "women's" (read "white women's") socialization. She notes that by embracing psychodynamic perspectives, no matter how seductively well they appear to represent women's (e.g., the usually white therapist and her usually white clients') internal reality, these feminist therapists have ceased to raise questions about the role of the father, of patriarchy, and of the reality of external oppression in favor of the psychodynamic focus on mother. Even racism in white women becomes reframed as "unconscious reenactment of oppression suffered as children at their mothers' hands" (p.22). Aside from the highly apolitical nature of this analysis, notice how it makes invisible the oppression children suffer at their fathers' hands, e.g., sexual and physical abuse! Racism is thus both trivialized into an intrapsychic wound suffered by white women and blamed on the insufficiencies of mothers in one fell swoop.

It is impossible to dismiss the feminist psychoanalysts. It is clear that their theorizing reflects a deep hunger among many feminist therapists for a more intrapsychic, more complex, more theory (as versus politically) oriented approach to feminist therapy. This has certainly been the source of my own ambivalent attraction to and relationship with such theories. I read the feminist psychoanalysts, rage at points, and yet resonate to the usefulness of their descriptions of internal experience when applied both to myself and to many of the clients with whom I work. After all, I and many of them are white North American women. Thus, a simple rejectionist posture will rob feminist therapy theory of a potential richness.

However, we must not be seduced by that which resonates for us, particularly if we are white women. Rather, our questions should be of how we could draw upon the models for theory building and development offered by such highly phenomenological traditional theories of personality and psychotherapy in order to develop a model that is both feminist and multicultural. Additionally, we must ask whether alternative models are available to us for the understanding of phenomenology and internal reality, a question increasingly raised by feminist family therapists (Bograd, 1986; Goldner, 1985; Lerner, 1988). It is to move forward that task that I will devote the remainder of this paper.

A first step towards a multicultural feminist therapy theory would be the development of a multicultural, non-white-and-non-Western feminist data base on the varieties of female experiences. A feminist consciousness must inform the way in which we frame our research questions and pursue our task of gathering information. At the same time, we must consciously avoid the trap of assuming that one woman's context is constructed in a manner equivalent to another's. We must particularly guard against imposing our own personal contexts, whatever they may be, upon the meaning and realities of women different from ourselves.

Additionally, by working from the feminist principle of respecting experience as it is defined by those within it, we must cease insisting on the primacy of gender as *the* issue in our examinations of the lives of women of color, poor women, women from non-Western cultures, and so on. A number of authors (Lorde, 1980; Kanuha, in press; Walker, 1983; Moraga & Anzaludua, 1981) have pointed out that for feminist women of color the requirement that sexism be chosen as the "ultimate" oppression negates the validity of their internal realities. In keeping with this reality, feminist researchers and therapists must not assume that gender and gender membership will be the variable of most importance in all women's lives. Feminist research towards developing a complete picture of all women's social contexts must guard against that tendency. While gender as an organizing variable is central to a feminist analysis and understanding of the data we collect, it may not be central to the women we study in all cases.

Thus, part of asking the questions regarding what it means to be socialized as female in a particular culture must include questions regarding the salience of gender as an organizing principle. We can then also ask about the meaning of differences between cultural groups in the power of gender as a social factor. The meanings given to the social expression and construction of female biology must and will vary, and those differences in meaning must be sought out and described. It will also be necessary to ask ourselves how various factors interact with one another to create different varieties of social context for women who may appear, from a white-or-middle-class-centered perspective, to be similar.

For instance, it is inappropriate to speak of "American Indian women" as a group in describing the experience of gender role socialization, since the experience and meaning of female gender membership will vary from one tribal tradition to another, and will be affected by such factors as the degree of acculturation of the particular woman's family, whether she is reservation or non-reservation raised, and so on. Similar fine-tuning must occur in attempts to examine any group, including ethnically different groups within the white population. White-Hungarian is different from White-Norwegian. When we generate this very diverse picture of the external realities of women's lives, feminist therapists will begin to have a picture of the many female socializations experienced by women within a broad variety of contexts.

Some of this data is already available to feminist therapy theorists in the work of feminist anthropologists, sociologists, political scientists and historians. Such an interdisciplinary knowledge base is essential to the creation of a multicultural feminist therapy theory. This is particularly so because of the tendency of North American psychology and related behavioral sciences to proceed as if other cultures and scientific traditions do not exist and the rigid overemphasis on the controlled, laboratory based experimental model for understanding human behavior (or as a member of a friend's tenure committee once said, "It's too bad you can't randomly assign your subjects to rape and no-rape conditions."). Bleier (1984) points out that feminist scholarship regarding the sociology of knowledge has had less impact within the canons of psychology and the related psychotherapy disciplines than anywhere else in the social sciences. Lerner (1988) reminds us of how imprisoned much of our thinking is in linear models of causality that obscure other paradigms from examination. Yet to create a multicultural theory we must ask questions regarding how we define knowledge (Ballou, 1988). To define the knowledge of our sister feminist social scientists as central to the development of feminist therapy theories would break through the tyranny of psychology's "affinity for positivism" to use Bleier's terminology.

This move is a risky one for the feminist researcher wishing to survive in the infertile soil of academe. While feminist behavioral scientists have proclaimed long and loudly the importance of developing different approaches to our research, that which reaches the daylight of publication tends to reflect the research methodology that is taught in most graduate research methods courses. Much of this reliance on the scientific method is necessary for that process of academic survival; researchers without tenure are less likely to be staying in academia and generating more data. However, we must be careful not to become so intent on surviving that we loose sight of alternative possibilities for the generation of knowledge. As Lorde (1979) points out, "The master's tools will never dismantle the master's house." Not only are we asking that truth be given to us from other intellectual traditions. We must also attempt to broaden ourselves so that the ways in which we ask questions and define truth will not simply be the work of feminists using the methods of masculinist social science.

In an odd way, what I am suggesting is that in order to develop this feminist psychology of all women's experience we will have to be more rigorous than usual in our pursuit of knowledge. Odd, because the use of non-conventional research methodologies and the borrowing from other disciplines' approaches is what is usually defined as non-rigorous. A feminist rigor, however, is one that does not draw conclusions about women in general from any one group's experiences, or about that group from only one age cohort or class group or sexual orientation within that larger group.

Simultaneous with this, we must create the theories of personality that reflect the internal realities that grow within these social contexts. I believe that the psychodynamic theories that have been attractive to some feminist therapists give us a model for asking questions about these internal realities. However, as feminist therapists, we must push beyond the answers and models given us by white European men such as Jung, Kohut, or Winnicott and ask how internal reality is shaped by diverse external experiences. Although phenomenology and introspection as tools of theory development have long fallen out of favor among North American psychologists, they may be the most effective methods available to us as feminist therapists for this task. For if we rely upon them, we will be asking women to define for themselves and for us the unique experiences of being female and. . . . Only then will we begin to meet the criterion of a theory that is diverse and complex.

In this, too, we have resources already available in the body of historical and/or autobiographical non-fiction literature and womanist (to use Walker's [1983] term) fiction that has grown dramatically in the last decade. Women of color have been vividly describing the experiences of being Black and female, Chinese American and female, Caribbean and female, Lebanese/Laguna Pueblo and female, and so on for many years. Freud, when asked what women want suggested (for lack of a better idea on his own part) that we turn to the poets. A similar course of action might be a first step for white feminist therapy personality theorists asking what it may be like to live inside the experience of being a non-white woman.

Take, for instance, social and familial realities of Morrison's novel *Beloved*. If we apply, as suggested by Chodorow (1979) the concepts of projective identification as a core construct of the development of self and identity in an infant to the generations of women who might come from this family we can start to ask ourselves how personality might develop in the line of women descending from one who has killed her child to save her from slavery. This leads to some new and startling notions about the nature of normalcy and pathology. At the very least such different questions will suggest that our notions of personality development, and thus our concepts about therapeutic intervention, will come to reflect an intergenerational understanding of the meaning of being female and the development of identity. If we follow Lerner's (1988) admonitions to look even further than the mother-child relationship, our paradigm expands further. What does it mean to be the child of a father who is killed for wanting to maintain and protect his family in the face of murderous racism? To be female in such a family? The richness of our understanding grows as our questions become more prolific.

Too, we must examine how cultural factors outside of the control of members of a particular group shape internal experience. Giddings' (1984) book title reflects the internal reality for Black women in America, quoting the Black American author of the 1890s, Anna Julia Cooper who stated, "When and where I enter, . . . then and there the whole race enters with me." What does it mean to the development of self to carry that knowledge and awareness, to be the embodiment of the symbolic representations of the dominant other? Even if we search for an archetype we cannot, as Bolen suggests (1984) turn to a Jungian typology of Greek goddesses to comprehend this experience, since such a typology resides solely within the dominant culture which has framed this context. While feminist therapy theorists have asked these questions about generic "woman" in relationship to generic "man" and generic "patriarchal culture," our answers fail to include the possibility of white women as the dominant other and the impact of that dominance both on white women's personalities and those of people of color.

Practically, this means that feminist therapists must both include significant numbers of women of color and significant numbers of therapists working with people of color among our ranks. My own experience of theory-building as a feminist therapist, and my reading of that process as experienced by other theory-builders, is that it takes the form of an extended conversation (often in writing) between colleagues about their work and their insights. If I am not interacting with feminist therapists of color, with culturally literate and white feminist therapists, with clients of color and with others who work with them, my "conversations" will remain limited in their scope and understanding.

If we do not soon undertake the process of making feminist therapy a multicultural theory, we may loose our chance and become yet another white, exclusionary system. Some therapists who are women of color and feminist in their theoretical perspectives have refused to take on an identification with feminist therapy in part because of its overly white bias, and in part because feminist political theory has seemed to deny to women of color the importance of their racial and cultural identities (Kanuha, in press). It is both inappropriate and racist to assume that women of color therapists will want to join in the development of feminist therapy theory in order to raise the consciousness of white feminist therapists; "it is not the duty of the oppressed to educate the oppressor" (Moschkovich, 1981). White feminist therapists and our theories must proactively seek to be anti-racist and multicultural so as to demonstrate our relevance to women of color, non-North American women, and so on. Perhaps one answer to the question often raised in feminist therapy organizations about where all the feminist therapists of color are is that they are reluctant to affiliate with these essentially white organizations unless and until white feminist therapists have demonstrated in concrete ways our commitment to valuing diversity and comprehending the lives of women unlike ourselves. Making our theories diverse and complex is one such concrete commitment.

What I am suggesting may seem monumental in scope; it is both essential and exciting in its realization. If now, at the initial stages of theory-building in feminist therapy we start with these new challenges to our old assumptions, we have the potential to develop theory that is not simply a female-centered revision of what has already been written. Rather, we have the opportunity to re-envision a broader reality and generate a deeper understanding of how human beings come to know themselves, and how pain and dysfunction develop and can be healed. We can question the paradigms by which we understand interpersonal and intrapersonal processes, and integrate the best of all disciplinary perspectives into our work. Should we miss this opportunity, we risk making feminist therapy yet another reaction against or re-writing of the concepts of orthodox psychoanalytic personality theory which have so imbued the Western social and behavioral sciences for the past century. To remain true to our own ethics, we have no choice but to plunge into the task.

REFERENCES

American Psychological Association (1987). *Accreditation handbook*. Washington DC: Author.
Ballou, Mary (1988, May). *Building feminist theory through feminist principles*. Paper presented at the Advanced Feminist Therapy Institute, Seattle WA.
Bleier, Ruth (1984). *Science and gender*. New York: The Pergamon Press.

Bograd, Michele (1986). A feminist examination of family therapy: what is woman's place? *Women & Therapy*, *5*, 2/3, pp. 95-106.

Bolen, Jean Shinoda (1984). *Goddesses in every woman*. New York: Harper Colophon.

Brown, Laura S. (1985). Women weight and power: Feminist theoretical and therapeutic issues. *Women & Therapy*, *4*, pp. 61-72.

Brown, Laura S. (1986a). Gender role analysis: A neglected component of psychological assessment. *Psychotherapy: Theory, Research, Practice, Training*, *23*, pp. 243-248.

Brown, Laura S. (1986b, August). Fat oppression and psychotherapy: A new look at the meaning of body size. In Esther Rothblum (Chair) *Women in Context: Disordered or Displaced?* Symposium presented at the Convention of the American Psychological Association, Washington DC.

Brown, Laura S. (1987a, May). *Training issues for white feminist therapists working with women of color*. Paper presented at the Advanced Feminist Therapy Institute, Woodstock IL.

Brown, Laura S. (1987b). Lesbians, weight and eating: New analysis and perspectives. In Boston Lesbian Psychologies Collective (Eds.) *Lesbian Psychologies Explorations and Challenges*. (pp. 294-310) Urbana IL: U. of Illinois Press.

Chernin, Kim (1985). *The hungry self: Women, eating and identity*. New York: Times Books.

Chodorow, Nancy (1979). *The reproduction of mothering*. Berkeley CA: University of California Press.

Dinnerstein, Dorothy (1976). *The mermaid and the minotaur*. New York: Harper Colophon.

Eichenbaum, Luise & Orbach, Susie (1983). *Understanding women: A feminist psychoanalytic approach*. New York: Basic Books.

Evans, Dorothy (1985). Psychotherapy and Black patients: Problems of training, trainees and trainers. *Psychotherapy: Theory, Research, Practice, Training*, *22*, 457-460.

Giddings, Paula (1984). *When and where I enter: The impact of Black women on race and sex in America*. New York: William Morrow and Company.

Gilligan, Carol (1981). *In a different voice*. Cambridge MA: Harvard University Press.

Goldner, Virginia (1985). Feminism and family therapy. *Family Process*, *24*, 31-47.

Greene, Beverly (1986). When the therapist is white and the patient is Black: Considerations for psychotherapy in the feminist heterosexual and lesbian communities. *Women & Therapy*, *5*, pp. 41-66.

Greenspan, Miriam (1983). *A new approach to women and therapy*. New York: McGraw Hill.

Jones, James M. (1985). The sociopolitical context of clinical training in psychology: The ethnic minority case. *Psychotherapy: Theory, Research, Practice, Training*, *22*, pp. 453-456.

Jordan, Judith V., Surrey, Janet L., & Kaplan, Alexandra G. (1983). Women and empathy: Implications for psychological development and psychotherapy. *Work in Progress*. Wellesley MA: Stone Center.

Kanuha, Valli (in press). The need for an integrated analysis of oppression in feminist therapy ethics. In Hannah Lerman and Natalie Porter (Eds.) *Ethics in Feminist Therapy*. New York: Springer.

Lerman, Hannah (1987). *A note in Freud's eye: From psychoanalysis to the psychology of women*. New York: Springer.

Lerner, Harriet Goldhor (1988). *Women in Therapy*. Northvale NJ: Jason Aronson.

Lorde, Audre (1979, September). The master's tools will never dismantle the master's house. Panel, *The Personal and the Political*, Second Sex Conference, New York NY.

Lorde, Audre (1980, April). Age, race, class and sex: Women redefining difference. *Copeland Colloquium, Amherst College*, Amherst MA.

Miller, Jean Baker (1976). *Toward a new psychology of women*. Boston: Beacon Press.

Miller, Jean Baker (1982). Women and power. *Work in Progress*. Wellesley MA: Stone Center.

Moraga, Cherrie & Anzaldua, Gloria (Eds.) (1981). *This bridge called my back: Writings by radical women of color*. Watertown MA: Persephone Press.

Morrison, Toni (1987). *Beloved*. New York: Alfred A. Knopf.

Moschkovich, Judit (1981). "But I know you, American woman." In Cherrie Moraga & Gloria Anzaldua (Eds.) *This bridge called my back: Writings by radical women of color*. (pp. 79-84). Watertown, MA: Persephone Press.

Orbach, Susie (1979). *Fat is a feminist issue*. New York: Paddington Press.

Orbach, Susie (1982). *Fat is a feminist issue II*. New York: Berkeley Books.

Orbach, Susie (1986). *Hunger strike*. New York: Norton.

Parlee, Mary Brown (1979). Psychology and women. *Signs: Journal of Women in Culture and Society*, 5, pp. 121-133.

Rosewater, Lynne Bravo & Walker, Lenore E.A. (Eds.) (1985). *Handbook of feminist therapy: Women's issues in psychotherapy*. New York: Springer.

Sayers, Janet. (1988). My mother, my therapist. *Women's Review of Books*, 5, 7, p. 22.

Sturdivant, Susan (1980). *Therapy with women*. New York: Springer.

Sue, Stanley. (1983). Ethnic minority issues in psychology. *American Psychologist*, 38, pp. 583-592.

Surrey, Janet L. (1984). Eating patterns as a reflection of women's development. *Work in Progress*. Wellesley MA: Stone Center.

Tyler, Forrest B., Sussewell, Deborah Ridley & Williams-McCoy, Janice (1985). Ethnic validity in psychotherapy. *Psychotherapy: Theory, Research, Practice, Training*, 22, pp. 311-320.

Walker, Alice (1983). *In search of our mothers' gardens: Womanist prose*. New York: Harcourt, Brace, Jovanovich.

Winnicott, Donald W. (1953). Transitional objects and transitional phenomena. *International Journal of Psychoanalysis, 34* pp. 89-97.

Wolfman, Brunetta R. (1983). Women and their many roles. *Work in Progress.* Wellesley MA: Stone Center.

Wyatt, Gail E. & Parham, William D. (1985). The inclusion of culturally sensitive course materials in graduate school and training programs. *Psychotherapy: Theory, Research, Practice, Training, 22,* pp. 461-468.

Approaching a Feminist-Principled Paradigm in the Construction of Personality Theory

Mary B. Ballou, PhD

SUMMARY. Five methods of generating and validating knowledge are presented and illustrated through selected psychology of women literature. The strengths and weaknesses of each method is discussed. Critiques within the psychology of women and feminist studies of logical positivism and phenomenology are referenced and drawn into a positioning of feminist principles and the epistemological assumptions of general systems theory as central to the development of a more adequate paradigm.

What is the nature of knowledge and how does it originate? This fascinating and important question has recently begun to interest feminist theorists. Classical philosophers have long been aware, and feminists have increasingly realized, that approaches to knowledge generation shape the reality found. Rejecting the common assumption that an unchanging reality exists and that differing approaches to its investigation are more or less powerful, complete and adequate, feminist researchers have begun to ask how we know what we know. In their ground breaking work, *Women's Ways of Knowing* (1987) for example, Belenky and her associates identified

Mary B. Ballou works in both academic and clinical settings. She is Associate Professor of Counseling Psychology at Northeastern University and has a private practice in both Keene, NH and Boston. Mary writes, researches, teaches, consults and counsels in her active professional life. As a tenth generation Yankee WASP, she struggles with her privilege yet fully enjoys the pleasures of a life split between the stimulation of the city and the tranquility of the country.

Correspondence may be addressed to the author at: Northeastern University, 205 Lake Hall, 360 Huntington Avenue, Boston, MA 02115.

five different cognitive processes that women use in dealing with the world and have shown the relationship of each to authority, sense of self, and reasoning. While Belenky and her colleagues have described individual epistemological positions resulting in different views of reality for their respondents, this article seeks to discuss the same phenomenon at the level of formal analysis. That is, the focus here is not on individual ways of knowing but on methods of knowledge generation and validation within mainstream and feminist psychology. It is my contention that methodologies impose severe limits on the reality which psychology constructs.

As a case in point, consider research on the effectiveness of consciousness-raising (C-R) groups. In a review of studies on this issue, I found that results (reality) depended on the method of knowledge generation and validation used (Ballou, 1979). Studies using experiential methodology, which accepted the notion that reality is in the experience or perception of the respondent, found C-R groups had an enormously positive impact on women participants. Studies using experimental methodology, which held reality to be objective and independent of experience and perception, found no significant impact from C-R group participation. Clearly, particular epistemological assumptions about the nature of knowledge and its validation of truth, legitimized through method, shaped the outcome of these studies.

This article examines five different methods of knowledge generation and validation that have been used within the psychology of women literature and by psychologists attempting to build a feminist personality theory. Each method — experimental, experiential, reason, appeal to authority, and nonrational knowledge generation is illustrated and set in its epistemological context, and its strengths and weaknesses are discussed. My argument is not that one method is better or more real than another, but that each has strengths and shortcomings in construction of reality.

The premise of this article is that the consensual principles of feminist therapy can be used to develop an overarching method of knowledge generation and validation for the creation of a feminist personality theory and continuing research on women's psychology. Given the limits of each methodology, none alone is equal to the task of constructing and describing reality. This article sets forth alternative paradigmatic structures consistent with and more appropriate to the task of the creation of a feminist personality theory within women's psychology.

FIVE METHODS OF KNOWLEDGE GENERATION AND VALIDATION

Experimental Method

The first and perhaps most widely used means of knowledge generation and validation is the experimental, or scientific method. Traditional psychology holds the experimental method as the normative standard through which knowledge is legitimized. The epistemological assumptions upon which this method rest include: single universal truth, objectivity (distant and nonrelated), historical- and context-independent phenomena, public and repeatable measurement, and the need for research designs in which all variables of interest are experimenter-designed and experimenter-controlled.

In the empirical C-R studies that I reviewed, researchers measured variables of interest to themselves using external instrumentation (self-concept tests, vocational interests, sex-role attitudes and ego strength), pre- and post-C-R group experience. They compared the results to control groups through statistical procedures involving comparison of group means. These studies, which found no significant changes in the women with C-R group experiences, shape a view of reality in which C-R group experiences are not associated with change among women participants.

Broverman, Broverman, Clarkson, Rosencrantz and Vogel's (1970) classic study on sex-role stereotypes in clinical judgement serves as a poignant example of the impact of experimental methodology. The researchers produced quantified evidence that mental health professionals were gender-role stereotypic in their clinical judgments and sex-role-biased in their normative criteria for mental health. Although ideas in their study were not new to feminists, they served to confirm and legitimize feminists' charges of sexism in clinical practice. Because this reality was constructed by means of an acceptable methodology, experimental method, mainstream psychology could not deny the findings, although at first the work was ignored or disclaimed by faulting specifics in design and measurement. Broverman's research has had an important impact in the psychology of women, not because it furthered conceptualizations of gender bias, but because it confirmed its existence in a manner acceptable to the mainstream of the discipline.

Logical positivism, or the scientific method, has been criticized extensively by feminist scholars. Harding (1983) through the philosophy of science, Keller (1985) through the genderization of science, Spretnak (1982) through radical feminist women's spirituality each offer important criticism in their areas, philosophy, science and spirituality. Within the psychology of women, Unger (1986) through values and personal epistemology in social constructionism and logical positivism, Sherif (1979) through multiple levels of bias against women in psychology, and Wallston (1979) through feminist challenges to research all presented careful analysis of the method's many limits and problems. They have criticized the arbitrary imposition of particular assumptions, the reshaping of phenomena being studied through measurement, the selection and definition of variables, the distortion of experience through experimental control and manipulation, the introduction of bias in hypotheses, and the tendency to ignore historical and contextual interactions.

Despite these valid critiques, the problem is not that research from a logical positivist stand is inherently wrong and to be rejected. As Broverman's work demonstrates, useful and important empirical work does exist. Rather *the issue is the domination of psychology by one epistemological method — a method rooted in the patriarchy*. Logical positivism does not deserve its normative criterion status as the most legitimate method of knowledge generation and validation nor its dominance in verification of reality. Just as a feminist perspective has altered the content of research on the status, nature and functioning of women, so too must patriarchal control of knowledge generation and validation through empiricism be explored and disempowered in the development of feminist psychological theory. The experimental method is not a priori more fitting or valid than other methods of knowledge generation and validation. In fact it may be less fitting for the purposes of feminist scholarship.

Experiential Methodologies

A second epistemological position, one that supports research within the psychology of women's literature, is phenomenology. This position holds that truth is in the experience or in the perception of the experience. While acknowledging that perceptions can and do vary independent of the phenomena (bias), phenomenology sees perception as the best source of reality and route to truth. The position stands in contrast to notions of universal laws and objective truths. Indeed, it claims that truth is in perception and that perceptions differ, which renders nonsensical ideas of truth beyond perception and all governing laws. The phenomenological position looks to perception of experience and induction from that base as the proper way to generate and validate knowledge.

It is understandable that phenomenology is being advocated by some feminists (Stanley & Wise, 1983) since its suppositions are quite in keeping with feminist sensibilities and its methods of knowledge generation have demonstrated themselves to be powerful. In C-R group research, for example, researchers who asked women to report their experience or who participated in the groups themselves found tremendous changes in attitudes, self-perceptions, vocational interests, sex-roles, and ego strength, as well as in sisterhood and social/political awareness. The results of these studies, which used questionnaires, participant-observation, observer rating and self-report, contrast markedly with the findings of the empirical studies described above. In fact, two studies (Ballou, 1979; Kunstel, 1979, unpublished), which employed both empirical and phenomenological methodology to assess the same women in the same experience found meaningful changes on several dimensions when data were gathered through observer ratings and content analysis of recorded participant narratives, while data obtained by pre-, post-, and follow-up standardized measures yielded no significant change among three experimental groups and one control group. In this study, the method of knowledge generation and validation controlled the findings; reality was truly determined by method.

The psychology of women literature offers strong descriptions of and inductions from women's experience. In Greenspan's (1983) work on feminist therapy, for example, she evaluated her own experience in both traditional and feminist therapy and induced from that a set of generalizations about feminist therapy. Her work was the first substantial articulation of the impact of sociopolitical forces in both the practice of therapy and self-perceptions of women clients.

Gilligan (1982) discussed with young women their experience and perceptions of moral conflicts and choices. Through this information she induced a theory of moral development that not only captured the experience of upper- and professional-class white women in the United States, but conflicted sharply with widely-accepted theories of moral development. Gilligan's work has had a profound impact on mainstream psychology because (1) it demonstrated gender bias in moral development theory and by implication cognitive development theory; (2) it showed that women have different experiences, perceptions, and values than those presented by men; and (3) it served to legitimize and confirm as useful a different methodology—one based upon a phenomenological philosophical base. While Greenspan draws from her own experience and Gilligan more formally on others' perceived experience, both have used methods of knowledge generation that assume that reality is in experience and that inducing generalizations from individual experiences is legitimate. Their methodology has enabled them to accomplish work that refutes traditional theories and provides an alternative view of reality.

Feminist paradigmatic considerations have progressed to the point of critiquing logical positivism and calling for an alternative. This alternative method has usually been phenomenology. Phenomenological epistemology is quite alluring because it has produced important refutations and set new directions, and because it is aligned with women's experience. Nevertheless, like logical positivism, it has weaknesses in its ability to construct and shape reality.

The main weaknesses of the phenomenological method is its potential for bias. The individual's perceptions of her experience and the cognitive schema she uses to organize and communicate those experiences, as well as the self structure from which she operates all may influence the experience. Bias can also be introduced by the one who listens to and then summarizes another's experience. Also, of course, generalizations from one woman's experience to every woman's is problematic. Overgeneralizing from one group's experience to all women without regard to factors which alter experience and perception, e.g., race, class, culture, age, physical status, generation, nationality and sexual preference is another destructive bias potential. Finally, if the data used in the generation of knowledge are experience, how can that knowledge be validated? The phenomenologist would answer, "by experience," but such reasoning is circular. Thus, while phenomenology has great potential for refuting old ideas and setting new directions, its epistemological limits constrain it from being a single adequate method for the generation and validation of knowledge.

Reasoning

A third approach to the generation and validation of knowledge, frequently used within the psychology of women literature, is reasoning. This approach uses consensual rules of logic and applies an adversarial method (Moulton, 1983) of analysis to suppositions, linking arguments, and conclusions. It can be used to refute existing analyses, theories, and interpretations, and to offer alternative explanations.

Hannah Lerman's (1986) critical analysis of psychoanalytic theory is a clear example of the reasoning approach. Similarly Laura Brown's (1987) critique of the literature on eating disorders from a lesbian feminist perspective is an outstanding example of the use of the method. Both authors employ a variety of forms of intellectual analysis, but centrally use the adversary method and rejection by counter example. Lerman reviews psychoanalytic thought regarding women and counters it with the view of contemporary feminist psychology. Brown rejects the suppositions and conclusions within the traditional eating disorders literature through lesbian and feminist counters to the suppositions and contextual arguments against the conclusions. Lerman's analysis is astute and comprehensive providing an essential refutation to psychoanalytic thought in personality theory. Brown offers a cogent and instrumental analysis, rejecting misogynist normative conception in mainstream clinical work. Both arguments can serve as models in the restructuring of mainstream psychological theory in personality and psychopathology.

While Brown and Lerman convincingly refute the adversary (here, traditional conceptualizations), neither is able to fully generate an alternative position. In their work, the method of reasoning reaches its limits: their wise alternative conceptualizations are simply neither as powerful nor convincing as their refutations of others' works. This is not a criticism of these authors, but rather a comment on their methodology. Reasoning cannot generate knowledge as competently as it validates or refutes existing theory. It is by no means incidental that Brown changes from a reasoning to an experiential approach in setting forth new positions for conceptualization and treatment of eating disorders.

Additional weaknesses of the reasoning method exist. It is dependent upon the idea, theory, or data which is used as a basis of argument. That is, if an untrue supposition is used to argue against an existing conclusion, the method falls apart. For example, were Kohlberg and Gilligan to argue about women's mortality, the differing suppositions about women's morality (Gilligan's, relational and responsible; Kohlberg's, application of objective principles) means the argument would be nullified because no consensual agreement exists between them regarding the initial, basic supposition. The method is also vulnerable to the possibility of an incorrect understanding of the positions against which the argument is directed. For example, when Reagan argues against abortion, he quite clearly does not understand women's rights positions. Finally, those using the reasoning method sometimes misdirect their attention to trivial implications stemming from fundamental concepts, rather than considering the concepts themselves. Thus, it is of little consequence to argue against men opening doors for women when the fundamental issue is women's devaluation.

In sum, the use of reasoning as an epistemological position is a powerful tool in the process of validating knowledge, but other methods are better suited for the generation of knowledge.

Appeals to Authority

The fourth epistemological method of knowledge generation and validation used in the psychology of women literature is that of appeals to authority. This method seeks to legitimize new ideas by derivation from or application of old accepted ideas. Such appeals are seen in the work of Chodorow (1978) and Dinnerstein (1977).

Chodorow, in her discussion of gender's causation and the necessities of change, appeals directly to psychoanalytic thought (Freudian, neo-Freudian, object relations, and a small amount of ego psychology). She asserts this construction of reality as true and affirms it by an appeal to authority. Chodorow's work has been enormously popular in contemporary American feminist theory, both within and outside of psychology, perhaps because it offers a nonsuperficial view of the gender development process where little existed before. However, the work does not escape many of the essential problems of psychodynamic theory, as it could not, given the use of appeal to authority as the basis for generating and validating knowledge.

Dinnerstein's work appeals to the authority of Freudian and Gestalt theory and uses the tensions between them as a dialectic to inform her construction of reality, one which centralizes sexual arrangements. Dinnerstein's work, while not as carefully descriptive as Chodorow's, is conceptually more interesting as she builds on tensions between authorities and draws upon nonrational, intuitive or personal methods of knowing (see discussion below). While Dinnerstein's method of dialectic appeal to authority allows her, unlike Chodorow, to escape the first order problems of Freudian and Gestalt constructions of reality, she is still constrained by the underlying assumptions in mainstream personality theory, e.g., the assumptions of the existence of functional, autonomous, internal psychic processes and individualism.

Chodorow and Dinnerstein have created new conceptualizations of phenomena in gender development and sex-role ascription, and, as such have added depth and sophistication to the psychology of women literature. Yet each has depended upon earlier theory and its authoritative status for validation of the knowledge they generated. Hence, while deepening the discussions of these topics, they have not escaped the constraints on reality of the original theory. Both

Chodorow and Dinnerstein have relied upon essentially unexamined phallocentric constructed personality theory. Ironically even while they have contributed to ideas of gender development, they have not uncovered the androcentric bondage within the reality constructs. Were the implication of their work followed in gender development the gender arrangement might be reordered but fundamental androcentric reality (here heterosexual, western, white, professional class) would continue unopposed, in fact perhaps be reinforced.

The adequacy of appeals to authority depends upon the merits of the original theories, whose central assumptions and reality structures are carried forward without examination. The method decreases the possibility of challenging the central assumptions of the original ideas since they assume the cloak of truth by virtue of their use as referent. The appeal to authority is a powerful method of knowledge generation, but it cannot validate the ideas it generates.

Nonrational Knowledge Generation

The last method of knowledge generation and validation is not well represented within the psychology of women's literature. This position is identified concurrently as mystical, essential forms, revealed truth, personal or tacit knowledge, spiritual, intuition, or nonrational. This position holds that reality is fixed and universal in principles and patterns and is quite independent of social and cultural constructions; science, logic, and human developments are irrelevant to universal patterns and principles. The task of knowledge is to become aware of the universal pattern and principles. Mander and Rush's early work, *Feminism As Therapy* (1974) with its implicit position of self-evident truth is one example. A second example is Dinnerstein's *The Mermaid and the Minotaur* (1977) with her short introductory statement, "Its method is to appeal to the reader's own experience: if the result feels in any way enlightening, the argument is validated insofar as it can be" (p. ix). As discussed earlier, Dinnerstein also uses arguments based on authority, but here she is also offering an essential form or personal knowledge, epistemological invitation. Some treatment modalities such as spiritual healing, meditation and body work, appear, to the extent that an epistemological bases can be inferred, to rely on transcendent universal patterns. Fuller, and in the end more convincing, examples of this way of knowing exist outside the boundaries of the psychology of women.

The work of Adrienne Rich (1979), Jane Roberts (1974), Mary Daly (1978), and Starhawk (1982) are compelling examples of the nonrational epistemological positions. All are feminists attempting to answer questions about knowledge generation and validation through the body sense or intuition. Knowledge, they believe, is consciousness of essential forms once the contamination of patriarchal systems is transcended.

Cross cultural work that rests on diverse cosmologies, world-views, and values offer a different expression of nonrational method of knowledge. For example, Reynold's (1976) work on Morita psychotherapy presents a radically different view of human nature and its relationship to the cosmos. Its aims are those of passive achievement of enlightenment—of inner experience, interdependence, and acceptance of harmony with one's environment. This therapy is derived from Zen Buddhism, which has a particular cosmology based upon revealed truths through enlightenment. Jackson (1985) writes of an Africentric way of thinking based upon

> an ontology of spiritual essence, collectivism, interdependence . . . oneness of being and an epistemology of affect, immersion in experience, flexibility, and complementarity of differences, preferred novelty, freedom and personal distinctiveness to a greater degree than did Euro-americans, based upon their belief in object-measure, observation of experience, rigidity, and duality of differences. (p. 234)

Each of these examples—the radical feminist and the culturally diverse—represent a method of knowledge at once challenging and threatening to Western, middle-class, patriarchally-trained minds. Yet each offers a method of knowledge generation and validation demanding disciplined approaches and leading to important constructions and appreciations of reality. This epistemological position uniquely requires use of other-than-intellectual dimensions of human capacities. It offers constructions of reality not available through other epistemological positions — realities that are profoundly important for inspiration, access to nonordinary dimensions, and a comprehensive understanding of life. It also offers potential of constructing personal theory based upon dimensions equally available to diverse peoples. Theory constructions which centralize human capacities are available to and applicable for all humans of all resources, colors, cultures, physical statuses, sexes and lifestyles. The knowledge generated through this epistemological position is profoundly confrontative to dominant power/knowledge hierarchies.

The weakness of this method aside from its devalued status is that it cannot be articulated and assessed. One must connect, find oneself spoken to and accept, or simply ignore. Just as the method requires other-than-intellectual dimensions of human functioning, it obfuscates rational analysis.

THE ALTERNATIVE

An alternative to arguing for a single replacement method of knowing is to use a multiple method based on feminist principles. Because particular methods of knowing shape the reality which is knowable and because each method of knowing has strengths and weaknesses in its validation of knowledge, the use of multiple methods as an epistemologic standard may produce constructed realities that better reflect the phenomenon under investigation.

Sutherland (1973) has suggested such an approach, contending that

> general systems theory can serve as a distinct epistemological alternative to the platforms which currently predominate in the social and behavioral sciences . . . strict empiricism, positivism, and phenomenology at one extreme of the continuum and, toward the other, intuitionalism, subjectivism, and rhetoric-idiographic preferences. (p. 6)

Arguing that reality will be misconstructed by adherence to any single epistemology or method of knowing, general systems theory proposes that the real truth (Reality) is to be found in the connective nexus among the many methods of knowing and their shaping of reality. The nexus of convergence and the multiple epistemological methods, then, is the call of general systems theory. Sutherland's work seems to escape Harding's (1987) recent criticisms of both relativity in method and single use of phenomenology. She argues eloquently about the limits within the phenomenological method which Stanley and Wise (1983) have proposed. She also argues against the relative position that all methods are equal in generating knowledge on a particular question.

It would seem then that feminist principles may be used as an organizing and normative base in confronting the questions of what is legitimate generation and validation of knowledge, and what are its implications for the shaping of reality? That is, the following feminist principles can, when applied to the philosophic, govern the content of what is knowledge, the process and structure of how it is generated, and conclusions about what is real: (1) valuing women's experience, (2) pluralism, (3) equalitarian relationships, and (4) external forces influencing causation. These principles, drawn from consensual aspects of feminist therapy, influenced by the women's movement and the current wave of feminism, can instruct and organize methods of knowing within personality theory in much the same way as Lerman (1986) suggests they be used evaluatively as criteria for judging existing personality theory.

The principle of valuing women's experience is central in feminist theory. It has evolved through various insights and analyses, starting from the notion of the "personal is political" (Gilbert, 1980; Sturdivant, 1980; Lerman, 1974), and expanded through liberal feminist analysis of discriminatory attitudes and actions toward women, socialist feminist analyses of division of labor and economic control, and radical feminist analysis of cultural patriarchal oppression of women (Donovan, 1985). As the analyses were extended further into information bases, the contamination of data about women and views of women in Western society became clear (Ballou & Gabalac, 1985; Weisstein, 1970; Sherif, 1979). The only and perhaps best recourse to valid data then became focusing on women's experience to achieve unbiased reconceptions of women. C-R experiences also helped women see their experiences not as their faults, deviations, or unique difficulties, but as the result of the external forces controlling women. Women's experience then became not only a valued data base, but also a guide to the analysis of social oppression and devaluation of women. Rather than being a measure of women's inferiority and pathology, women's personal experience became an important source of information for seeing the sexism in external forces and for reconceptualizing women's strengths.

In feminist therapy the principle of valuing women's experience has come to mean separating the internal from the external and validating the female experience. Women's experience as felt, lived, and processed is a valid method of knowing. While potential bias is acknowledged and serious attempts must be made to clarify and articulate the experience, there must be a fundamental reliance on women's experience. In a multi-method approach to epistemology and theory building, the feminist principle of reliance on women's experience guides away from eclectic relativism (Harding, 1987) to a position of placing the connective nexus of the multiple knowledges in women's experience. Valid knowledge would be seen as that which is overlapping through many methods and grounded in women's experience. Hence information and concepts, derived from multiple methods, would be judged legitimate as they fit with one another and illuminated women's experience.

Pluralism is a second feminist principle that should guide the positions taken in legitimizing knowledge and its shaping of reality within feminist epistemological approaches. Pluralism is a principle of equally valid differences. In this discussion, it is the recognition that dominant systems (logical positivism and Western, white, middle-class males) have established the goals, rules, and criteria of judgment. Rather than being real, right and true, these systems are value-laden and arbitrary. Thus, the dominant method of knowing results in a shaping of reality that supports and maintains the dominance of those in power. Pluralism, then, with its position of *equally valued differences*, when applied to epistemologies and many methods of knowing, would legitimize all methods of knowing. Logical positivism, phenomenology, reasoning, appeal to authority and intuition, in an epistemology guided by pluralism all would hold equal value in their different methods of knowing. The differential strengths and weaknesses would be seen; yet the different shaping of reality through each method of knowing would be valued. The connective nexus, where they came together or overlapped, as grounded in women's experience would be valid knowledge and substance of the shaped reality. The conflicts would be the starting points for further investigation.

These two principles — women's experience and pluralism, when joined by a third, egalitarianism, outline an exciting paradigm for theory development. Egalitarianism is a particular prescription for power relationships. That is, it requires a sharing of power. Applied to this discussion, it means that the existing hierarchical domination of logical positivism is an unacceptable epistemology. Broverman et al.'s (1970) empirical demonstration of sex-gender bias within mainstream mental health would not have been possible had not other women experienced, perceived, reasoned, intuited and referred to other theories of oppression. Broverman's method spoke in mainstream forms, but was certainly not alone in making sex-gender bias real.

In addition to transforming the attribution of power from selected methods of knowing to all methods of knowing, egalitarianism changes power relations among the levels of knowing. Experience, connecting, description of experience, comprehending theory, creating hypothesis, designing experimentation, analyzing data or theory and deducing or inducing through reason are not in ascending order of value. Each share power, each has value in defining methods of knowing and the right to bargaining in the shaping of reality.

Sharing power among levels and methods legitimizes all ways of generating and validating knowledge. Knowledge then becomes that which is the overlapping results of many methods of knowing grounded in women's experience, in an epistemology directed through feminist principles. Women's experience must include all women's experience not just the group of (white, Western, middle-class, able-bodied, heterosexual) women, who most nearly fit reality construction of traditional theory. Hence the consensual principles of feminist therapy can guide epistemology as feminists struggle to create a paradigm within which feminist theory building can occur. While this discussion has occurred at a philosophical level, clinical practice illustrates its concrete functioning.

Within the therapeutic setting, therapists already use that which is discussed here as formal positions regarding epistemology. The feminist therapist believes the women's descriptions of her own experience while at the same time thinking about the possibility of the clients' perception distortion and need for sex-role analysis and cognitive restructuring. Simultaneously the therapist questions her own ability to hear accurately what the client is saying, given her own values, limited contextual experiences, and particular attributions of meaning. The therapist guides her sense of accuracy in understanding the client through a nonrational process of connection with the client through the changes felt in empathic connection. Then too, in deciding on responses to the client and the conceptualization of the client's difficulties, the therapist considers and uses ideas gained from both mainstream and women's psychology through empirical studies, reasoned analysis, respected authors, and her own experiences. Hence, in therapy the therapist uses and integrates ideas drawn from many methods of knowing while basing her interaction in the client's experience and connection among women. She also mediates her values and conclusions by vigilance in equally valuing differences and in sharing power between herself and her client.

Feminist principles have informed therapy and should be implemented in the generation and validation of knowledge in theory building. If feminist personality theory is to be developed, it must be built within a paradigm which is at once consistent with feminist principles and inclusive of multiple methods of knowing and their consequent shaping of reality. The building of feminist personality theory must occur within a paradigm which both allows nondominant knowing and equalizes the power accorded to all methods. If personality theory which conceptualizes women's experience, diversity, unique strengths, and externally caused damage is to be built, then knowledge, other than logical positivism's epistemology, must be included and equally legitimized. In short, feminist, not sexist paradigms, constructs, and methods of knowing must inform theory construction.

REFERENCES

Ballou, Mary & Gabalac, Nancy (1985). *A feminist position on mental health.* Springfield, Illinois: Charles Thomas.

Belenky, Mary, Clinchy, Blythe, Goldberger, Nancy & Tarule, Jill (1986). *Women's way of knowing.* New York: Basic Books.

Broverman, Ingrid, Broverman, Donald, Clarkson, F., Rosencrantz, P. & Vogel, S. (1970). Sex-role stereotypes and clinical judgement of mental health. *Journal of Consulting and Clinical Psychology, 34,* 1-7.

Brown, Laura (1987). Lesbians, weight, and eating: new analyses and perspectives. In Boston Lesbian Book Collective (Eds.) *Lesbian Psychologies* (pp. 294-310) Urbana: University of Illinois Press.

Chodorow, Nancy (1978). *The reproduction of mothering: psychoanalysis and the sociology of gender.* Berkeley: University of California Press.

Daly, Mary (1978). *Gyn/Ecology: The metaethics of radical feminism.* Boston: Beacon Press.

Dinnerstein, Dorothy (1977). *The Mermaid and the Minotaur.* New York: Harper and Row.

Donovan, Josephine (1985). *Feminist theory.* New York: Ungar Publishing Company.

Gilbert, Lucia (1980). Feminist therapy in Brodsky, Annette and Hare-Mustin, Rachel (Eds.) *Women in Psychotherapy.* (pp. 245-266). New York: Guilford Press.

Gilligan, Carol (1982). *In a different voice: psychological theory and women's development.* Cambridge: Harvard University Press.

Greenspan, Miram (1983). *A new approach to women and therapy.* New York: McGraw-Hill Publishing Company.

Harding, Sandra (Ed.) (1987). *Feminism and methodology.* Bloomington: Indiana University Press.

Harding, Sandra & Hintikka, Merrill (1983). *Discovering reality.* Dordrecht, Holland: Reidel Publishing Company.

Jackson, Gerald (1985). Cross-cultural counseling with Afro-Americans. In Pederson, Paul (Ed.), *Handbook of Cross-cultural Counseling and Therapy.* (pp. 231-238). Westport, Connecticut: Greenwood Press.

Jackson, Gerald (1982). Black psychology: an avenue to the study of Afro-Americans. *Journal of Black Studies, 12,* 241-260.

Kunstel, Ingrid (1979). *An Evaluation of an audio-tape leaderless c-r group-outcome,* Unpublished doctoral dissertation, Kent State University, Kent, Ohio.

Lerman, Hannah (1986). *A mote in Freud's eye.* New York: Springer.

Lerman, Hannah (1974). What happens in feminist therapy? In Cox, Susan (Ed.) *Female psychology and the emerging self.* (pp. 378-384) Chicago: Science Research Associates.

Mander, Anica & Rush, Anne (1974). *Feminism as therapy*. New York: Random House.

Reynolds, David (1976). *Morita psychotherapy*. Berkeley: University of California Press.

Rich, Adrienne (1979). *On lies, secrets and silence*. New York: W.W. Norton.

Roberts, Jane (1974). *The nature of personal reality*. Englewood Cliffs: Prentice-Hall.

Sherif, Carolyn (1979). Bias in Psychology. In Julia Sherman and Evelyn Beck (Eds.), *The prism of sex. Essays in the sociology of knowledge*. (pp. 34-47). Madison: University of Wisconsin Press.

Spretnak, Charlene (1982). *The politics of women's spirituality*, Garden City: Anchor Books.

Stanley, Liz & Wise, Sue (1983). *Breaking out: feminist consciousness and feminist research*. Boston: Rutledge.

Starhawk (1982). Consciousness, Politics, and Magic. In Charlene Spretnak (Ed.) *The Politics of Women's Spirituality*, (pp. 172-184) Garden City: Anchor Books.

Sturdivant, Susan (1980). *Therapy with women, a feminist philosophy of treatment*, New York: Springer.

Sutherland, John (1973). *A general systems philosophy for the social and behavioral sciences*. New York: George Braziller.

Unger, Rhoda (1984). Hidden assumptions in theory and research on women. In Clare Brody (Ed.) *Women therapists working with women*, (pp. 119-134) New York: Springer.

Wallston, Barbara (August 1978). (Presidential Address to Division 35) *What are the questions in psychology of women: a feminist approach to research*. Annual meeting of APA, New York.

Weedon, Chris (1987). *Feminist practice and poststructuralist theory*. New York: Basil Blackwell.

Weisstein, Naomi (1970). Kinde, kuche, kirche as scientific law: psychology constructs the female. In Robin Morgan (Ed.), *Sisterhood is Powerful*. (pp. 205-220). New York: Vintage.

Paths Toward Diversity:
An Intrapsychic Perspective

Susan E. Barrett, PhD

SUMMARY. The life experience of an individual woman has an impact on the ideas she contributes to feminist therapy theory. One critical dimension of her life is her personal journey of identifying as a member of a minority group and learning self-value as a result. The Minority Identify Development Model developed by Sue (1981) and Atkinson, Morton, and Sue (1983) is used here to describe a process of self-valuation. The connection between self-valuing and the development of feminist therapy theory is explored, with emphasis placed on the need for diversity in the development of a feminist theory.

Womanist is to feminist as purple is to lavender
          —Alice Walker (1983, p.xii)

Diversity in feminist therapy theory means incorporating, appreciating, and building on the differences among women. Any feminist theory, to be truly representative of women in the United States, must be based on the experiences of all women. Otherwise, the predominant theory is that of middle class white women. Women of color or other classes are not any better represented by it

Susan E. Barrett is in private practice as a psychologist in Atlanta, GA. She was a co-founder and member of Karuna, a women's counseling collective from 1974 to 1981. Her primary experiences as a member of a minority group stem from being a woman, a lesbian, and a member of a bi-racial family.

Author note: "Thanks to Carol M. Aubin for her contribution to the ideas presented in this paper. Thanks also to Belenky et al. for introducing me to Elbow's work in their workshops and book."

Correspondence may be addressed to the author at: 1904 Monroe Drive NE, Suite 200, Atlanta, GA 30324.

than women in general are represented by theories of therapy developed by men.

Diversity also means being pluralistic. This is opposed to being assimilated or "melting into one pot." The melting pot metaphor is the model of one culture resulting from all others contributing to it. Assimilation is a model in which minority cultures are absorbed into the dominant one. Obviously, both of these ideas destroy the unique aspects of the subgroups involved.

In contrast, pluralism values all people contributing to society. It serves to maintain the uniqueness of each culture, while sharing common elements of a larger one (Atkinson, Morton, & Sue, 1983). Our society, at varying times viewed either as a melting pot or as an assimilated culture, values white, male, middle class, Protestant, heterosexual, able-bodied, etc. as the norm. It is designed to devalue other ways of being. People belonging to any of the devalued categories are oppressed and must learn to value themselves in order to contribute to a true cultural pluralism.

LEARNING TO VALUE ONESELF IN A WORLD WHICH DEVALUES YOU

Learning self-value in a world which devalues you is a tremendous strength that can be gained by individuals who are oppressed. Sometimes valuing can come naturally through support of a family and a community in which one is raised. More often, however, people are raised in an environment which devalues their minority characteristics, or they are valued in one context but not in another. Then they must go through a process of learning to care for themselves with regard to their minority status.

The most recent wave of change for minority groups in this country occurred first with Blacks in the Civil Rights and Black Power movements of the '60s. Other oppressed groups, including women, gay men and lesbians, and other racial minorities have had similar experiences over the last two to three decades. Common themes emerge in the process of overcoming internalized oppression. One model which is useful in understanding these themes is the Minority Identity Development Model developed by Sue (1981) and Atkinson, Morten, and Sue (1983). The model presents the themes in sequence, though the authors acknowledge that the process is not always unidirectional. In reality, the themes provide an understanding of an individual at a particular point in time and may or may not be part of a pattern.

The Minority Identity Development Model has five stages. In Conformity, the first stage, individuals

> are distinguished by their unequivocal preference for dominant cultural values over those of their own culture. . . . Those physical and/or cultural characteristics that single them out as minority persons are a source of pain, and are either viewed with disdain or are repressed from consciousness. (Atkinson et al., 1983, p. 35-36)

Conforming depends upon denial and disparagement to exist. Atkinson et al. (1983) use the terms depreciation and shame. A lesbian in this stage, for instance, is often well closeted, keeping her preferences hidden from all but a few friends. She accepts the belief that her choice of sexual partners has nothing to do with the rest of who she is. She lives in the mainstream as though she were single, for example, leaving her partner on holidays to join her family of origin. She doesn't deal with the pain and anger about the need to keep her lifestyle a secret, or the resignation that this is her only choice. She often believes something is wrong with her wishing she could be heterosexual. She is threatened by and often highly critical of "out" lesbians. Early identification with other homosexuals may be with gay men, or she may identify with a male way of being in the world, disparaging women in the process. It is impossible to be in so much denial about a central part of one's being and still value oneself.

In Dissonance, the second stage, individuals are aware of aspects of their existence shared with other members of their minority group, while still strongly being influenced by the views of the dominant culture. Confusion and conflict over values and beliefs exist, resulting in alternating feelings of shame and pride (Atkinson et al., 1983). Intrapersonally, this may manifest as the coexistence of fear and hope. Now, in the 1980s, with so much positive attention being paid to differences among people in some parts of the country, a person has reason to be excited about learning new and joyful ways of viewing herself. However, as with any major conflict, attempts to change are met with resistance and fear. The known often seems safer than the unknown. At this point, a lesbian, for example, may reach out to other lesbians in a tentative manner. She may want to read books about lesbianism from a feminist perspective, but have difficulty actually going to a bookstore and buying them. She may want to attend lesbian events, but be afraid of being rejected by others she may see as strident in beliefs she is just coming to believe may be possible. Her behaviors are fraught with trepidation. Anxiety alternates with excitement. Dissonance may be a temporary stage or a constant theme in the life of a lesbian. Having the opportunity to pass as straight reinforces the conflict between hiding within the dominant culture and being known as a lesbian.

In Resistance and Immersion, the next stage, an individual "endorses minority-held views and rejects the dominant society and culture. Desire to eliminate oppression of the individual's minority group becomes an important motivation of the individual's behavior" (Atkinson et al., 1983, p. 36). This stage is a separatist one, with people living separatism in differing degrees. Developing a positive identification with a minority group, and thereby learning, creating, and valuing common bonds, is important to the development of a positive sense of self.

At this stage, the very aspects of oneself that have been denied and disparaged are brought to the forefront of awareness to be positively chosen and cherished. Atkinson et al. (1983) state that an individual moves toward pride and honor and away from shame and disgust. Returning to the example of a lesbian, she, at this point, identifies the positive aspects of loving women, seeing her preference in more than sexual terms. She broadens her view of herself, while she explores the valuable personal consequences of being a lesbian. She often immerses herself in lesbian culture through reading, socializing, and listening to music, for example.

Intrapsychically, the positive part of this stage is the turning inward and toward like others, either emotionally, behaviorally, or both. As part of turning inward, an individual also must turn away from the dominant culture. The dominant culture has devalued the very part of herself she is now learning to value and she cannot choose both beliefs. Separation from the dominant culture ranges from disavowing only the negative beliefs about a particular minority group to being critical of and separate from many aspects of the dominant group.

The value of the Resistance and Immersion theme in self-valuation cannot be overstated. Countering the internalized oppression of the larger society is not only an extremely difficult process, but one that is almost impossible to do alone. Separate time, space, and energy with members of a like group allows an individual to see herself reflected clearly and positively. Books, films, music, language, and art focusing on the positive aspects of the minority status are often helpful. The personal strength derived from valuing oneself is essential in connecting with those who are different.

Each individual and group of people comes to terms with the form of oppression she or they feel most intensely. Individuals who are part of more than one minority group will sometimes shift focus from one group to another (Espin, 1987). Throughout this process, a sifting and winnowing of ideas and beliefs occurs.

The difficulty of not having a clear minority group with whom to identify is very evident to bi-racial individuals and to children adopted by parents of a different culture or race. They belong to both groups, not fitting fully in either place. The same process of self-valuation must occur, but separation may not be achievable or advisable as it necessitates a devaluing of another aspect of self (Root, 1988). Bisexual women, another example of people who claim two cultures, often experience being outsiders in both the dominant, heterosexual world and the minority lesbian community. Some women have begun to develop bisexual communities for support (Shuster, 1987).

During Introspection, the fourth stage, an individual feels the constraints of minority identification. Not all aspects of herself can be met by focusing on the minority group alone and personal autonomy becomes more important than in the Resistance and Immersion stage (Atkinson et al., 1983). Intrapsychically, people feel confined, wanting to resist being part of a mold. A lesbian may, for example, choose to develop her professional life even though it is not related to her lesbianism. She may expand her contacts with straight friends or be involved in activities that focus on her interests, needs, and desires that are not met within the lesbian community. As with the other themes, this one may be ongoing in the life of a lesbian as she attends both to her minority status and aspects of herself, such as her particular talents, that are not part of being a minority.

Finally, Synergetic Articulation and Awareness is the time when an individual experiences a sense of self-fulfillment with regard to cultural identity. "Desire to eliminate *all* forms of oppression becomes an important motivation of the individual's behavior" (Atkinson et al., 1983, p. 38). Certainly, this is a time when a sharp awareness of the connection between various forms of oppression, and therefore, the critical need for change at all levels exists. An individual at this point brings with her all the positive values and beliefs from earlier experiences as well as her own individual being and is able to use her full self in the world.

Internally, the individual feels whole. Weaving together all the threads of her being she creates a fabric that is both unique to her and shared with other people. Individuals often report being at peace with themselves with little worry about what others think. Continuing the example of a lesbian, her preference for women is moved from foreground to part of the fabric of her life. It just *is*. Her friends and often her family know she is a lesbian. She creates a space for herself, surrounding herself with people who value her, while maintaining a clear awareness of how the larger culture can still be dangerous. She feels ties with members of other minority groups while being respectful of the differences between them.

Once a sense of integration is reached, time alone with other minority group members may be essential to a person's health — a time to rejuvenate. Each minority needs the respite that comes from being out from the view of the dominant, often hostile, culture. These times offer people a place where they can assume some common base of understanding while leaving certain things unsaid.

Many women, whether Black, Latina, Native American, Asian American, or white, and lesbian, heterosexual, or bisexual are at the same evolutionary step of wanting to extend their lives beyond their particular minority group(s) while maintaining the ties and strength they get from their minority identification. Other women, either new to the process of valuing themselves or choosing to live within the framework of their minority group, may find their way eased by those who have followed similar paths over the years. However, each woman must travel on her own journey and will need separate space and time for her travels.

THE DANGER OF SEPARATION FOR DIVERSITY

Separation, when practiced by members of the dominant culture, is totally different from when it is practiced by members of a minority culture. Due to differences in power, value, and visibility between dominant and minority cultures, separation by members of the dominant culture has inherent dangers and is, in fact, a basis for oppression.

Certainly, for specific periods of time and for given reasons it can be helpful for dominant group individuals to focus on their special situation. Examples of this include white women working on their own racism and men meeting to discuss the impact on them of living in a sexist society. However, in these situations, separate space is not needed to focus on feeling devalued specifically because one is a member of the dominant group. Rather, it is necessary for exploring one's own dominant group membership in order to change one's own collusion with oppression.

Aside from such particular situations, dominant groups meeting alone become exclusionary. The clearest example of this within feminism is all-white groups. White feminists organize around specific issues, as defined by our particular perspective, often oblivious to the impact on women of color (Yamada, 1981; Davenport, 1981; Lorde, 1981). Members of such all-dominant groups are often unaware/uninvolved in either building organizations across racial groups or in widening the base of connections with members of minority groups. The power and privilege that come with being part of the dominant culture so pervades our awareness that we unthinkingly act as though our experience is shared by all. Living within a dominant culture only, it is very easy to avoid seeing or knowing other groups.

Conversely, minority group members rarely lose their knowledge of the two different cultures in which they live (Boyd, 1988). Even while being turned toward their particular minority group, they cannot ignore the dominant culture. To varying degrees, they live in it daily (Moraga & Anzaldua, 1981).

Separatism, although critical for minority group members, can also be dangerous. Separation can become an end in itself. Rather than being used as a time to value and sustain oneself for a *"lifetime of struggle and change"* (Bunch, 1987, p. 63), separatism can become a way of being, without further meaning. It can become a place of stagnation rather than growth.

PERSONAL JOURNEYS AND POLITICAL THEORIES

Understanding the connection between separation and diversity on a personal level is critical to understanding the development of diversity in feminist theory building. People develop theories. Women at varying points in their personal and professional journeys are thinking and writing about their experiences. Therefore, "the knower is an intimate part of the known" (Belenky, Clinchy, Goldberger, & Tarule, 1986, p. 137).

Women in different stages in the process of self-evaluation contribute to theory building from that particular perspective. A woman immersed in the Conformity theme of Sue's model (1981) will filter information through a lens that accepts the dominant culture's view of minorities. A woman in Resistance and Immersion would likely wax eloquently about the psychological status of women in the particular group(s) with which she identifies. She may not make connections with the experiences of women from other minority groups. A woman in Synergistic Articulation and Awareness is most likely to truly understand that she writes from her own perspective and that, at this point in time, that is all she can do.

Theory building is like observing a construction site with a tall wooden fence around it. The peepholes in the fence are at different heights and directions. Construction in this case is the psychology of women and feminist therapy. The women looking through the holes vary in what they see as foreground, depending on their own life experience and for what they are looking. None of us, as yet, has the full picture.

Since who we are affects our conceptualizing, it is important to identify ourselves in context as we contribute to feminist theory. It is equally important, as we read or listen to theory by others, to attempt to identify the context of the theorist. In so doing, we can look for the unique piece of the total theory which each woman has to offer.

THE CHALLENGE AHEAD:
FEMINIST THERAPY THEORY BASED ON PLURALISM

The development of feminist therapy theory is the bottom line around which we join forces. We want to develop an inclusive theory which begins by identifying the context within which questions are asked. We then must ask the questions and do our best to provide answers. It is essential we do this in a pluralistic manner, i.e., having many forms of conceptual frameworks, definitions, areas of interest, experiences, and ways of addressing problems with all groups of women equally valued.

When I think what might be possible, I am reminded of Charlotte Bunch's comment on coalitions. Bunch says that "Coalitions are possible, but they are only effective when you have mutual respect; when you have a clearly articulated bottom line; and when you have your own group mobilized for action" (Bunch, 1987, p. 74). Though we are talking about theory building and not a coalition, her points hold true.

Often, women who have several aspects of the dominant group as part of their identity, e.g., white, middle class, and heterosexual, lose sight of the fact that race, economic status and sexual preference, for example, are extremely relevant to how we view ourselves. Too frequently the voice of white women, both heterosexual and lesbian, is the dominant one presented. Women of differing racial and cultural backgrounds may have less access to more mainstream press (Brown, 1988) and white women do not necessarily go searching for literature/information from women of color (Moraga & Anzaldua, 1981).

As feminist therapists, we absolutely must facilitate the flow of information from theorists who look at the experience of minority women as well as those who focus on women of the majority. We also have the difficult task of incorporating information from women who are conforming to the dominant culture, women who are separatists, and women who integrate their internal sense of their minority status with other groups.

As bits and pieces of a theory of feminist therapy emerge, we need to approach them both believing and doubting, probably in that order. In the "believing game" (Elbow, 1973), the idea is to search for what is believable in the ideas, connecting as much as possible with them. Especially when the ideas come from a woman with a different life experience than ours, we need to look toward our environment to verify the truth of what she is proposing. This will allow for our own experience to be widened. Then, we need to apply our capacity to doubt, to think critically about the ideas. This is the process of critical thinking and is based on separating from the ideas as much as possible (Belenky et al., 1986). This "doubting game" (Elbow, 1973) looks for the flaws and imperfections in the theory, including its limitations beyond a small group of women.

Too often, we doubt before we believe and thereby lose something of importance. Women well trained in traditional academic settings where doubting and critical thinking are the modus operandi are often especially vulnerable to skipping the believing portion of theory development. To not believe others, we risk losing essential information. The only possible outcome of this is an inadequate theory. To not critically evaluate them, we risk perpetuating sexist, racist, etc. beliefs and accepting poorly considered or superficial ideas.

Minority women spend part of their theory building time countering the racism, etc. of white, heterosexual theories and part of their time developing ideas related to their particular group. Both functions are critical. Dominant group women need to be able to hear the important information contained in both styles and not minimize or generalize. Just as some men hear any statement of feminism as being anti-male rather than pro-female, some women hear any description of how life looks from the inside to a minority woman as being anti-white and so on.

Slowly, we are building toward a theory of feminist therapy that can be culturally pluralistic. We will have to search for a common language that reflects our diversity. For example, Alice Walker uses *womanist* as a term for a Black feminist. We will need to widen the very frameworks we use, so that we also include the experience of women whose cultural backgrounds involve the family, instead of the individual, as the basic social unit. We have to assume that *feminist* comes attached to other descriptive words, like black and white, as well as lesbian and heterosexual. It is essential for us to trust and value the women who, out of their own experience, bring ideas that will be different from ours.

In creating feminist therapy theory, we are individuals from a wide variety of backgrounds involved in a collective process. Each of us has something to add from our own particular perspective. Our personal journeys of self-valuing influence who we are as individuals. This in turn influences how we create theory. The theory we are working toward cannot be less than representative of all women. All of us together must be held responsible for the overall inclusiveness of that which we develop. Together, we will explore purple, lavender, and all other colors as well.

REFERENCES

Atkinson, Donald, Morten, George, & Sue, Derald Wing (1983). *Counseling American minorities*. Dubuque, IA: Wm. C. Brown Company.

Belenky, Mary, Clinchy, Blythe, Goldberger, Nancy, & Tarule, Jill (1986). *Women's ways of knowing*. New York: Basic Books, Inc.

Boyd, Julia A. (1988, May). *Ethnic and cultural diversity—keys to power*. Paper presented at the Advanced Feminist Therapy Institute, Seattle, WA.

Brown, Laura (1988, May). *The meaning of a multicultural perspective for theory-building in feminist therapy*. Paper presented at the Advanced Feminist Therapy Institute, Seattle, WA.

Bunch, Charlotte (1987). *Passionate politics*. New York: St. Martin's Press.

Davenport, Doris (1981). The pathology of racism: a conversation with Third World wimmin. In Cherrie Moraga and Gloria Anzaldua (Eds.), *This bridge called my back: Writings by radical women of color* (pp. 85-90). Watertown, MA: Persephone Press.

Elbow, Peter (1973). *Writing without teachers*. London: Oxford University Press.

Espin, Oliva (1987). Issues of identity in the psychology of Latina lesbians. In Boston Lesbian Psychologies Collective, (Eds.), *Lesbian psychologies* (pp. 35-55). Chicago: University of Illinois Press.

Lorde, Audre (1981). An open letter to Mary Daly. In Cherrie Moraga and Gloria

Anzaldua (Eds.), *This bridge called my back: Writings by radical women of color* (p. 94-97). Watertown, MA: Persephone Press.

Moraga, Cherrie & Anzaldua, Gloria (Eds.) (1981). *This bridge called my back: Writings by radical women of color*. Watertown, MA: Persephone Press.

Root, Maria P. P. (1988, May). *Resolving "other" status: The process of identity development in biracial individuals*. Paper presented at the Advanced Feminist Therapy Institute, Seattle, WA.

Shuster, Rebecca (1987). Sexuality as a continuum: the bisexual identity. In The Boston Lesbian Psychologies Collective (Eds.) *Lesbian psychologies* (pp. 56-71). Chicago: University of Illinois Press.

Sue, Derald Wing (1981). *Counseling the culturally different*. New York: John Wiley and Sons.

Walker, Alice (1983). *In search of our mothers' gardens*. New York: Harcourt Brace Jovanovich.

Yamada, Mitsuye (1981). Asian Pacific American women and feminism. In Cherrie Moraga and Gloria Anzaldua (Eds.), *This bridge called my back: Writings by radical women of color* (pp. 71-75). Watertown, MA: Persephone Press.

On Creating a Theory of Feminist Therapy

Marcia Hill, PhD

SUMMARY. Feminism implies, and comes out of, a phenomenological philosophy. This means that we know what is true not by the "givens" of society, but by listening to our inner experience and that of others. The fundamental political act is the same as the fundamental therapeutic act: it is the process of joining another person's experience in a way which enables that person to make explicit her internal knowledge of what is real. The therapeutic stance, which implies a belief in the basic rightness of a person's way of being in the world, is what makes this kind of experiential knowing possible.

To carry our thinking and practice of feminist therapy forward in an authentic way, we must approach ourselves and one another from a therapeutic stance. From this we can begin to formulate a reality which encompasses the experience of those who have thus far been invisible and silenced. This article uses the problem of boundary violations as an example of a current issue in feminist therapy that can be explored from an experiential perspective. The questions that come out of this perspective can inform our creation of a therapy and society that is truly pluralistic.

How do we create a theory of feminist therapy that is authentic when we live in a world that is largely antagonistic to female reality? In this article, I will explore what we know about the process of transformation (i.e., change at the level of the meaning and basic experience of an issue) as it occurs in therapy, and use this knowledge to describe a method of developing a theory of feminist ther-

Marcia Hill is a feminist therapist in private practice. Her ancestry is partially unknown (her maternal grandmother was adopted). Otherwise, .she is of fourth generation Irish Catholic and German background, as well as the descendant of English people who came to this country in the 1600s.

Correspondence may be addressed to the author at: 25 Court Street, Montpelier, VT 05602.

apy. Boundary violations (i.e., ethical violations which involve stepping outside of the therapeutic relationship on the part of the therapist) are an example of a current theoretical issue that can be approached in this way. I am choosing boundary violations to serve as an example because this problem, in spite of the careful thought it has received, remains very difficult to solve (Brown, 1989). Its tenacity as a serious concern suggests to me that our ways of understanding and approaching the issue have thus far been inadequate.

Since we cannot create that which we cannot imagine, the first step in creating theory is the process of knowing and describing a feminist reality. This means that the essential act of change must somehow come out of what has until that point been unarticulated because, like air, it has been invisible, pervasive, and taken for granted. To speak of the unspeakable is no easy task. As Audre Lorde (1984) describes it:

> The possible shapes of what has not been before exist only in that back place, where we keep those unnamed, untamed longings for something different and beyond what is now called possible, and to which our understanding can only build roads. But we have been taught to deny those fruitful areas of ourselves. (p. 101)

Feminist thought tells us that most of what we take for granted — our language, our vision of morality, our sexuality, our spiritual practices, our communities, our ways of learning, and our concepts of work and play — are all based in fundamental ways on the experiences of white men (Daly, 1978; Belenky, Clinchy, Goldberger, & Tarule, 1986). We have barely begun to articulate how profoundly the world, as defined in this way, fails to reflect the spirits of the rest of us.

THE PROCESS OF TRANSFORMATION: POLITICAL

Consider the process of change as it has unfolded in the recent period of feminism. Some of the first steps of this era have been based on believing women when they said that they had been battered, raped, or sexually abused. Because feminists assumed that these reports were true, we began to question what this meant about the nature of what we had thought was reality. We began to know certain things about the world that had previously been unknowable, unsayable, and invisible. We began to look more deeply within ourselves as a way to discover what is true. The personal became political.

We are still only beginning to hear what women have to say, not just about our factual experiences, but also about our internal, vaguely sensed knowing of what is real. This process is not easy. Paradoxically, we cannot know what is true until it is possible to say it, nor say the truth until it is possible to know it. But we hear murmurings of other visions of reality: that perhaps there is no such thing as scientific objectivity (Ballou, 1988; Levinson, 1988); that perhaps the capacity for relationship is at least as important as the capacity for individuation (Bradshaw, 1988; Miller, 1976); that it may be possible to live and work together in a way that makes dominance and hierarchy irrelevant.

Thus, when we look at political change, we see that transformation does not come simply from doing something about rape or battering or any of the multitude of "women's issues," important as that action is. Nor does it spring only from including women and people of color more actively in a world that is informed primarily by the experiences of white men. Political transformation comes from challenging and reconceptualizing the very foundations of patriarchal thought. We must appreciate what a profoundly radical thing it is to fully explicate the inner knowing of those whose reality does not come out of the existing Weltanschauung.

THE PROCESS OF TRANSFORMATION: THERAPEUTIC

Consider the way that change works as it occurs in the process of therapy. As I see it, there are three main elements in therapeutic change. Initially, we approach the client from a therapeutic stance; secondly, we use a process that assists the client in making explicit the meaning inherent in her experience; and finally, there are ways in which that new meaning is carried forward in the person's life. I will describe the first two of these more completely, since these elements are especially applicable to the creation of a theory of feminist therapy as well as to the actual process of therapy. What I am calling the therapeutic stance is a set of assumptions familiar to us as feminist therapists: a belief in the basic rightness of the client's way of being in the world, i.e., an understanding that people choose the best level of adaptation available to them (Wycoff, 1980); the knowledge that health means the increased becoming of who one is most deeply (Miller, 1976). This is in striking contrast to a traditional model that emphasizes the "pathology" of the client's way of being. The therapeutic stance is a reframing of the meaning of the client's "symptoms." It describes the client as a success rather than a failure. It enables both the client and the therapist to look at the client's way of being in the world and to say, "Well, no *wonder!*" Only in an atmosphere of appreciation for the client and her efforts at solution can we expect to see the unfolding of the inner knowing that is the basis for any significant change. Only through an experiential knowing that she is *right*, given the context of her situation and resources, can a client regain the power that has been stolen from her by a society that defines her as wrong in so many subtle ways.

However, therapeutic change requires more than hearing the other from the vantage point of the therapeutic stance; we must enter the experiential world of the other. By this I mean that the essential therapeutic act (as well as the essential political act) is the process of joining another person's experience in a way that enables that person (in the case of therapy, this means the client) to make overt her pretheoretical, unclear knowing of what is real. A number of theorists, most notably Eugene Gendlin (1978), have described this aspect of therapy. Essentially it is a way of carrying the client-centered approach a step further, by helping clients to transform implicit meaning into explicit knowing. From a feminist perspective, this kind of approach is critically important if one is to avoid the danger often inherent in traditional therapies of distorting the client's truth by viewing it through the lens of the therapist's reality or the prevailing definition of reality. If we wish to assist our clients in experiencing a reality which is truly theirs and not externally imposed, we must be guided by an ethic of respect. This implies that we make room for meaning to be created out of the living experience of the person before us. We do not make assumptions about what that meaning should or might be. In the most general sense, this means that we do not assume that the person of Japanese heritage will have the same experience of family, for example, as the individual with an Eastern European ancestry, or that the complexities of the issue of dependency will be the same for a client regardless of gender. But more specifically, this means that we are wary of easy understanding. It may be more important for the client to be able to articulate her experience in a specific and finely nuanced way than to have her particular sorrow or joy shared by the therapist. Understanding can sometimes be a way to comfort the therapist and silence the client when an articulation of differences is too uncomfortable.

APPLICATION TO THEORY

In both therapy and politics, transformation means finding a way to give voice to the unheard, to embody the invisible. Until we make possible the internally generated creation of meaning, we cannot even guess what shape the world would take in the hands of a woman. We cannot even imagine the language of meaning as it would be spoken by a person of color in a white-dominated culture. The possibilities are, as yet, unthinkable. Yet an ethic of respect means that we make the unthinkable an honored guest. The process that I have described as intrinsic to both political and therapeutic change can also be used in the creation of a theory of feminist therapy. However, the honoring of the unthinkable that we bring — at our best — to our work with our clients is less easily maintained when we turn to face one another. Feminist thought also tells us that the process we use to create change becomes the change we create. If we hope to change the traditional therapeutic matrix of authority to one of respect, then we must do so respectfully. I would like to elaborate on this using the example of handling ethical violations; in particular, boundary violations when committed by feminist therapists. The therapeutic relationship is one in which the therapist, as caregiver in an emotionally charged and intimate exchange, has inherently greater power than the client (Rawlings & Carter, 1977). As a result, the therapist is responsible for maintaining a clearly defined role, or boundaries, with the client. Failure to maintain this clarity of boundaries is a replication of the incest paradigm. In this situation the person in power (parent or therapist) uses the trust, dependence, and idealization felt by the person with less power (child or client) to reverse the caretaking role in some way. With such a significant power difference, the client is not able to give freely; the therapist who allows the client to caretake her in this way can be thought of as taking something from the client without any meaningful consent on the client's part.

Responding to ethical violations, especially boundary violations, is difficult at best. It easily elicits an authoritarian mode: we want to lay down the law, to judge the offender. As feminists, we find ourselves confused and distressed by boundary violations. Are not such problems a matter of abuse of power? Yet with all our information about power dynamics, we still find ourselves seeing such ethical violations in our colleagues who are feminists: knowledge has not solved this problem. How can we use respect as a foundation for our responses to problems of ethics? What might the problem tell us if we listen to it in a therapeutic way? We must start with assuming a therapeutic stance toward the issue of boundary violations. Let me make an attempt to speak to this issue from such a stance.

Example: Boundary Violations
from a Therapeutic Stance

Boundary violation is the result of wanting something reciprocal, of asking the client to be or give us something of themselves that is not part of the implicit or explicit therapy contract. Sex is the most obvious type of violation, of course, but so is wanting friendship, or affirmation as a good therapist, or any kind of caretaking from the client. Feminist therapists are particularly at risk in this area because we choose for philosophical and political reasons to be *people* (with human vulnerabilities, pain, and needs) as well as therapists with our clients (Kaschak, 1981). It is hard to let our human selves be present, and to be in contact with that aspect of self, and yet refuse to allow the other person to take care of it. Perhaps we find it easier, at times, to avoid the risk of wanting our clients to give to us by denying to ourselves or to them that we do have needs or unhappiness, as traditional therapists often do.

We are also at risk because as a group it is probably a fair generalization to say that we are too good at giving and not good enough at taking. Those of us who are really talented have probably been honing those skills since we were two years old, caretakers in our families of origin as well as in our work as adults. We have learned to get satisfaction from the contact and the power of the helping role. And though we may be conscious of, and relatively adept at, "taking care of ourselves," we are often in some subtle way living our scripts as the caretaker, the competent one, the giving mother, the problem-solver: all roles that emphasize giving to everyone but taking little. So we often live in a world of low-level emotional deprivation. Therapy is lonely work. It is also very intimate, and because we get so much intimacy, we may overlook that the intimacy is one way and that one way relationships are fundamentally lonely, especially for the giver. Even if we do well at letting colleagues and friends and lovers nurture us, it takes a lot of nurturing to balance the intense emotional giving of a week's worth of 25 to 30 people in pain, week after week.

It is easy, in our identification with our clients, to be envious of them — envious of the fine nurturing they are getting (from us!). We empathize with their hurt, which means we draw on our knowledge and memory of our own hurts to some extent. With that hurt awakened in both us and our clients, it is the client's needs and longings that get spoken to with the quality of our presence and responsiveness. Our own needs and echoed hurt are put aside. Yet we ask ourselves to caretake in a way that's fully empathic, knowing that we must not wish for caretaking in return. Another risk factor has to do with the nature of therapy. It is our job — and most of us do this part quite well — to see and value the client: both who she is now and her possibilities. It is our job to "prize," as Rogers (1961) puts it: to love the client, her triumphs, the miraculous forward movement of her spirit, the unique beauty of who she is. No wonder we find it easy to imagine what a fine friend our client would make, to notice how much we have in common with her (we often see others as more similar to us when we know them more fully). It is difficult and wearing work to love without expectation of return except for the joy of giving and the satisfaction of watching the person move forward. What parent does it, really? Even the best of parents hope for gratitude, for children who are a credit to them, and often more. Conversely, because we are more accessible as people than traditional therapists, the client is in a position to see for herself what she does in fact have in common with us, what elements of personality she enjoys or responds to separate from the fact of our relationship with her. Only, of course, it is never entirely separate: the client's natural liking is magnified by her good feelings about being well cared for. We all have known clients who liked us in a way that was clearly linked to the one-way nature of the relationship — sometimes so obviously that she might imagine similarities about us that we knew to be untrue. But we also have all known clients with whom we had a clear, and clearly mutual, appreciation, friendliness, pleasure in one another's company, in addition to whatever might be going on in terms of transference. These are the people who could have been friends or even lovers if we had come to know them in a different context. By choosing to be clear about boundaries in these relationships in particular, we experience a loss: the loss of a potential. Few of us would describe ourselves as so rich in personal relationships that we would not be glad for one more, so the loss of potential is a real one.

Here we are, mere human beings, in intimate relationships with people we genuinely like. Our job is to stay at this wonderful banquet of relationships and yet to taste none of it, no matter how hungry we may be. It is not so surprising that boundary violations happen, given the nature of therapists and the nature of therapy, particularly feminist therapy. It is more a tribute to the profession's integrity that such violations do not happen more often, that for most of us they are limited to the "venial sins" of unnecessary self-disclosure, or irritation when a client has a relapse, or vaguely thinking that a friendship with a client would be nice. This is not to say that such things do not count or should be dismissed. On the contrary, the ability to be respectful about boundaries in a consistent way is absolutely essential to doing good therapy as well as to avoiding doing harm. But, as we appreciate how our client's symptoms come out of who they are and the context of their lives and their efforts to get what they need, we might also appreciate that the same is true for us. As we well know from our work, only in an environment of acceptance—which is *not* the same as approval—can a person freely examine her behavior, her motives, and their repercussions. When it comes to the complex issues surrounding the ethics of boundaries in therapy, it is not enough to work to get more nurturing in our lives, important as that is. We also need to develop a therapeutic attitude toward ourselves and our colleagues: an attitude that understands what we are up against and values our efforts in a difficult situation, while still holding us in a loving challenge to be the best that we can for ourselves and the people whose lives we touch.

Example: From Experience to Ideas

This is what boundary violations might look like from the viewpoint of the therapeutic stance. *Like all symptoms, boundary violations are an effort at solution.* The problem being solved varies somewhat from therapist to therapist, but probably has the central element of desire for caretaking in a context of a heightened need and an easily available caregiver. How can we use this experience to make available a deeper level of knowing, a knowing about the issues, meanings, assumptions that underlie the particular "symptom" of boundary violations? Let yourself sense the unarticulated hurts that lie underneath this picture. What questions or new ways of seeing emerge? For me, there are several thoughts.

I consider the need for response that the therapist puts aside and wonder what, if anything, is legitimate for the therapist to expect in return from the client (besides payment!)? Therapy is not just a service, it is a relationship. What is the client's responsibility in this relationship? While expecting caretaking is inappropriate, expecting respect and a responsive acknowledgement of oneself as the partner in a very human enterprise strikes me as not only appropriate, but necessary, at least as a goal for therapy. In fact, it seems that we may be in danger of doing the client a disservice if we allow that relationship to proceed in a way that fails to appreciate the humanity of the therapist. After all, the therapist and the therapeutic relationship are models for the client as well as catalysts for change.

Another thought is that perhaps there is something inherently wrong with the model of professional healer, especially when it comes to emotional healing. It certainly does seem that there is a cost to the power that the therapist carries, as, I suppose, with any power. In part this is the argument of the radical therapists (Agel, 1971), who point out that a relationship of unequal power cannot be used to heal distress that arises out of the abuse of power. But there are other flaws in the model as well. The use of a professional healer could easily dilute the individual's sense of responsibility for, and power to accomplish, her healing process. What kind of a society is it in which average people are so lacking in skills to assist themselves and one another in the ordinary business of emotional healing and growth? Does our willingness to assume the role of professional healer only enable an emotionally impoverished society to ignore its deficiency?

The other issue that emerges for me comes from noticing that feminist therapy has meant a change in accepted boundaries for what we see as appropriate for the therapist to give (a change toward more personal presence). We have responded to this by noting that feminists have a particular responsibility for clarity about separation from clients. Is there anything else that is implied by these shifts in the handling of boundary issues?

THE CREATION OF THEORY

This is an example of the inception of an experiential process: the use of an ethic of respect as a way to begin to make visible the meanings inherent in experience. The issues outlined above are the first that happen to emerge for me; another person might move in other directions. They are statements of beginnings; much more exploration would be needed to make their possibilities clear. But this serves as an example of how an experiential process can be used to create a meaningful theory and practice of feminist therapy. It is the same experiential process that can be used to create meaning and change with our clients, and the same process that can be used to make possible the profound political change that would accompany the articulation of a truly alternative reality.

We cannot create a theory of feminist therapy by simply adapting or changing the ideas that have come out of a white-dominated patriarchal model. We also cannot create feminist therapy theory solely by using the methods that are part of the dominant culture. As Audre Lorde (1984) reminds us, *"For the master's tools will never dismantle the master's house.* They may allow us temporarily to beat him at his own game, but they will never enable us to bring about genuine change" (p. 112). Genuine change, whether in politics or therapy or theory, will only emerge from that which we know intuitively, bodily, experientially, before and beneath the knowledge that we have been fed by white patriarchal culture. This knowing will emerge more easily if we can develop a process to assist its articulation. We already have such a process. We know it from political change, but we know it even more fully as the process we use to create transformation in therapy. In this process, we enter into the experience of the self or the other in a way that enables the expression of a new knowing that is deeper and perhaps more true than that which had already been known.

To create feminist therapy theory, we can use such a process to examine issues or problems with a respectful vision, which is what Marilyn Frye (1983) calls "the loving eye." She describes this in part as follows:

> The loving eye knows the independence of the other . . . It is the eye of one who knows that to know the seen, one must consult something other than one's own will and interests and fears and imagination . . . The loving eye seems generous to its object, though it means neither to give nor to take, for not-being-invaded, not-being-coerced, not-being-annexed must be felt in a world such as ours as a great gift. (pp. 75-76)

From this standpoint, we can begin to tell one another the questions and concepts and possibilities that are the authentic expressions of our reality. This means that we must recognize that theory cannot be based on unidimensional constructs: the vision of one group of people may not match that of another. It is crucial that we recognize and honor the visions of many kinds of people if we ever hope to shape a theory of therapy that is multidimensional and responsive to us all.

CONCLUSION

Feminism implies, and was born of, a phenomenological philosophy (Boukydis, 1981). We know what is real by trusting our own experience and that of others; we know what is true because of a bodily response that says, "yes!" To create a society that is pluralistic, we must hear and appreciate the reality of those whose experience has thus far been silenced and invisible. Further, we must live a response to that reality which embodies the very thing that we are hoping to create. We will create change only by living in a way that is already changed.

This means that our "therapeutic stance" — which for most of us represents our most respectful possibilities — cannot be reserved only for our clients. The process of change that works for our clients in therapy is the best tool we have for creating a theory of feminist therapy that is truly revolutionary. This suggests that we need to approach one another with the same therapeutic stance that we use with clients. It also suggests that we must work to help one another articulate the meaning that is implicit in our experience of healing and of pain. We can, and should, expect the best from ourselves and one another in the dangerous work that is psychotherapy. But we can do so in a context that honors *all* of who we are. When we honor our clients, they transform themselves. If we respond to ourselves and one another out of an ethic of respect, we can expect to see transformation. Who knows the shape of the world we will create?

REFERENCES

Agel, Jerome (Ed.) (1971). *The radical therapist*. New York: Ballantine Books.
Ballou, Mary (1988, May). *Approaching a feminist principled paradigm in the construction of personality theory*. Paper presented at the Seventh Advanced Feminist Therapy Institute, Seattle, WA.
Belenky, Mary Field, Clinchy, Blythe McVicker, Goldberger, Nancy Rule & Tarule, Jill Mattuck (1986). *Women's ways of knowing*. New York: Basic Books.
Boukydis, Kathleen McGuire (1981, March). *Existential/ Phenomenology as a philosophical base for a feminist psychology*. Paper presented at the Association for Women in Psychology conference, Boston, MA.
Bradshaw, Carla (1988, May). *A Japanese view of dependency: What it can con-*

tribute to feminist theory and therapy. Paper presented at the Seventh Advanced Feminist Therapy Institute, Seattle, WA.

Brown, Laura (1989). From perplexity to complexity: thinking about ethics in the lesbian therapy community. *Women & Therapy, 8*, 13-26.

Daly, Mary (1978). *Gyn/Ecology*. Boston: Beacon Press.

Frye, Marilyn (1983). *The politics of reality: Essays in feminist theory*. Trumansburg, NY: The Crossing Press.

Gendlin, Eugene (1978). *Focusing*. New York: Bantam Books.

Kaschak, Ellyn (1981). Feminist psychotherapy: The first decade. In Sue Cox (Ed.) *Female Psychology* (pp. 387-401). New York: St. Martin's Press.

Levinson, Rascha (1988, May). *The seamless web: A feminist world-view for the future*. Paper presented at the Seventh Advanced Feminist Therapy Institute, Seattle, WA.

Lorde, Audre (1984). *Sister outsider*. Trumansburg, NY: The Crossing Press.

MacKinnon, Catherine (1987). *Feminism unmodified*. Cambridge, MA: Harvard University Press.

Miller, Jean Baker (1976). *Toward a new psychology of women*. Boston: Beacon Press.

Rawlings, Edna I. & Carter, Dianne K. (Eds.) (1977). *Psychotherapy for women*. Springfield, IL: Charles C Thomas.

Rogers, Carl (1967). The interpersonal relationship: The core of guidance. In Carl R. Rogers & Barry Stevens, *Person to person* (pp. 85-101). New York: Pocket Books.

Wycoff, Hogie (1980). *Solving problems together*. New York: Grove Press.

A Japanese View of Dependency: What Can Amae Psychology Contribute to Feminist Theory and Therapy?

Carla K. Bradshaw, PhD

SUMMARY. White American culture celebrates independence, self-reliance, and individual choice as hallmarks of healthy mental and emotional functioning. However, from a feminist perspective, the disproportionate emphasis on independence in American culture reflects the predominance of the white, middle-class, male point of view; appropriate models for healthy dependency have been neglected. This paper offers an alternative view of dependency from the perspective of Japanese culture. The structure of Japanese society is predicated on subordinating the needs of the individual to that of family or community and interdependency is highly valued. A psychodynamic theory proposed by Doi (1973) is used to explain the role of dependency in Japanese society. The concept of *amae* is examined as the central organizing dynamic and its influence on Japanese psychotherapy is also discussed. The Japanese emphasis on amae is often misunderstood by Western thinkers and one example of a racist interpretation of Japanese behavior by a prominent

---

Carla K. Bradshaw is a clinical psychologist in private practice in Seattle, WA. She is Amerasian, born of a Japanese mother and a caucasian father. Her childhood years were spent both in parts of Japan and the United States giving her an appreciation for the richness and unique aspects of both cultures. Her current interests lie in women's issues, biracial identity development and problems of assimilation, cross cultural therapy, feminist therapy and theory, and family therapy. She recently became mother to her first child.

Author note: "I thank Maria Root, Laura Brown, and Christine Ho for their support, patience, thoughtful comments, and gentle editing. Their support helped to sustain and inspire me through the process of clarifying and translating my thoughts into writing."

Correspondence may be addressed to the author at: 22370 N.E. Woodinville-Duvall Road, Woodinville, WA 98072.

Western theorist is critically reviewed. Lastly, some suggestions are made regarding applications of amae psychology to feminist theory and therapy.

White American culture celebrates self-sufficiency, self-reliance, liberty, and individual choice. Erik Erikson (1950), whose developmental stage theory has enjoyed prominence and wide support suggests in his classic work, *Childhood and Society*, that "The process of American identity formation seems to support an individual's ego identity as long as he can preserve a certain element of deliberate tentativeness of autonomous choice. The individual must be able to convince himself that the next step is up to him" (p. 286). Essentially, Erikson views the focal issue in American identity formation to be the preservation and idealization of separation and individuation. Achieving separation from parents and family is axiomatic in the definition of the well functioning, fully mature American individual. Interpersonal interactions are predicated upon preserving separation/independence while attempting interrelatedness. Encroachments upon another's independence are considered intrusive, immature, or overly dependent. This view of healthy interpersonal functioning is characteristic of Western cultures and particularly of the American culture.

In this paper the preeminence of individualism in American society is challenged and some of the consequences of idealizing separation and individuation are outlined. Japanese views of dependency are then examined for an equally valid yet less pejorative perspective on dependency. James Masterson's work (1985) which has pervasive, significant impact on American psychology is also examined as an example of an ethnocentric, racist application of Western ethos to non-Western cultures. Last, some comments are offered regarding ways in which non-Western thinking about dependency may inform and enrich feminist theory and therapy.

Erikson (1950) theorizes that the particular emphasis on self-determination reflects an ideological bias that whether or not a choice exists, "the individual must be able to convince himself (herself) that the next step is up to him (her)" (p. 286). The ability to maintain this perception and to act upon it would constitute (according to Erikson) an important aspect of a mentally healthy American. However, there are many Americans, (women, the economically disadvantaged, the disabled, people of color, the elderly, and children) for whom the opportunities for self-determination are more constrained and for whom the limits on independence are external and very real. To predicate mental health status upon the ability to convince oneself that a choice exists when it may not, or when actualizing the choice may be very difficult, constitutes a subtle but damaging injustice which is in fact a form of oppression. From a feminist perspective, it may be argued that the American emphasis on independence without appropriate models for dependency reflects the disproportionate influence of the white, male perspective. Kaplan (1983) offers some thoughts on this:

> DSM-III does not mention the dependency of individuals — usually men — whose mental illness rates are higher when they are alone than when they are married (women's rates are higher when they are married than when they are alone [Gove, 1972]). In short, men's dependency, like women's dependency, exists and is supported and sanctioned by society; but men's dependency is not considered sick, whereas women's dependency is. (p. 789)

This indicates that incorporating more flexible norms around the expression of dependency, interdependency, and affiliation needs is of particular importance to American women who are more likely than American men to be diagnosed for a mental disorder (Chesler, 1972). Furthermore, some of the diagnoses reported in the third edition of the *Diagnostic and Statistical Manual of Mental Disorders* (DSM-III) as more prevalent in women than in men may tend to be those which represent stereotypes of femininity: e.g., Dependent Personality Disorder, Histrionic Personality Disorder, and the spectrum of Affective Disorders (Kaplan, 1983). If women are particularly vulnerable to such diagnostic labeling based on sex biases and people of color are similarly vulnerable to diagnostic labeling based on race biases (Sue, 1983), women of color may stand in double jeopardy both as a function of gender as well as race. A standard for healthy mental functioning informed by the diverse experiences of women, people of color, the aged, and the economically and physically disadvantaged would be likely to incorporate the value of dependency upon others and the ability to affiliate.

Jean Baker Miller (1976), addressing the lack of a coherent theory of female development, said "the parameters of the female's development are not the same as the male's and the same terms do not apply" (p. 86). She further comments that the absence of a language for describing women's sense of self, "organized around being able to make and then to maintain affiliations and relationships" (p. 83), impedes recognition of more affiliative ways of living. With respect to American culture, the goals of interpersonal separation and individuation have taken on disproportionate importance. The pervasiveness of these constructs in American personality theory contributes to the unfortunate inhibition of a socially valid, interpersonally powerful means for expressing dependency and interdependency needs.

Expanding the repertoire for expressions of dependency and the need for other people offers the opportunity for a deeper sense of belonging and interpersonal intimacy. Perhaps we can borrow from the wisdom of other cultures to inform our own about alternatives to the overemphasis on independence and self-reliance.

A JAPANESE VIEW OF DEPENDENCY

In traditional Japanese society there is a highly developed sense of interdependency which provides the basis for social structure. The cultural norm is to subordinate individual needs to the needs of family and society. Japanese philosophy stresses that individuals are indebted to the efforts of their parents and family for having become as they are. A Japanese is discouraged from excessively referring to the self, and therefore, is unlikely to refer to one's development as "who one has become," rather would use the less personalized "as one is." Essentially, the Japanese individual would consider herself the product of nature and family. This heavy emphasis on the interrelationship between people serves the aim of maintaining harmony through a proper attitude of deference and etiquette but also places the individual in the context of a family.

This notion of family extends both forward and backward in time and is the source of one's sense of honor and belonging (Shon & Ja, 1982).

This sense of indebtedness pervades the culture and affects the ways in which interpersonal exchanges are conducted. One body of literature uses exchange theory to account for differences in expressed dependency (Akiyama, Antonucci, & Campbell, 1987; Shon & Ja, 1982). These authors suggest that American interpersonal relationships are primarily of a contractual form between theoretically free individuals or groups. In contrast, the Japanese apply two clearly distinct exchange rules, one for the "inner circle" of family, spouse, and relatives and another for the "outer circle" composed of the public, strangers, and foreigners (Doi, 1973). The exchange rule for those in the outer circle is similar to the American one involving contractual agreement. The period of time in which repayment should occur, amount of repayment, and conditions of the agreement are understood at the outset.

In contrast, relationships within the inner circle are organized around reciprocity and indulgence. This indulgence in a cultural context may be translated as "presuming on some special relationship that exists" (Doi, 1973). Though obligation exists, the conditions for repayment are more ambiguous. Within the closest of relationships (parent to child) there may be a notable lack of obligation, and instead, indulgence is shown on the part of the parent toward the child. The child, in return is expected to treat the parents with deference and respect. There is an understood, but unspoken obligation to repay the debt of gratitude to the parents, but the criteria for fulfillment of this debt are ambiguous. Therefore, one is never free from this sort of obligation in the way an American would consider a debt repaid when the contractual obligation is fulfilled. Consequently, one is not expected to be psychologically independent.

The Japanese concept of indulgence is best described by example. In my own experience with my Japanese grandmother in Japan, I remember a very special relationship with her in which she allowed me to go with her nearly everywhere if I wished. It seemed to me in retrospect that I had a great deal of latitude about what I wanted to do and she would accompany me. On many summer mornings she would take me to a public exercise class ("Radio Taiso") at 6 a.m. where many members of the community would congregate on a field for a radio broadcast calisthenics session. I was often still sleepy on the way there and my grandmother would carry me there on her back. Over a period of years I had become accustomed to being carried on her back as is customary for Japanese to do with their children. On the way there one morning a friend of my grandmother's saw us and she exclaimed, "such a big girl to be on the grandmother's back . . . look! Your feet nearly touch the ground!" Till this point I had not realized how big I had become at five years of age and that my grandmother at four feet of height was not much taller than myself. I had felt so nurtured by her that I had indulged in a fantasy with her of still being nearly an infant. It was not until this friend mocked me in her kindly but critical way that I realized what a comical scene we must have presented. I do not recall feeling that my grandmother was shamed or embarrassed by her friend's comment. Rather it was I who felt some shame and stopped indulging myself in this way. I do not know when I would have stopped riding on her back or when she would have begun to object, but I suspect she would have allowed this until I was ready to stop on my own. Within this special relationship my grandmother indulged my need to retain an infantile dependence on her.

The indulgence I have just described illustrates the fundamental Japanese concept of "amae" (Doi, 1973). Doi feels it describes a basic human phenomenon roughly similar to Balint's notion of "passive object love" (1965) but for which there is no exact translation in the Western culture. Amae refers to the feeling presumed "to arise first as an emotion felt by the baby at the breast towards its mother, . . . it corresponds to that tender emotion that, arising in earliest infancy, was labeled by Freud 'the child's primary object-choice'" (Doi, 1973, p. 20).[1] Doi finds the concept so central to Japanese psychology that he suggests that amae "is a key concept for the understanding not only of the psychological makeup of the individual Japanese but of the structure of Japanese society as a whole" (p. 28). In considering the psychological prototype of amae, Doi suggests that the concept

serves as a medium making it possible for the mother to understand the infant mind and respond to its needs, so that mother
and child can enjoy a sense of commingling and identity . . .
one may perhaps describe amae as, ultimately, an attempt psychologically to deny the fact of separation from the mother.
(p. 74)

From a psychoanalytic perspective, Doi suggests that the amae
mentality offers the opportunity to re-experience ''oneness'' such
as that between mother and child. To interpret amae psychology
exclusively as a defense against separation anxiety or abandonment
without appreciation for the positive function would be onesided
and reflects a Western ideological bias. Doi also sees amae more
positively as an affirmation of tolerance, respect for nondiscrimina-
tion and equality. Taken positively, amae thought is linked to the
Zen spirituality in which there is indivisibility of subject from object, self from other. Doi quotes Suzuki Daisetsu (cf. Doi, 1973) a
Zen spiritualist:

At the basis of the ways of thinking and feeling of the Westerner there is the father, it is the mother that lies at the bottom
of the Oriental nature. The mother enfolds everything in an
unconditional love. There is no question of right or wrong.
Everything is accepted without difficulties or questioning.
Love in the West always contains a residue of power. Love in
the East is all-embracing. It is open to all sides. One can enter
from any direction. (p. 77)

Thus, it can be said of amae psychology that it provides a social and
spiritual structure for coping with the fact of separation by providing conditions in which it is possible to nurture and indulge the
child within without incurring shame or guilt.

At this point, a word about Japanese shame and guilt would seem
in order. The use of shame to help reinforce societal mores has been
widely written about in the literature on Asian culture and families.
The phrase ''loss of face'' is considered synonymous with shame
and indicates a sense of being exposed to the public in a way which
would bring negative attention upon oneself or family. It is experienced as the withdrawal of the community's and family's support.

To a Japanese for whom social identity and interdependency are so focal, to have one's sense of belonging to family, or in a larger context, to community jeopardized, is significant. In the amae psychology which operates on the trust that there are others on whom to rely for coping with the existential anxiety of being truly alone, the withdrawal of the warm arms of indulgence is a powerful motivator for conformity.

It is sometimes mentioned that the American culture is based on guilt while the Japanese is a culture of shame. There is implicit in the statement that guilt and shame are exclusive, or at least significantly different. Benedict (1954) postulated that a culture of guilt places emphasis on inner standards for behavior while shame is more concerned with outer standards. It seems for heuristic purposes that sharp distinctions are made between such highly related abstract feelings. From the point of view of the experiencer, the feelings are often simultaneous and confused. Doi in contrast to Benedict proposes that for the Westerner, guilt is an inner problem for the individual while for the Japanese there is a sense of betrayal of the group to which she/he belongs. Here again the underlying ideological differences would contribute to how a feeling is interpreted. The American may also experience guilt as a sense of betrayal, but it is betrayal of oneself as opposed to one's group or community. Therefore, it would seem that the distinction is less one of guilt versus shame, but one having to do with the locus of one's sense of belonging.

What then is the relationship between shame and social obligation as it operates in Japanese culture? There are many words in the Japanese language referring to the nuances of dependency and obligation and this attests to the importance of these concepts to life among the Japanese. The Japanese term "giri" loosely translates to social obligation. There is a related term "ninjo" which translates roughly to mean human feeling in the context of obligation. Ninjo refers to the spontaneous feelings of closeness which arise between parent and child, among siblings, or close blood relatives. Giri relationships on the other hand involve teacher to student, friends, more distant relatives, etc. Doi (1973) explains that giri relationships are those in which ninjo does not spontaneously occur, but in which it is permitted to experience ninjo. It is thus said that "giri aspires to ninjo.'' Under conditions of family strain, ninjo may also take on a giri-like quality. Therefore, giri involves both an opportunity to show affection and gratitude and to incur it. When shame occurs, it is often in the context of giri in which one fears one may not have properly repaid the amae incurred. Shame does not occur in the context of ninjo because within these close relationships there is a great deal of latitude and indulgence, i.e., closer to the ideal amae relationship.

ONE WESTERN VIEW OF DEPENDENCY: RACISM CLOAKED IN PSYCHOLOGICAL JARGON

The Japanese emphasis on amae has been misinterpreted by Western thinkers who are culturally biased toward seeing individual freedom and separation as being developmentally more mature than reliance on the group and interdependency. In a recent book entitled *The Real Self*, James Masterson (1985) considers the role of the mother in the development of the child's "real self." He theorizes that for the child's self to fully emerge from the symbiosis between mother and infant and assume the unique characteristics which signal individuation, the parents must have the capacity to perceive the child's emerging self and respond in a "positive, supportive manner, and treat with respect the child's unique temperament" (p. 29). Furthermore, Masterson states that parental failures to foster this development lead to the production of narcissistic or borderline personality disorders. Though he gives passing mention to the role of parents (including fathers) his subsequent focus is on the role of mothers. In light of his thesis he wonders "Is all this emphasis on maternal libidinal availability really necessary for the development of the self?" He offers evidence that the answer is affirmative by considering Israel and Japan as cultures in which the maternal attitude toward the child is quite different than that of American mothers.

Israeli kibbutzim were used to illustrate the effects of the absence of maternal influence when socialized child care systems are the primary child rearing modality. He concluded that de-emphasis on the early mother-child tie leads to deficiencies in the essential human qualities of intimacy, creativity, and autonomy. He concludes that in Israel the failure to emphasize maternal libidinal availability for the emerging self results in adults who function "not unlike a higher-level borderline patient in this country" (United States) (p. 100). He then turns to the Japanese society in which the mother, in his view, rewards and indulges grandiosity and childhood omnipotence without inflicting "phase appropriate frustration" to curb the development of a "fixated intrapsychic structure, a self representation which is grandiose, omnipotent and self-centered—what we call narcissistic personality disorder" (p. 96). Masterson then compares pathologic narcissistic displays in the United States which he suggests are expressed by exhibitionism to the Japanese mother's shaming of exhibitionism. He suggests that shame is a key affect of Japanese culture which prevents the direct expression of narcissism resulting in "closet narcissistic personality disorder" (p. 97). He asserts that "the indirect expression of one's grandiosity and narcissism in indirect hidden behaviors through others became the keystone of Japanese behavior" (p. 96). He cites Doi's work on amae as evidence that in object relations terms the Japanese individual seeks fusion with others to relieve internal distress over the inability to gratify self-centered grandiosity. He proposes that the self-sacrificing behavior observed of the Japanese indicate the attempt to cull gratification of personal needs by evoking guilt in the other. About the Japanese adult, Masterson concludes they function "like the local variant of the narcissistic personality disorder" (p. 100).

These are serious allegations, it seems to me, to diagnose in a pejorative manner whole cultures as having either pathologic borderline or narcissistic personality disorders wholly based on an ethnocentric "American" point of view. Masterson ignores variants of fully functioning adults and implies that the best functioning adults of the Israeli and Japanese cultures are still disordered compared to American counterparts. He states in his text that the term "real" is "synonymous with healthy or normal" and that the real self provides an "internal repertoire" for blending "the need for real self-expression with the external roles required by adaptation" (p. 24). He derives the capacities of the healthy self by noting those which are impaired in the borderline or narcissistic disorders. The resulting clinical scheme for a healthy self is as follows:

1. *Spontaneity and aliveness of affect.* This refers to the capacity to experience affect deeply and spontaneously.
2. *Self-entitlement.* The sense that the self is entitled to appropriate experiences of mastery, pleasure, and to the environmental input necessary to achieve these objectives.
3. *Self-activation, assertion, and support.* The capacity to use autonomous initiative and assertion to express individuative wishes in reality and to support them when under attack.
4. *Acknowledgement of self-activation and maintenance of self-esteem.* The ability to acknowledge to oneself that one's self had coped with an affective state, to autonomously fuel self-esteem.
5. *Soothing of painful affects.* The ability to autonomously limit, minimize, and soothe painful affects.
6. *Continuity of self.* The experience of "I" is continuous over time.
7. *Commitment.* The ability to commit the self to an objective or relationship and to persevere to attain that goal.
8. *Creativity.* The ability to use the self to change old, familiar patterns into new ones. (p. 26)

Inspection of these criteria indicates that the healthy, normal individual is autonomous in all of these respects. Little mention is made of how the healthy adult relates to and derives support from others. In fact, implicit in these criteria is the notion that the less one relies on others to support self-esteem, soothing of painful affects, etc., the healthier. Based on his observations of American infants and adults, Masterson feels justified to diagnose the Japanese and Israeli adults as narcissistic or borderline. In light of Masterson's powerful status as a theorist on narcissistic and borderline disorders he is particularly responsible to know the limits of his knowledge and to guard against the misuse of his authority. His diagnoses of Japanese and Israeli culture are highly ethnocentric, fail to recognize legitimate ideological differences among cultures, and are essentially racist. For example, the Japanese would not consider it healthy to spontaneously display affect to a stranger. However, such displays among relatives or family may be more permissible. Thus, from an outsider's point of view the Japanese appear "inscrutable" when in fact they display all of the affective range but within a different context than do Americans. Masterson is not comparing child rearing practices. Rather he is indicting cultural practices from the idiosyncratic point of view of the Westerner for whom the self and the individual is paramount. Furthermore, without examination of this a priori assumption, he imposes his standards upon other cultures. He does not suggest that in these cultures there are fully functioning individuals who may also serve as models for furthering clinical understanding of human nature. Rather, he assumes that the Western (more accurately the American) practices on which his theory is based and confined comprise human nature as it should be and serve as the ideal to which other cultures should aspire. *This is racism cloaked as psychological theory.*

Interestingly, Masterson does not derive an independent definition of the real self, but instead defines it in light of what is impaired in a narcissistic or borderline person and what Masterson observed happening in the process of "repair." There are several difficulties with this approach to defining adaptive functioning. First, he does not attempt to draw from multiple examples of adaptive responses to the "real world" and to cull from this a full definition of what is healthy or normal. Clearly culture, society, family, environment, and politics all constitute forces to which a healthy individual must adapt. There is a rich variation of these forces among cultures and a paucity of understanding in psychology regarding the meaning and significance of other cultural experiences. Is it then just to derive a definition of adaptive, normal functioning from the myopic position of one particular culture? It would be interesting to subject the criteria listed above to clinicians representing various cultural perspectives for validation of the construct "healthy" as represented by that list. Second, the process of treatment and evaluation of its outcome is value-laden. Therefore, Masterson's procedure of deriving the norm for healthy functioning based on the outcome of his borderline and narcissistic cases is not based on objective criteria but on the subjective perspective of the therapist. It would perhaps be fairer to use Masterson's formulation to describe the American and generously the Western view of a healthy, male adult. Given current understanding of human nature it is fallacious to apply this as a standard against which to diagnose other cultures.

Curiously, Masterson comments that the main impediments to the development of the real self in the American culture is the lack of extended families, the instability of the family unit, and the decline in the influence of religion. Significantly, it is precisely the function of amae psychology to maintain the extended family and family stability. This comes, however at some expense to the individual but not at the expense of the self. This distinction between the individual and self is important to illustrate that there may be many pathways to actualizing the self contrary to the "American" notion that self reliance is equivalent to self actualization. Masterson fails to explain how the strong currents of disruption could have developed in American society which presumably corners the market in healthy selves. He only suggests that

> negative social forces have a far greater impact in those with a disorder of the self than on those with a healthy self since the less intrapsychic structure an individual has, the more he turns to seemingly stable factors in the external world for stability to help him contain and adapt. (p. 110)

The deterioration of family and religious ethic in American culture (if we agree that this is so) may be attributed to the extreme application of the assumption that individuals are free and that self reliance is the preeminent goal. Taken to an extreme, such a philosophy would advocate disaffiliation, competitiveness, and the commitment to self before commitment to others.

This critique of Masterson's work is an effort to illustrate that it is as yet premature to generalize about adaptive human functioning from knowledge of one culture. Rather the job before us now entails taking a broad perspective which embraces differences and attempts to draw from the diversity the ingredients for constructing a knowledge of human functioning. From the narrow, linear view of only one perspective much of what is valuable in other cultures will be lost.

JAPANESE PSYCHOTHERAPY

Naturally, the amae psychology or permissiveness toward dependence does not insulate members of the culture from showing emotional pathologies. It seems possible, however, that there may be a tendency toward certain types of pathologies as a function of the social structure. Morita therapy is probably the most widely recognized therapy of Japanese origin and Morita's theory of neurosis is considered uniquely Japanese. Originally it was devised for those suffering from strong feelings of fear, apprehension, or shame. Given the social prohibition against expressions of feelings to strangers, patients frequently somatize psychological pain and present with physical complaints. The Morita perspective on somatizing and disabling self-consciousness is that the symptoms result from a disorder of attention such that attention concentrated on a particular sensation heightens it and sets in motion a vicious circle in which sensation and attention interact on each other. Morita hypothesizes that an obsessional preoccupation occurs and that it is this which must be stopped. Though originally designed for the obsessive-compulsive, somatizing, and/or neurotic dispositions, the approach has also been used successfully to treat depression as well as other conditions (Reynolds, 1987).

Upon initial reading several years ago, I recognized that Morita theory and therapy embraces a strong Eastern philosophical contribution which gave it a very different perspective than Western psychotherapies. There are several fundamental tenets:

1. There is value in unpleasant feelings because they remind us of our basic purposes and desires whereas pleasant feelings are not as compelling.
2. Feelings fade over time if left as they are when behavior does not restimulate them. Feeling-based life is volatile, while purpose-based life is more stable and satisfying.

3. Neurosis is a learned disorder of the mind and can be un-learned.
4. Acceptance of reality as it is involves a passive element of noticing feelings and fantasies but taking no action on them, and an active element of constructive, moral action.

The treatment advocates a lifestyle change and is guided by supervised journal writing, individual or group discussion, experiential tasks, and work therapy. Some typical questions for self examination may include pondering matters such as one's indebtedness to one's parents, the people who have contributed to one's life, and the people toward whom one had shown insufficient gratitude. The therapist would point out one's place in the web of family and community and confront the client about the selfishness of her/his self centered preoccupation. The theory, as I understand it, advocates interrupting obsessive ruminations by reviving feelings of belonging and gratitude toward the family or group and restoring the desire to work and repay obligation. The Morita approach uses a Zen philosophy which stresses awareness of feelings but does not permit feelings to disrupt what one must do. This seemed to me the crux of the work of therapy: to learn that feelings do not dictate one's actions and to be aware of even trivial acts as an opportunity for character development.

From an amae point of view, Morita therapy restores the ability to treat others with the same gratitude and indulgence thought to be missing in one's own life (Doi, 1973). Though Morita does not say this, it would seem that obsessive or neurotic difficulties arise out of the frustrated desire to be indulged (for amae) such that one becomes wholly concentrated on attaining amae, forgetting the essential ingredient that one must also give amae, as it were. Work plays an integral part of reawakening the joy of selfless giving. Therefore, in Morita therapy a client may be asked to make tapes of books for the blind anonymously, to experience pure giving. Often menial tasks are assigned such as weeding large gardens for the experience of deriving joy out of simplicity, doing for the process of doing rather than for results, and to learn the line between thoroughness and unconstructive perfectionism. In summary, the techniques for constructive living advocated by Morita therapy seem very consistent with amae psychology in its emphasis on the interdependency among people.

There seems some similarity between the Morita focus on gratitude and Alcoholics Anonymous' (AA) step program and use of personal inventories. In both approaches, one attempts to turn concentration from oneself to one's personal community consisting of family, friends, and AA. Both approaches also make use of gratitude toward significant people in one's life as a catalyst for encouraging social contact and mending broken relationships. In a way it seems that the success of AA may partly be attributed to the establishment of a supportive, warm community in which one's mistakes would likely be forgiven. In Japanese terms it is creating a "giri" situation with a high likelihood of "ninjo"; that is, dependency upon the group is encouraged and the rules for dependent conduct are clear. In this context I wonder whether the need for people to show interdependency is being met in American society through belonging in social clubs and organizations. What has been lost in extended family and consumed by the needs of work can be partially regained through a limited but intimate contact.

AMAE PSYCHOLOGY AND FEMINIST THEORY

In the preceding pages I have tried to convey how the amae world view permeates Japanese culture. A brief description of one mode of Japanese psychotherapy has been presented to illustrate how amae psychology could effect some cultural differences in treatment. I hope to have shown that the word dependency alone is an insufficient translation for a concept that pervades private, public, and even political behavior among the Japanese. Relative to Japanese, the American language has fewer words referring to the nuances of dependency and interrelationships. This absence of a vocabulary is a disadvantage as we try to develop a better understanding of connectedness, try to depathologize dependency, and try to incorporate interdependency into ways of living that are uniquely American and feminist. It would not work to simply apply the Japanese structure to our own American culture ignoring the national ethos, social context, and political climate in which we live. But, what can we take from another cultural perspective that may be useful to us?

As I sifted through the many Japanese expressions and words for dependency and indulgence, I came to realize that the Japanese view of dependency is not linear. It is circular, having shades of meaning and application. For the Japanese this complexity is not troublesome and many words were developed to refer to the nuances of dependent behavior, attitude, and mood. There is a word for the dependency one feels toward a parent and it is a different word than the one describing dependency toward an employer. There are even words to describe the various pathologies of dependency such as the person who unreasonably expects to be indulged when no right to indulgence exists within the relationship, or the person who presumes too much of a relationship even though there is a right to presume to some extent, or the one who acts indifferently toward someone who deserves indulgence, etc. The awareness of the various levels in dependency seems missing in our language. The current feminist effort toward recognizing the importance of interdependency (Gilligan, 1982; Green, 1988; Miller, 1976) is also a way of creating a language for talking about these issues which have come to be largely neglected in the body of Western professional psychology.

The absence of English words for the subtleties of dependency is merely an inconvenience. Clearly, the absence of such words does not imply that the phenomena described in Japanese do not exist, only that they have not been valued and subsequently labeled in this culture. Doi (1973) understands this concept well and his thinking parallels feminist thinking that linguistic characteristics reflect the world of meaning and to some extent conditions the thinking of those who use it. Therefore, it would seem that feminist practitioners are in a particularly advantageous position to observe and develop a lexicon for processes which are occurring but remain obscured. Why are feminist therapists in a particularly advantageous position? First, it is only from a position of understanding oppression that the power dynamics within relationships are revealed.

Amae psychology is intimately related to issues of power because amae refers precisely to feelings of vulnerability. Doi (1973) observed that American psychiatrists were notably slow to detect the "amae" (need for passive love) in their patients and were "extraordinarily insensitive to the feelings of helplessness of their patients" (p. 21). From a feminist perspective this is not a surprising observation. By overtly attending to the power dynamics within therapeutic relationships and even more broadly other social exchanges, types of dependency and changes in dependency over the course of the relationship will become clearer. From such observations more discrete descriptions of adaptive and maladaptive forms of dependency should emerge.

Second, amae psychology supports feminist theory and practice from an "other" cultural view. It suggests some additional psychodynamic explanations for the empowering effect of recognizing, validating, and working with a client's helplessness (e.g., victimization). The amae psychology validates (versus pathologizing) helplessness either as it originates from real events or from intrapsychic events related to separation and differentiation. It is likely that Americans are not spared the desire for amae, but lack the language and cultural support for expressing these dependency needs. One possibility is that "enmeshed" family systems result from frustrated amae and that the intervention might consist not of imposing separation, but of heightening gratitude thereby allowing members to loosen their grip on one another. I hope that by seeing amae in a positive light, feminist therapists will feel more free to examine the forms of dependency which arise in the lives of our clients, in the therapeutic relationship, and in our own lives.

Last, I have tried to convey the idea that amae behavior may not have a direct translation in English but that it is nonetheless a universal feeling that even animals show. The puppy that cannot get close enough to its owner and squirms and rolls into a warm ball on the lap is just as good an example of amae and is a feeling that everyone can recognize. The difficulty seems to lie in the fact that the American culture offers very few situations in which one is allowed to indulge someone else the way one might a puppy and also be indulged. Ideally this condition would exist in the family, but as therapists already know too well, the impediments to intimacy are many. Our work, our children, our partners, our selves all compete for our energy and attention. But I think the main problem lies in the fear of weakness. Somehow, through years of socialization we have come to be afraid to be weak or vulnerable. Unfortunately, vulnerability is the crux of intimacy and dependency. *To defensively hide weaknesses behind the armor of self-reliance robs us from acknowledging the universal human weakness and the sense of belonging that can come out of sharing our strengths. In some sense, the task of creating a language and environment for dependency or interdependency means talking about weakness and risking putting it out where it can be seen.*

NOTE

1. I recognize the difficulties this definition may present in light of current effort to address "mother blaming" or "momism" tendencies in developmental theorizing caused by exclusive focus on the mother-child dyad. However, the significance of the mother's place for having positive impact is at issue here. This aspect of the female role is devalued in our current culture and psychological theories. Doi's definition though arising out of traditional Western psychoanalytic training and also out of the vertical social hierarchy which exists in Japan in which the mother remains the primary domestic influence still celebrates the powerful influence of a strong, positive identification with the mother. I also concur with Lerner's (1988) perspective that even an absent father impacts the development of the child and a systems perspective likely would give a more rounded view by accounting for the influences of all family members. However, this particular issue is beyond the scope of this paper.

REFERENCES

Akiyama, Hiroko, Antonucci, Toni C., & Campbell, Ruth (1987). Rules of social support exchange: The U.S. and Japan. *Asian American Psychological Association Journal, 12*, 34-38.

Balint, Michael (1965). *Primary love and psychoanalytic technique*. New York: Liveright.

Benedict, Ruth (1954). *The Chrysanthemum and the sword*. Tokyo: Tuttle.

Doi, Takeo (1973). *The anatomy of dependence*. Tokyo: Kodansha International.

Erikson, Erik H. (1950). *Childhood and society (2nd ed.)* New York: W. W. Norton.

Gilligan, Carol (1982). *In a different voice*. Cambridge, MA: Harvard University Press.

Gove, W. R. (1972). The relationship between sex roles, mental illness and marital status. *Social Forces, 51*, 34-44.

Green, Dorsey G. (1988, May). *Is separation really so great?* Paper presented at annual conference of the Advanced Feminist Therapist Institute, Seattle, WA.

Kaplan, Marcie (1983). A woman's view of DSM-III. *American Psychologist, 38*, 786-792.

Lerner, Harriet Goldhor (1988). A critique of the feminist psychoanalytic contribution. *Women in therapy*, Northvale, NJ: Jason Aronson.

Masterson, James F. (1985). *The real self: A developmental, self, and object relations approach*. New York: Brunner/Mazel.

Miller, Jean Baker (1976). *Toward a new psychology of women*. Boston: Beacon Press.

Reynolds, David (1987). *Water bears no scars. Japanese pathways for personal growth*. New York: William Morrow.

Shon, Steven P. & Ja, Davis Y. (1982). Asian families. In M. McGoldrick, J. K. Pearce, & J. Giordano, eds. *Ethnicity and family therapy*. New York: Guilford Press.

Sue, Derald W. (1981). *Counseling the culturally different*. New York: John Wiley & Sons.

Sue, Stanley (1983). Ethnic minority issues in psychology. *American Psychologist*, May, 583-592.

Is Separation Really So Great?

G. Dorsey Green, PhD

SUMMARY. This paper challenges the validity of current male, Western psychological theories which state that separation and autonomy are prerequisites for mental health. The author argues for consideration of theories that envision individual development as occurring within the context of relationships. Lesbian couples are used as a focus for this discussion. Examples from communities of color in the United States and Eastern cultures are also discussed.

Current psychological theory posits separation, individuation, and independence as signs of healthy emotional development. One of the problems with this definition of health, however, is that it equates separation and independence in interpersonal relationships with a strong sense of self or secure ego boundaries.

The goal of this paper is twofold. It challenges the almost universal, Western assumption that psychologically healthy people are defined by their autonomy or independence and that mastery of tasks that are not relationship oriented is more important than care of relationships. The second goal is to explore the definition of the construct, healthy ego boundary. Within this new definition, which

G. Dorsey Green is a psychologist in private practice and the co-author of *Lesbian Couples* with D. Merilee Clunis. Dorsey is white and has a combination of Puritan and Quaker ancestors in her predominantly English background. She grew up on the Eastern Shore of Maryland which is mainly rural, agricultural, and politically conservative. She discovered feminism and a broader world view in Michigan where she was working as a small college administrator. Dorsey now lives with her life partner and their two sons in Seattle.

The author wishes to thank Merilee Clunis, Sandra Coffman, Ginny NiCarthy, and Margaret Schonfield for their feedback and editorial suggestions.

Correspondence may be addressed to the author at: 521 19th Avenue East, Seattle, WA 98112.

assumes interdependence, the paper will examine how autonomy and ego boundaries are connected. Lesbian couples will be the focal context for understanding this dynamic because there is no better place to see this dynamic at work than in an examination of couples made up of two women. There are also examples from communities of color in this country and from non-Western countries, so as to demonstrate the culture bound nature of this concept of separateness.

WOMEN'S ROLES AND DEVELOPMENT

Jean Baker Miller (1976) points out that women have been made the "carriers" (p. 23) of emotion, nurturance, empathy, and other relationship enhancing skills. She theorizes that men are threatened by any feeling or behavior that identifies them with women and, thus, makes them appear less masculine. The famous Broverman study of therapists' definitions of mentally healthy women, men, and adults found that therapists viewed women as emotionally healthy when they were dependent and emotional; women were viewed as unhealthy if they were assertive, active, or otherwise emotionally strong, even though that was the therapists' definition of a healthy adult or a healthy man (Broverman, Broverman, Clarkson, Rosenkrantz, & Vogel, 1970). A follow-up to this initial study (Broverman, 1984) showed that therapists' attitudes about what constitutes healthy men and adults had changed. They placed more value on being aware of feelings. However, the therapists had not changed their ideas about women.

Clearly, "healthy" women are supposed to be immersed in finding, developing, and maintaining intimate relationships. However, this focus on relationships is not seen by therapists, and I suspect most other people, as important, valuable, or appropriate for healthy adults (i.e., men). Our efforts to maintain the connectedness and integrity of our networks are devalued (Blumstein & Schwartz, 1983).

Men's refusal to attend to relationships is one way that women's skills at relationship nurturing have been ghettoized. The bind for women comes because relationships must be nurtured if they are to thrive. If men refuse to nurture relationships, and women do not compensate by taking full charge of relationships, then relationships will suffer and fail.

Irene Stiver, a feminist theoretician, discusses the connectedness typical of female relationships as valuable (1984). She defines dependency as "a process of counting on other people to provide help in coping physically and emotionally with the experiences and tasks encountered in the world, when one has not sufficient skill, confidence, energy and/or time" (p. 10). She sees dependency as a natural, ongoing *process* and not a single, static *event*. She also believes that people are "enhanced and empowered through the very process of counting on others for help" (p. 10). I would broaden her statement and say that she actually describes a truly *interdependent* society.

If we look at life as a continuum, it is obvious that all of us are dependent on someone at all times whether or not we wish to acknowledge it. If, as infants, we are not taken care of, we die. As clinicians, we know that people who were not able to trust and count on others as infants and children have difficulty with intimacy as adults. Yet mainstream society and mainstream psychology have seen "dependent" people as weak and less emotionally viable than so-called "autonomous" individuals. However, if everyone behaved as if dependence and interdependence were immature and to be outgrown, we would have few lasting relationships.

What is not always obvious is that all of us are dependent for different things throughout our lives, even wealthy men who hire out mundane tasks. Because they are busy making money in the world of high finance, such supposedly "autonomous" men are dependent on others for keeping their households, offices, and stores running smoothly. Perhaps this myth of male independence is perpetuated by the notion that if we are dependent on someone who is of lower status, then we are "independent"; if we are dependent on peers or people of higher social status, then we are "dependent." The reality is that we are all dependent and interdependent. For some reason the illusion of independence is an integral part of Western culture's definition of masculinity. One of the best places to see how this myth is maintained is in the typical Western stories and movies and in popular romance novels. The hero in Westerns is most often a white man who is somewhat of a loner and depends only on his horse and on a faithful follower who is rarely a peer. This man rides into a town that is in some kind of trouble, fixes it, and then often rides out again, leaving boys and women who vow never to forget him.

Two studies explore differences between men and women in how they relate to people, and may shed some light on why dependency has become such an important issue. Pollak and Gilligan's study (1982) of images of violence that appear in white, college students' stories using the Thematic Apperception Test (TAT) highlights men's discomfort and fear of closeness and relationship building. The TAT is a projective test that requires people to make up stories about a series of ambiguous pictures. The theory is that clients will project their fears, assumptions, and values onto the characters in the pictures. Pollak and Gilligan found that men reported violence as the figures in the pictures moved closer together. The women reported violence as the figures were in what appeared to be work related situations. Thus, Pollak and Gilligan hypothesized that men seem more likely than women to avoid close, intimate relationships out of fear of what will happen to them. Women seem more likely to avoid situations where they are more successful than their peers. They fear that they will become isolated as a consequence of their success. Because of the race of their participants, their data can only be generalized to white college students and may tell us nothing about how men and women of color would view the same situations.

Janet Lever's study (1976) of play behavior of boys and girls observed that boys were likely to play games with clearly delineated rules and often with large numbers of participants. Girls on the other hand, were more likely to play in dyads and have more diffuse guidelines. The boys would have long disagreements about the rules of the game and happily continue play; the girls would end play rather than have conflict. Lever does not indicate the race of the participants in her study, so one is unable to assess whether findings are generalizable to one or more races.

There is no better place to see women's fear of and discomfort with isolation than in an examination of their adult relationships with other women, particularly in lesbian couples. In their book about friendships between women Eichenbaum and Orbach (1988) address how hard it is to maintain friendships in the face of differences and disagreements. In this author's experience, lesbian couples most often seek out therapy to deal with the issues of separation, being different, how to engage in conflict without ending the relationship, or how to end the relationship without conflict. In general, women seem to be willing to change rules rather than lose relationships (Gilligan, 1982). This is clearly demonstrated by the fact that many lesbians' social networks include their ex-lovers (Becker, 1988).

THE WHITE, MALE PERSPECTIVE

The psychological description of the world has been written predominantly by white, middle class men from Western cultures, as they see and experience it. Their experiences are reflected in society's theories of individual development. These theories do not even take a different but equal perspective. Instead they maintain that any way of relating to the world other than that of male, singularly defined accomplishment of separation and individuation is unhealthy. In contrast, people in all of the undervalued groups (women, people with disabilities, people of color, gays and lesbians, working class, etc.) have developed interdependence as a way of life; the numbers of people valuing interdependence by far outnumber the white males in Western cultures. Yet, theories have still remained void of valuing interdependence. With no exception, members of undervalued groups are seen by white, male society as "making do" out of weakness. We always hear about the "self-made man" not the one who made it with the help of his friends. While I was growing up as a white, upper middle class girl in a small southern, segregated town, the adults around me inferred that women could not achieve the pinnacle of health because they were born deficient, that people from other cultures did not know any better, and that people of color in this country were not bright enough or did not work hard enough. I assume that I am not the only one who received these teachings. It is narcissistic and quite parochial for the white, Western, privileged society to assume that if others were truly strong, they would forego interdependence and choose to be "independent" as defined by current, Western psychological constructs.

If we look for them, there are a myriad of examples of how real life is different than the way white, male theories would have us believe. When I was in a training group years ago for social workers from Big Brothers/Big Sisters around the country, we played the game of what we would do if we had a million dollars. The Black men and women in our group all gave large portions to family members; none of the white participants did. It never even occurred to the whites to give some of it to our families; charity outside the family, yes, sharing with the family, no. Familial interdependence appears to be less ingrained in the white culture. This goes beyond the sharing of financial resources and extends to interpersonal support as well. For instance, lesbians and gay men of color often have more trouble deciding to come out to their families than their white counterparts because they do not want to risk losing the support that has been so important to their survival in a hostile society (Espin, 1987; Zitter, 1987; Moses & Hawkins, 1982).

A BROADER PERSPECTIVE

Eastern cultures also do not have the same preoccupation with autonomy as the white West does (Bradshaw, 1988; Protacio Marcelino, 1988). One Chinese woman did a linguistic search in her language and could not find the word autonomy in a Chinese dictionary; she did find it listed in an American translation (E. Chan, personal communication, April 28, 1988). In, Japan, mental pathology is often treated by the patient's being encouraged to rejoin the mainstream through an examination of how one fits in "the web of family and community . . ." (Bradshaw, 1988). The illness is the person's inability to be one with community and interdependent. Extended families are still in existence in many countries; nuclear families are in daily contact with extended family members through work and shared childcare responsibilities even if they do not live together. These examples raise the possibility that white, Western psychology represents a minority viewpoint. Those who see "independence" as the only healthy option may not be taking into account the practices and values of the majority of the world.

The prevalence of the belief that separation and individuation equals mental health has served to keep undervalued groups as less than healthy. A Native American man, for instance, who has his parents living with him may be seen as immature by the white man's values but perfectly normal by his tribe's culture. When people of color, women, people with disabilities, and gays and lesbians as groups began to assert their rights for equal treatment under the law, they also began the process of challenging the stereotypes that have held them psychological prisoners. Asking for equality under the law also begins the process of making the white, male culture take seriously these groups' values about interdependence as well.

Lever's study (1976) and personal experience suggest that men are more likely than women to play by the rules (whatever they are in a given situation) even if it means the end of a relationship. A sarcastic comment on this can be found in Gary Trudeau's *Doonesbury* cartoon strip (1984). Mark Slackmeyer's father is talking to his business partners about a man named Fred who is trying to buy their company's stock. The men begin to plan an unfriendly takeover of Fred's company. Mark asks, "What did Uncle Fred ever do to you?" His father's response is "This is no time for sentimentality! The economy's at stake here!" Obviously, takeovers are part of the business game and hurting a family member is a secondary issue. For all we know Uncle Fred expressed little sense of betrayal at having his company taken over by a family member, his pain might be seen as an admission of vulnerability, a prerequisite for interdependence (Bradshaw, 1988), and therefore, unmasculine.

PSYCHOLOGICAL DEVELOPMENT

Does Mr. Slackmeyer's brand of independence imply a healthy ego boundary (the intangible border where a person senses the differentiation between self and other)? Unfortunately, judging the health of a person's ego boundaries upon whether that person is dependent or independent in her or his relationships can be confusing. Someone who appears to be independent or separate in her/his interpersonal relationships is also often assumed to have intact ego boundaries (American Psychiatric Association, 1987).

Women typically have more flexible ego boundaries which allows them to move close, pull back, and then move closer again. Men tend to have more rigid boundaries and maintain more distance in their interpersonal contacts (Chodorow, 1978). The question is whether women's flexibility is due to an undifferentiated ego state, as has been the assumption of most psychological theories, or whether it is due to a sense of self that is not threatened by flexibility. Society seems to have equated rigidity with strength when it may in reality be indicative of a fragile sense of self. This belief has supported the male oriented notion that flexibility means fragility and weakness. As a result a valid analysis of male and female psychological development is not possible within the current mainstream psychological theories where "different but equally valuable or healthy" is a foreign concept.

What is a healthy sense of self? My definition revolves around physical, psychological, and affective interpersonal boundaries. Does a person have ths ability and the experience of being able to contain her/his own feelings within her/his own boundaries? Clunis and Green (1988) see a boundary as:

> that intangible bubble that surrounds each of us at our core. This bubble contains our sense of self, and separates what is "me" from what is "not me." The outside world, other people, skills and traits I don't have are all examples of "not me." Someone who is *not* afraid of heights is different from me — "not me."

Can someone be empathic with another person who is not afraid of heights without losing her/his sense of self? Jordan (1983) theorizes that empathy requires the basic ability to recognize another person's affective cues. Empathy also implies "temporary identification with the other's emotional state" and that the empathizer regain a sense of "separate self that understands what just happened" (Jordan, 1983). Another word that describes this temporary identification is merger.

Merger

Merger by adults is most often described as an unhealthy event in psychological literature. However, it is used here to describe a *process* that is often positive. By this definition, merging results when two people experience themselves as one; their boundaries overlap, and they are unable to tell the difference between each other's feelings. There are at least three times in one's life when merger is healthy and developmentally appropriate. The first is when we are infants. We are merged with our primary caretaker, and we cannot differentiate ourselves from her/him. This phenomenon is crucial to our development and we should be supported in moving through this stage at our own pace. Another time in our lives when merger is healthy is when we are in the early stage of a romantic relationship. We tend to minimize difference and maximize sameness. We have that feeling of wanting to crawl under our lover's skin and it is very hard to tell where one person's feelings end and where the other's begin. The third time we may feel merged is when we are focused intensely on each other, usually for brief amounts of time. This is most common during some experiences of love making, but people can also experience merger at other times of intense togetherness such as during air raids, kidnapping, or working hard together on an important task.

While merger is used for all three above examples, there is a crucial difference in context among these examples that needs to be mentioned. When an infant is merged with her or his caretaker, it is because she or he has no differentiating ego boundaries. The infant has no choice but to be merged. When a healthy adult experiences merger, during love making, for instance, it is because the adult has chosen to let go of her/his boundaries for a finite amount of time. The experience of being merged may be similar for infant and adult (i.e., feeling as one with the other), but for the adult there really are interpersonal boundaries and for the infant there are none.

An adult who does not experience her or himself as having intact boundaries may respond to the possibility of merger in one or both of two ways. She or he may be terrified of getting too close and being swallowed up by the other. Or she or he may be terrified of becoming too distant and being abandoned. Both possibilities are too much like the original parent/child relationship, which for the adult whose dependency needs in childhood were not met, was not safe the first time. For such a person the prospect of merger means reliving the terror of infancy. It is important not to confuse the reaction to merger of adults who have healthy boundaries with that of adults whose dependency needs have not been satisfied.

I believe, as does Beverly Burch (1985), that problems occur not because of the process of merger but because a person is unable to differentiate enough to feel separate. She or he experiences the merger as a condition over which there is little control. There is no sense that it is a choice to merge one's self with another's self, even temporarily. For the sake of clarity, I will refer to being involuntarily *stuck* in closeness as fusion and the *process* that happens when people's boundaries temporarily overlap, as merger.

There are other ways of being with someone else in addition to merger. Contact results when two people are together, focused on something else instead of each other, such as a game of cards. Separateness is when the people are focused on different things. A healthy person can be in a relationship with someone else and be merged at times, be in contact, or even separate from the other at different times during the relationship (Clunis & Green, 1988). Someone who is unable to tolerate these changes in distance has some sense of fragility in her or his sense of self.

The Definition of Personal Success and Health

Girls are reared to believe that being in a relationship is the only way to be a healthy woman. Boys are reared to believe that success as an *individual* (usually in business and sports) is the sign of health (Doyle, 1983). Many men, however, do report feeling very close to other men with whom they have shared an intense experience, such as in certain sports competitions and in wars. Most men may be so defended against closeness or merger that it takes extraordinary situations for them to relax their defenses against feeling close to someone else or to feel that they have permission to experience closeness. It may be that what men feel in these situations is the equivalent to the closeness women experience on a more day to day basis. It may be that most men need the rules they develop for business and sports in order to feel safe enough to feel connected to another person. Without the rules most men keep their boundaries rigid to protect against possible closeness and merger.

Chodorow (1978) hypothesizes that boys realign their identification from mother to father or, female to male. They thus need to defend against their original experience of merger, which was with their mother, to prevent them from becoming confused about their identity. This may also extend to their avoiding behaviors and feelings that seem too "feminine."

Psychological theories, instead of seeing the male response to the developmental dilemma as one piece of what is true for our species, have elevated men's experience as the only normative path of health. Men who stay home with their children may be seen as less masculine and, thus, less healthy. The corollary of this, that women who are successful in business or sports are less feminine and less healthy, does not seem to be as prevalent. This is likely due to society's overvaluing male role behavior. Anyone who crosses lines to be more like a man may be seen as a little strange but not as pathological. Someone who engages in the undervalued female role behavior is seen, however, as pathological (Lynn, 1966). People, typically, are not encouraged to incorporate the two extremes of the merged-distanced continuum into their sense of self because it may raise the spectre of role and gender confusion for men.

Generally, however, I think women have managed to incorporate more facets of the whole range of human behavior than men have, because society as a whole has considered women less important. We have not been seen as the standard bearers of our culture, and therefore are not as noticed or censored when we are "aberrant."

WOMEN IN RELATIONSHIPS TOGETHER

While Merilee Clunis and I were working on our book about lesbian couples (Clunis & Green, 1988), we kept returning to the concept that if most lesbian couples have a similar experience, it might be that such an experience is normal no matter how different it is from heterosexual norms. We talk about the dynamic of merger that is likely to be an issue in lesbian couples. We say that heterosexual couples give the illusion of stability because one half of the couple is more distanced (usually the man) and one half of the couple is more attached (usually the woman). This balance can look like intimacy from the outside. Lesbian couples have no man or gender difference to introduce distance between the individuals. Both partners have been reared to value connectedness and to work hard on maintaining an intimate relationship.

Women are socialized to be convinced that we must be in a relationship to be worthwhile. As a result, many lesbians frequently consider themselves to be in a relationship before the third date, long before they know enough information about the other woman to decide whether they really want to be in a relationship with her. Then, one or two years later when the romance wears off, they are in the position of ending a relationship that should have been limited to a few dates. That is the bad news. The good news is that lesbians in couples usually do put a lot of "quality time" into their relationships. They work hard to design a life that nurtures both women and the couple. They are both usually willing to admit their dependency on each other and other people. This is, of course, affected by how out of the closet the women can be and how easy it is for them to find people who are supportive of their lifestyle (Clunis & Green, 1988).

Because we are women, lesbians have also been enculturated to believe in the necessity of being in a relationship and are more aware of and desirous of strong interpersonal networks. Instead of looking for the Mr. Right that the culture says we need, we are looking for Ms. Right. A lesbian relationship has two partners who tend to be relationship focused and who have the emotional skills necessary to nurture the couple.

> When two people are involved in a healthy couple relationship, it is rather like two bubbles moving through the flow of contact, merging, and separateness. One complete bubble contacts the other, edge meets edge, differences are recognized and appreciated. In the merging experience, there is often the wonderful feeling of "losing oneself." However, the boundaries of the individual bubbles remain intact, rather than becoming blurred, even when the couple is in the merging phase of the relationship. (Clunis & Green, 1988, p. 31-32)

COUPLE DEVELOPMENTAL STAGES

It might be useful at this point to discuss couples from a developmental perspective in order to illustrate how the concepts of conflict, separation, and ego boundaries intersect. After the initial Romance Stage, most couples usually enter the Power Struggle (Campbell, 1980) or as Merilee Clunis and I call it for lesbian couples, the Conflict Stage (Clunis & Green, 1988). At this point the partners' sense of difference and separateness reasserts itself after the initial merger of early romance. This happens in all couples but in heterosexual couples the distancing of most men and the desire most women have for closeness often keep the issue from surfacing as much. A heterosexual couple with this dynamic can continue the illusion that they are experiencing intimacy, when it is really an imbalanced and unacknowledged form of interdependence. Gay male couples also experience similar dynamics when faced with conflict but due to their training as men, they are not likely to confront openly their issues around dependency and closeness. They are also usually more comfortable than women with the distance and separateness that comes with conflict (Pollak & Gilligan, 1982).

In my clinical and personal experience, lesbian couples often reach the conflict stage of their relationship between years one and three. When a couple is healthy, conflict becomes a normal piece of the relationship and each partner is able to tolerate disagreements without feeling personally threatened. Sometimes a couple is not healthy and gets stuck in the merged position that began in the Romance Stage of their relationship. When this fusion happens, one or both partners tries to avoid conflict as one or both of the women do not have a sense of separateness or of individual wholeness; they feel complete only when they are merged.

> If a person has not developed a strong sense of self and clear boundaries, it is as if her boundary bubble has a gap, or weak spots. We might imagine this bubble as a "C" shape. . . . the boundary that separates this person from others is not complete. There is a gap. When a person with a "C" shaped boundary gets involved in a relationship, the boundaries between the two individuals in the couple may become blurred. (Clunis & Green, 1988, p. 31)

Fusion

Difference or conflict forces the issue out into the open of whether the women have a sense of wholeness or a sense of incompleteness. A lesbian couple with incomplete boundaries feels like they will explode when the conflict stage arises and may try to contain the explosion by forcing sameness and discounting the emerging differences. Even a couple with intact boundaries may try to discount the conflict because as women they have not been encouraged to develop conflict resolution skills. Thus, lesbian couples may try to avoid conflict out of either lack of skills or out of fear of being separate. Since women are encouraged by society to value relationships and to focus much of their attention on these relationships, it is quite likely that a lesbian couple will have a tendency to merge. And since women are not taught how to be separate and how to feel good about being separate within a relationship the lesbian couple who merges also has a good chance of becoming stuck and, hence, fused.

Another pressure that facilitates fusion is society's hostility which discredits and disallows lesbian coupling. This struggle with the outside world has the effect of forcing the two women even more inward as they try to stay coupled. It is hard for any couple in these circumstances to feel comfortable with conflict and to flow easily between merger, contact, and separateness.

If healthy women can get fused, imagine how likely it is for women who do not trust their ability to maintain their sense of themselves. The societal pressure on women to be relationship focused, the historical punishment of women who dare to push into other areas of interest, and the hostility towards lesbian couples put a tremendous amount of pressure on weak boundaries. It is very tempting to find a relationship and then hang on.

In spite of the potential problems for a couple who gets fused, merger for these women can be part of the healing process for them. A woman with a damaged sense of self "can find nurturance that was withheld from her as a child" (Burch, 1985). Obviously, she cannot replace what she did not get but being merged in a relationship with a lover can affect her sense of her self-image and her feelings of loveableness. "It can, in effect, enlarge her capacity to receive" (Burch, 1985). Such a couple also needs to learn how to move in and out of merger, contact, and distance, but being merged is one of the ways a person can begin the process of healing. Without merger as part of a couple's repertoire of ways of being together the individuals risk losing the opportunity to grow in the context of a relationship.

When a lesbian couple comes into my office they are often asking for help in learning how to be separate within their couple or how to end the relationship without feeling like failures as women. They do not know how to do either one and still feel good about themselves. As in Pollack and Gilligan's study (1982), women tend to feel scared when they think about being isolated. This fear, coupled with a sexist and homophobic society (for many women this is also compounded by racism, classism, and paternalism towards women with disabilities) and little encouragement to learn conflict resolution styles, leaves many women terrified of conflict in their important relationships. The wonderful aspect of a lesbian couple's seeking therapy is that they are often looking for a way to heal not only the couple but themselves as individuals as well. Thus, a couple who is coming out of the merging process into conflict can strengthen their boundaries which in turn allows more individual flexibility and health. Beverly Burch (1985) puts it well when she says:

> The experience of merger can be a part of this process of growth: finding one's self inside the merger and keeping one's self through the transition back out of it. Trust in the self is built by learning that one can love deeply and not have one's self devoured or abandoned. (p. 107)

Intimacy and Interdependency

When a lesbian couple is healthy the two women feel separate from one another and yet able to give good attention to the relationship. They have separate and mutual friends, both as individuals and as a couple. They are able to maximize woman's value of interconnectedness and weave a strong network that nurtures and yet supports stimulation. In the case of a biracial lesbian couple, for instance, each woman has her separate cultural/racial identity in addition to her identity as part of their couple. The woman of color may spend time with other women of color as she maintains her identity as a person of color. The white partner may choose to gather with other white women who are in biracial couples. And both of them may spend time with other biracial couples for support and understanding.

A difference that often shows up between women of color, white, working class, and middle class women is the amount of money and time they devote to their families. Women of color and working class women are often criticized by white, middle class partners for spending too much time and/or money on their families of origin. So, even in a couple with healthy boundaries, one partner may feel that her partner is not sufficiently differentiated from her family of origin. This provides an example of the two kinds of separation. The women may have sufficiently secure boundaries to have a flexible, separate-yet-together relationship (ego boundary separation). Yet they may still believe the white, upper class myth that we have to be independent from our families or other people in order to be healthy (interpersonal relationship separation).

Some cultures are more mutually interdependent than middle class, white United States (Bradshaw, 1988; Protacio-Marcelino, 1988). I think this demonstrates more ego flexibility and, hence, better mental health as regards ego boundaries. This does not mean that such cultures are not sexist. Almost all cultures are sexist and seriously impair women's development. If men in Eastern cultures have been better able to be close and acknowledge their interdependence, then they have developed some of the health that Western men have missed. But Eastern men still see women as less worthwhile and not significant or privileged enough to do what men do in those cultures. These men, too, have restricted their own growth in some of the same ways Western men have. While women across the world may have developed more flexibility in our ego boundaries, and by my definition, more health, we have also been so conditioned to see ourselves as "less than" and so restricted that we have developed other problems that affect our sense of self and, therefore, our mental health (Phyllis Chesler, 1972).

CONCLUSIONS

Luise Eichenbaum, Susie Orbach, Jean Baker Miller, Carol Gilligan, Merilee Clunis, and I all write about essentially the same issue even if our language varies. We are all examining the idea that women's ways of being in the world are valid and healthy. We acknowledge the struggle that women face as we learn how to be separate and individuated within the context of a relationship. This is particularly crucial for women because relationships are where we strengthen our sense of ourselves as individuals and derive our energy to create. It is clear that theorists have to look at development within context. People of color in this country have evolved in their own cultures and as oppressed groups. Their development cannot be evaluated just from the white male perspective. Eastern cultures likewise cannot be evaluated from a narcissistic Western perspective. Every culture, and this includes women, needs to be seen as viable options, not as second rate alternatives. To do this we need to learn the language, the strengths, and the context of that development. Then we will have the beginnings of what individual human development on this planet is all about.

REFERENCES

American Psychiatric Association (1987). *Diagnostic and statistical manual of mental disorders* (3rd Ed, Revised). Washington: American Psychiatric Association, 353-354.

Becker, Carol (1988). *Unbroken ties: Lesbian ex-lovers*. San Francisco: Allyson Press.

Blumstein, Philip & Schwartz, Pepper (1983). *American couples*. New York: William Morrow and Company.

Bradshaw, Carla (1988, May). *A Japanese view of dependency: What can it contribute to feminist theory and therapy?* Paper presented at the Advanced Therapy Institute Conference. Seattle, WA.

Broverman, Inga K. (1984, August). Sex role stereotypes and clinical judgments of mental health: An update. Paper presented at the annual meeting of the American Psychological Association.

Broverman, Inge K., Broverman, Donald M., Clarkson, Frau L., Rosenkrantz, Paul, & Vogel, Susan R. (1970). Sex role stereotypes and clinical judgments of mental health. *Journal of Consulting and Clinical Psychology, 34*, 1-7.

Burch, Beverly (1985). Another perspective on merger in lesbian relationships. In L. B. Rosewater & L. E. A. Walker (Eds.), *Handbook of feminist therapy* (pp. 100-109). New York: Springer Publishing.

Campbell, Susan M. (1980). *The couple's journey*. San Luis Obispo, CA: Impact Publishers.

Chesler, Phyllis (1972). *Women and madness*. New York: Avon Books.

Chodorow, Nancy (1978). *The reproduction of mothering: Psychoanalysis and the sociology of gender*. Berkeley, CA: University of California Press.

Clunis, D. Merilee, & Green, G. Dorsey (1988). *Lesbian couples*. Seattle, WA: The Seal Press.

Doyle, James A. (1983). *The male experience*. Dubuque, IA: William C. Brown.

Eichenbaum, Luise, & Orbach, Susie (1988). *Between women*. New York: Viking.

Espin, Oliva (1987). Issues of identity in the psychology of Latina lesbians. In the Boston Lesbian Psychologies collective (Ed.) *Lesbian psychologies*. Urbana, IL: University of Illinois Press, 35-55.

Gilligan, Carol (1982). *In a different voice*. Cambridge, MA: Harvard University Press.

Jordan, Judith (1983). Empathy and the mother-daughter relationship. *Work in Progress*. No. 82-02, Wellesley, MA: Wellesley College.

Lever, Janet (1976). Sex differences in the games children play. *Social Problems*, 23, 478-487.

Lynn, David B. (1966). The process of learning parental and sex-role identification. *Journal of Marriage and the Family, 28*, 466-470.

Miller, Jean Baker (1976). *Toward a new psychology of women*. Boston: Beacon Press.

Moses, A. Elfin, & Hawkins, Robert, Jr. (1982). *Counseling lesbian women and gay men*. St. Louis: The C. V. Mosby Co.

Pollak, Susan, & Gilligan, Carol (1982). Images of violence in Thematic Apperception Test scores. *Journal of Personality and Social Psychology*, 42(*1*), 159-167.

Protacio-Marcelino, Elizabeth (1988, May). *Towards understanding the psychology of the Filipino*. Paper presented at the Advanced Feminist Therapy Institute Conference. Seattle, WA.

Stiver, Irene P. (1984). The meanings of "dependency" in female-male relationships. *Work in Progress*. No. 83-07, Wellesley, MA: Wellesley College.

Trudeau, Gary B. (1984). *Doonesbury: The Reagan years*. New York: Holt, Rinehart and Winston.

Zitter, Sherry (1987). Coming out to mom: Theoretical aspects of the mother-daughter process. In the Boston Lesbian psychologies collective (Ed.) *Lesbian psychologies*. Urbana, IL: University of Illinois Press, 177-194.

Towards Understanding the Psychology of the Filipino

Elizabeth Protacio Marcelino, PhD

SUMMARY. This article describes the development of a new consciousness in Philippine psychology called "Sikolohiyang Pilipino" (Filipino Psychology). It attempts to give national form and substance to the scientific discipline of psychology by critically examining the strong influence of American psychological models in Philippine psychology and explains how the practical applications of "Sikolohiyang Pilipino" in therapy differ from the Western methods. It presents an alternative framework of looking at human behavior particularly in the context of non-Western cultures and identifies key concepts in understanding the Filipino's mind, personality, and behavior. It elaborates on indigenous research methods that are more relevant and appropriate to Philippine realities.

I am often confronted with the question, "Is there really such a thing as Filipino Psychology?" At a very simple level, one could say, "There is a Filipino Psychology as long as there are Filipinos." But that is begging the question and further leads to another question, "Who is the Filipino?"

If one turns the pages of Western history books, it is written that

Elizabeth Protacio Marcelino is Assistant Professor of Psychology at the University of the Philippines where she teaches Psychology of Language and Filipino Psychology. Together with other colleagues, she helped develop these courses after many years of teaching in the native language. She also heads a rehabilitation center which provides therapy for child victims of political violence. A Filipino in heart and mind, she is actively engaged in promoting, both in her academic and practical work, a psychology that is relevant to the needs and aspirations of the Filipino people.

Correspondence may be addressed to the author at: Department of Psychology, CSSP, University of the Philippines, Diliman, Quezon City, Philippines.

there were no Filipinos before the Spaniards came to our shores in 1521 (Constantino, 1975). The term "Filipino" did not exist until the latter part of Spanish colonial rule. When first used, "Filipino" did not refer to the people inhabiting the archipelago in general, but to the "creoles" or the Spaniards born in the Philippines. It was, then, an elitist term used to distinguish a group of persons who were above the natives but not quite equal in status with the "peninsulares" or the Spanish officialdom and the clergy.

One could answer the above question in a legal sense and define the Filipino on the basis of geographical origin, birth, or blood. Though very convenient and simplistic, this definition would be far from adequate from a psychological perspective. One could simply enumerate the many and varied traits and characteristics possessed by the Filipinos, but these would not say much either. There may be other groups of people who also possess these traits and characteristics, differing only in the labels attached to them. In this case there is little significance in calling them uniquely "Filipino." Perhaps one can loosely state like Munoz (1971) that "A Filipino is one who thinks, feels and says he is." This definition, although broad and all encompassing, does not face the issue head-on.

A BRIEF HISTORY OF PSYCHOLOGY IN THE PHILIPPINES

To approach the problem of Filipino identity from the point of view of psychology, it is necessary to seriously consider the history of psychology in the Philippines. Psychology in the Philippines has both a long and short history. One finds indigenous psychology cataloged in a written history even before the Spaniards came among the "babaylans" and the "catalonans" (high priest and priestess) (Enriquez, 1977). However, one can only share the despair and anger of many Filipino scholars in reading Chirino's account (1604) of how members of the Jesuit order destroyed hundreds of Tagalog manuscripts—an act which after more than 300 years is still unforgivable.

Psychology as an academic discipline started in the Philippines about the turn of the century when the United States as colonizer came to the country and established a comprehensive educational system using English language as the primary medium of instruction (Lagmay, 1984). It is important to note that all other Philippine institutions developed concomitantly within the framework of the English language.

The spread of American culture and the Westernization of Philippine education led to the assumption that the Americans brought psychology to the Philippines together with their policy of "benevolent assimilation." If we accept this claim, psychology, then, is a direct importation from the West, from theory to method to practice. It is no surprise then that Americans (Sechrest & Guthrie, 1974) feel at home writing about "psychology of, by and for the Filipino" without being immersed in the native culture and without making an effort to learn the local language.

As a scientific discipline, psychology is generally viewed as a continuation of the development of psychology in the West. Historians of psychology, wittingly or unwittingly, drop the word "Western" when they write about the history of Western psychology. On the other hand, "Asian psychology" is always properly designated as such. This is understandable if the audience consists exclusively of Western scholars and readers. These above assumptions could also spring from a well-meaning interest in the people of a former colony. But the fact remains that the history of a relevant psychology, like the history of all colonized peoples, has to be rewritten. Alternative perspectives from non-Western psychologies should be seriously taken into consideration.

SIKOLOHIYANG PILIPINO:
A NEW CONSCIOUSNESS IN PSYCHOLOGY

"Sikolohiyang Pilipino" (Filipino Psychology) began in the early '70s initially as a protest against Philippine psychology's colonial character and the uncritical acceptance of American psychological models. With American textbooks in psychology, Filipinos began learning not only American psychology but a new culture. A major basis for perpetuating the American orientation of psychology in the Philippines is the use of English language in teaching and research. Psychology graduates who generally uphold and are dependent on American theories and methods are unable to perceive the limitations of the English language. They have no chance at all to think in the Filipino language and to formulate theories based on the Filipino people's experiences. A vicious cycle is thus formed as they pursue their careers in and out of the academe, further reinforcing the American orientation. This has resulted in a psychology that is elitist, i.e., limited to an elite group who can hardly communicate with the larger non-English speaking mass of people.

While theories and methods all over the world may be somewhat similar, real life settings of behavior vary radically from one cultural group to another. There is nothing wrong in studying foreign theories and methods and updating oneself on the developments in psychology in other countries. But these should only serve as guides and should not be mechanically adopted and applied. These psychologies are valuable as they inform the reader of the culture within which they originate. Acceptance of American psychological theories and methods as universal has obscured the necessity of examining the applicability of these theories to the objective realities and nuances of Filipino life and culture. While it is true that psychologists in academia are no longer contented with research on sophomore students or white rats, this is not enough data to develop a truly indigenous psychology. Field research and cross-cultural research, although important in generating a broader data-base, are still far from adequate in establishing a universal psychology.

"Sikolohiyang Pilipino" is an attempt by some Filipino psychologists to examine the ways in which one can give national form and substance to the scientific discipline of psychology. Giving a national character to psychology in the Philippines not only meets the requirement of fully appreciating Philippine life and culture, but it is also a contribution to the goal of evolving a universal psychology. This is the only way that psychology can be relevant to the needs and aspirations of the Filipino people, as all sciences should be.

As a commitment to this goal, "Sikolohiyang Pilipino" urges Filipino psychologists to confront social problems and national issues as part of their responsibility as social scientists. Thus, "Sikolohiyang Pilipino" emerged among those who criticized the American orientation of education in the Philippines and the use of English in teaching and research. As Enriquez and Marcelino (1984) strongly articulated:

> The colonial relationship between the USA and the Philippines demonstrate that language is power. With the imposition of the English language, the country became dependent on a borrowed language that carries with it the dominant ideology and political-economic interests of the USA. With the dependence of the country on a borrowed language, it became dependent, too, on foreign theories and methods underlying the borrowed language, thus, resulting in a borrowed consciousness. The people's values were then more easily modified so that they equate foreign interest with national interest. Thus, it became easier for the USA to further subjugate the Filipino people and impose its will on them.

THE IMPORTANCE OF LANGUAGE IN PHILIPPINE PSYCHOLOGY

Language is not merely a tool for communication nor a neutral system of signs and symbols. Each language is partisan to the values, perspectives, and rules of cognition of a particular class of society. One need not completely agree with the Sapir-Whorf hypothesis (1940) to be convinced of the clear connection between language and culture. It is for this reason that one's faith in language leads to the belief that meaningful concepts of understanding society and human behavior are probably most identifiable in language.

Take the case of sexism in language. In the last three decades, the feminists, particularly in the West, have created considerable furor over sexism in the English language. Anyone who tries to learn

German, Spanish, or Japanese, to name a few other languages, soon realizes the biases in these languages favor the male gender.

In an extensive and revealing study, Estrada (1981) showed that the original Tagalog language (one of the eight major languages spoken in the Philippines) does not contain sexist biases and reflects the equal treatment given to both male and female. Unfortunately, however, Spanish and American influences slowly introduced sexism in the language as Tagalog and other Philippine languages assimilated a sexist bias in favor of males.

To illustrate the former point, Estrada (1981) makes the observation that most Filipinos, even those presumably well-schooled in English, frequently interchange the use of he/she, her/his in ordinary conversation. This curious phenomenon can be explained by the fact that Tagalog does not have equivalents for the English he/she, etc. Tagalog only has "siya" or "kanya" or the formal "sila" or "kanila." She further elaborates that the other major languages spoken in the Philippines also do not have he/she or her/his equivalents either.

Moreover, Estrada (1981) asserts that if sexism was an element at all in the language, it would manifest itself in the realm of kinship. Tagalog has no specific sex-linked terms for the most important kin. For example, there is only one word "pamangkin" to mean niece or nephew. The sex of the person referred to may be established by attaching the proper qualifier "babae" (female) or "lalake" (male) to the kinship term. From the entire system of interlocking kin for which there is precise terminology only two are gender-marked and are not borrowed and these are primary ones, "ama/ina" (father/mother).

She goes on to prove her thesis that Tagalog is generally nonsexist by showing examples in the various domains of Philippine life and culture specifically focusing on the following: forms of address, terms of endearment, sexual terminology, professions/occupations, learning in early childhood, swearwords/curses, mythology and folk medicine. If Tagalog does show bias, it is more ageist than sexist.

To illustrate the latter point, the terms "lolo/lola" and their derivative "lelong/lelang," "tiyo/tiya" and their derivatives tiyuhin/tiyahin are from the Spanish "abuelo/abuela, tio/tia" respectively.

The term "maybahay" now commonly used to mean housewife formerly referred to either husband or wife (Santiago, 1977). The marking of "maybahay" as feminine is an instance of what Estrada sees as the increasing chauvinization of Tagalog.

VALUES AND THE CONTINUING MIS-EDUCATION OF THE FILIPINO

Earlier work on Philippine values identified some important concepts in understanding Filipino behavior. Lynch (1964) proposed the construct of "smooth interpersonal relations" as acquired and perceived through "pakikisama" (adjustment to the will of the majority). Kaut (1961) singled out "utang na loob" (debt of gratitude) as a key concept in Tagalog interpersonal relations. "Hiya" was interpreted by Fox (1956) as "self-esteem," by Bulatao (1964) as a kind of anxiety and fear of being left exposed, and by Silbley (1965) as "shame" — just to name a few of many other frequently mentioned values.

However, Enriquez (1977) pointed out that in spite of the token use of the language in previous studies, the methods used were still patterned after American models. The conclusions derived were still premised on English categories of analysis governed by the structure of American culture. The studies themselves were still written in English, reflecting only a limited description of the Filipino psyche. In spite of the indigenous material used, the resulting theory could not truly reflect Philippine social realities. In fact, it perpetuated a further subtle distortion of reality and to borrow Constantino's (1982) much quoted phrase, "the continuing mis-education of the Filipino."

Take for example, "pakikisama" (adjusting to the will of the majority), as a supposed Filipino value. One tends to overlook the fact that this is only one among the many levels or modes of interaction in Filipino indigenous psychology (see below). Although "pakikisama" should be accepted as a value in one level of interpersonal relation, one should carefully consider the context in which "pakikisama" is used. How does one label a person, for instance, who will not take part in corruption? He/she is identified as "walang pakikisama" (not adjusting to the will of the majority) simply because he/she insists on being honest. Is it a value then, in this case, to reward docility and conformity? What image does this create of the Filipino? The logical consequence is that they are considered negative and do not register a value in the sphere of "pakikibaka" (social protest) (Navarro, 1974).

The concept of "hiya" has been loosely translated by Sibley (1965) to mean "shame" when the Filipino experience tells us that it is simply "a sense of propriety." Referring to someone as "nahihiya" (ashamed) does not mean that she/he has lost face. However, if one is "nakakahiya" (shameful), it means that one has no manners. In this case, it is important to pay attention to the prefixes "na-" and "nakaka-." The Filipino language has an elaborate system of affixes which English lacks. The erroneous interpretation shows a lack of consideration for the importance of the local language and its subtleties and nuances. Sometimes, the token use of the language is even more dangerous than not using it at all!

What is notable in Kaut's (1961) analysis of "utang na loob" (debt of gratitude) is the insufficient attention given to the role of language in the formation of a concept. "Utang na loob" is only one of the many concepts that relate to the theoretically fertile concept of "loob" (inner core). Why choose "utang na loob" alone? Could it be convenient in perpetuating the colonial status of the Filipino in being grateful for American aid? Is it not more productive for the Filipino to highlight the concepts of "lakas na loob" (risk-taking behavior) and "kusang-loob" (initiative)? Using the native language could, in fact, reveal other psycho-social concepts that relate to "loob." Samonte (1973) needed no less than three pages to list the lexical domain of this particular concept.

KEY CONCEPTS IN SIKOLOHIYANG PILIPINO

"Sikolohiyang Pilipino" has embarked on the very difficult task of identifying key concepts for understanding a people's mind, personality, and behavior. The basic assumption is that such a concept already exists or can be discovered through a process of concept formulation. It is strongly believed that discovery of concepts and theories significant to Philippine society and culture is more important than blind translations of Western ideas, no matter how faithful one is to the original. It is interesting to note, therefore, that a whole new body of literature has emerged through the use of the native language as a tool in delineating and articulating Philippine realities.

This brings us back to the original question of the Filipino personality. Loosely translated, one could say "personalidad" to refer to the characteristic and typical patterns of behavior of a person. Filipino identity, however, is not simply the stereotype or projected image of the self. More specifically, one should use "pagkatao" which refers to being human, while "personalidad" is closer in meaning to the Western concept of personality. One may change his/her "personalidad" just like the change involved in wearing a mask. However, his/her "pagkatao" is not only the face he/she shows to people but rather the totality of being human.

An analysis of social interaction in the Philippine setting is a good starting point for understanding of the Filipino character. The Filipino language provides a conceptual distinction in several levels and modes of interaction. Santiago and Enriquez (1976) identified eight levels:

1. pakikitungo (transaction/civility with)
2. pakikisalamuha (interaction with)
3. pakikilahok (joining/participating with)
4. pakikibagay (in conformity with/in accord with)
5. pakikisama (getting along with)
6. pakikipag-palagayang-loob (having rapport with)
7. pakikisangkot (getting involved with)
8. pakikiisa (being one with)

According to the authors, the distinctions among the eight levels go beyond the conceptual and the theoretical. They are more than just interrelated modes of interpersonal relations. More importantly, they are levels of interaction which range from the relatively uninvolved civility of "pakikitungo" to the total sense of identification in "pakikiisa." They further elaborated that the different levels are not just conceptually but also behaviorally different. Five behaviorally recognizable levels were discussed under two general categories:

"Ibang-Tao" or Outsider Category

Level:
   pakikitungo (level of amenities)
   pakikibagay (level of conformity)
   pakikisama (level of adjusting)

"Hindi Ibang-Tao" or Insider Category

Level:
   pakikipag-palagayang-loob (level of mutual trust)
   pakikiisa (level of fusion, oneness, full trust)

The foregoing is ample evidence for the claim that the domain of interpersonal relations is theoretically fertile and lexically elaborate in Filipino.

Kapwa: A Core Concept in Filipino Social Psychology

In a conscious search for a core concept that would explain Filipino interpersonal relations, Enriquez (1977) was struck with the superordinate concept of "kapwa." According to him, it is the only concept which embraces both categories of "outsider" (ibang tao) and "insider" (hindi ibang tao). Similarly, "pakikipagkapwa" cuts across all levels of both categories. Enriquez (1977) explains the meaning of "kapwa":

When asked for the closest English equivalent of "kapwa," one word comes to mind, the English word "others." However, the Filipino word "kapwa" is very different from the English word "others" because "kapwa" is the unity of the "self" and the "others." The English word "others" is actually used in opposition to the "self" and implies the recognition of the "self" as a separate identity. In contrast, "kapwa" is a recognition of shared identity.

A person starts having "kapwa" not so much because of a recognition of status given him by others but more so because of his awareness of shared identity. The "ako" (ego) and the "iba sa akin" (others) are one and the same in "kapwa" psychology which says "hindi ako iba sa aking kapwa" (I am no different from others). Once "ako" starts thinking of himself as different from "kapwa," the self, in effect, denies the status of "kapwa" to the other.

Presumably, because of the importance of "kapwa," the Filipino language has two pronouns for the English "we"; an inclusive "we" (tayo) and an exclusive "we" (kami). "Tayo" includes the listener while "kami" excludes him.

Brislin (1977) noted that all cultures distinguish between the "in-group" and the "out-group," the "members" and the "non-members," or the "insiders" and the "outsiders." He surmised that this might be an example or a "universal" or "etic" distinction as opposed to "emic" or "culture-specific." Yet there seems to be at least one culture that does not fit into this mold perfectly. For the Filipino, the "ibang tao" (outsider) is "kapwa" in the same manner that the "hindi ibang tao" (insider) is also "kapwa" (unity of the self and the other).

The concept of "pakikipagkapwa," therefore, is very important psychologically as well as philosophically. It is much deeper and more profound in its implications because it has a moral as well as a normative aspect as a value and a "paninindigan" (conviction) which is another equally important concept in Philippine social psychology. "Pakikipagkapwa" means accepting and dealing with the other person as an equal and with respect and dignity. It is definitely inconsistent with exploitative human relations. As Santiago (1976) would put it, "pakikipagkapwa" refers to "humaneness" at its highest level.

The great importance of "kapwa" in Filipino thought and behavior is expressed in the negative reaction to one who is "walang kapa tao." If one is "walang pakisama" (not adjusting to the will of the majority), one could still be forgiven because that is the individual's prerogative. If one is "walang hiya" (lacks a sense of propriety), one can still be tolerated because one will eventually learn. However, if one is labelled "walang kapwa-tao," then one is the worst human being. As a Tagalog proverb says: "Madaling maging tao, mahirap ang magpakatao" (It is easy to be born a human being, but it is not easy to act like one).

Before one gets the impression that the Filipino is all smiles and all giving, it is equally important to discuss how the Filipino responds when treated unfairly or when his/her "pakikipagkapawa-tao" is abused. For example, how does the Filipino react to frustration and exploitative relations? It is wrong to assume that the Filipino accepts his/her fate with resignation and fatalism ("bahala na'') (Guthrie 1968). If one really tries to understand the concept of "bahala na" in Philippine culture, it implies an element of faith in a god (bathala) that goes with a sense of optimism and responsibility for one's action. While it is observed that Filipinos when provoked do not very easily display their emotions verbally, it is a distortion of the Filipino response to say that their reaction is essentially that of silence or "pagtitiis" (quiet desperation). One should not forget the adeptness of the Filipino to nonverbal cues known as "pashiwatig" or the elaborate art of "pakikiramdam" (feeling or sensing through) in everyday life.

For example, from the imperceptible expression of "tampo" (very mild hurt feelings) to "hinanakit" (resentment) and "sama ng loob" (deep grudge), one sees the transformation of the emotion of "galit" (anger). Initially expressed indirectly, covertly and non-verbally, the frustration progresses until it leads to direct, overt and verbal aggression or retaliation. As the Filipino saying goes: "Ang tapayan kapag napuno ay umaapam" (A jar when full overflows).

The Filipino knows the meaning of "pagbibigay" (giving deference to the other), but he/she also knows that "pakikibaka" (to struggle or fight) is a valid aspect of "pakikipagkapwa" in the face of injustice and exploitation. While it is "pakikipag-kapwa" that moves him to respect the dignity and rights of others, he/she also knows how to protest (makibaka) when his own rights are violated. It is with great pride that we remember that Magellan (who Western historians say discovered the Philippines) did not make it in Mactan (an island in the southern part of the Philippines) because Lapu-Lapu (a native hero) was there to resist Spanish colonization.

PROBLEMS IN WESTERN RESEARCH METHODOLOGY

In criticizing American psychological theories and models as well as presenting alternative views as embodied in "Sikolohiyang Pilipino," it is inevitable that one is confronted with the problems inherent in and created by Western research methodologies. One cannot ignore the growing dissatisfaction among a number of Filipino social scientists who have experienced great difficulties in using Western research methods because of their inappropriateness and inapplicability to the Philippine setting.

Because of the relatively few locally developed tests, American and other English language tests have been used and widely borrowed. It was initially assumed that the inadequate relevance of these tests or psychometric devices were merely due to problems of translating test instruments and developing local norms for the target population. However, personality inventories and other similar tests were found to have high culture-specific loadings (Lagmay, 1984), and therefore, simplistic adjustments failed to recognize the importance of the socio-cultural context. Furthermore, most practitioners soon realized that people from the rural areas and lower socio-economic groups did not have a good grasp of the English language in which most tests were being administered. These instruments, therefore, were not interpretable for the purposes of diagnosis or counseling.

One aspect of the relevance and usefulness of traditional psychometric devices that is often ignored is the issue of response styles. Felipe (1968) noted that the same inventory statements might not be perceived as equally socially desirable in the United States and the Philippines. Emphasis on "pakikisama" or smooth interpersonal relations makes the Filipino prone to give answers experimenters expect or desire and refrain from using the lower end of evaluation scales (Lynch, 1973). Similarly questionnaire surveys can be confounded by the Filipino tendency to say "yes" rather than "no" (Arkoff, Thaver, & Elkind, 1966). In addition, Hare (1969) found that Filipinos gave higher ratings of satisfaction with experimental participation than several other cultural groups.

Several studies further indicate that some traits and behavior constitute different constructs and may predict or interrelate differently in the Philippines as opposed to other cultures. For example, in a study of ethnic prejudice among university students, Weightman (1964) found that various social distance items (e.g., willingness to eat with, dance with, or have a relative marry members of different ethnic groups) did not interrelate in the way they do in American studies of prejudice.

With regards to the methods of data-gathering, Hendershot (1968) feels that certain assumptions about the interviewer-respondent relationship and the interview setting are more consistent with prevalent value themes and environmental realities in the United States than in the Philippines, e.g., universalistic and egalitarian relationships, efficient performance orientation, affective neutrality, privacy, and the absence of distraction from others. In contrast, some illustrative data from a Population Institute survey on migration and fertility is presented as evidence that the goal of privacy is rarely achieved in a Manila survey due to such conditions as the large number of people per household, small number of rooms, and other cultural factors related to privacy.

Feliciano (1965) drawing on considerable experience with survey research in the Philippines calls attention to similar problems in the implementation of Western research methods especially in the rural areas. She stressed the necessity of a less rigid structure in planning social research because of the limited amount and poor quality of locally available resources, difficulties in recruiting and training interviewers, and problems related to questions about time, distance, and precise quantities typical of Western or more urban settings. Guthrie (1968) similarly noted such problems with questionnaires as difficulties in translations, dubious cross-cultural validity, cultural differences in response styles, and the easy influencibility of responses by such factors as sex and ethnicity of examiner.

PROBLEMS IN THE APPLICATION
OF WESTERN MODELS IN THERAPY

In the field of practical work in psychology, psychiatrists, guidance counselors, and corporate psychologists have been the main practitioners of Freudian psychoanalysis, client-centered therapy, and behavior modification techniques despite recognition by many that these techniques may not be equally applicable for Filipinos. In principle, there is really nothing wrong in subscribing to a particular school of thought in psychology. What is being questioned here is its wholesale adoption and uncritical application in the Philippine setting.Navarro (1974) points this out emphatically:

> To the extent that the Filipino psychologist after the end of his academic training, tries to explain away the problems of the Filipinos according to the white man's concept of the etiology of mental illness, he continues the miseducation process. Take Western psychology, for instance, it generally takes the position that the individual is mostly to blame for his psycho-

logical problems. The sooner he accepts his problems, the faster the psychological intervention is provided, thus facilitating adjustment to his environment. A Filipino psychologist who subscribes to such a tenet by itself is ignorant of his country's history and lacks a total grasp of the psychosocial and political problems of Philippine society.

Western techniques largely assign the locus of control for behavior change and decision-making to the individual. This assumption may be less appropriate for more situation and group-centered cultures where the individual is defined not separately from the family and where a more dependent or external orientation is valued and accepted (Sue, 1978). In fact, it is strongly suggested that significant members of the family or group be involved in therapy and that use of the native language is critical (Salazar, 1976; Varias, 1963).

Reservations about using psychiatric or psychological services among Filipinos also reflect in part greater reliance on extended family, peer, and other social networks for emotional support and problem-solving (Bulatao (1980). It was also found that there was a greater preference for traditional "folk healers" especially for treatment of neuro-psychiatric or mental symptoms (Galvez-Tan, 1977; Valencia & Palo, 1979).

Conceptualizations of culture-relevant therapies draw on some findings to say, at least initially, that: (1) since Filipinos are more passive and modest with authority figures, the therapist may need to be more active and directive in the initial stages of therapy (Bulatao, 1978; Cuizon & Zingle, 1968), and (2) since Filipinos are more sensitive, have strong needs for acceptance, belonging and security in a relationship, the therapist may need to be closer and more paternalistic rather than non-directive (Varias, 1963).

SIKOLOHIYANG PILIPINO:
INDIGENOUS RESEARCH METHODS

Attempts at "indigenization" of Philippine psychology have taken a variety of forms. Enriquez (1977) has coined the terms "indigenization from without" (culture-as-target) approach versus "indigenization from within" (culture-as-source approach). Theoretically, the culture-as-target approach aims to demonstrate the universality or cross-cultural generality of existing constructs. In contrast, the culture-as-source approach identifies constructs that are truly indigenous. As Enriquez (1976), Salazar (1976), and Enriquez and Marcelino (1984) have repeatedly stressed, the native language provides a very rich source for the discovery of indigenous concepts. Many such concepts have not been studied because of dependence on the English language.

Enriquez and Marcelino (1984) went on to describe several indigenous concepts not found in any book on American psychology but which are meaningful concepts in Filipino psychology. An example is the concept of "saling-pusa" which refers to an individual who is included in an activity only in an informal or unofficial sense because he or she cannot be outrightly excluded without hurting his or her feelings. Another example is the concept of "pikon" which refers to someone who cannot take a joke or being teased — something that is particularly significant in Philippine culture where joking and teasing are frequent. As stated in the preface to their book *Neo-colonial Politics and Language Struggle in the Philippines*, Enriquez and Marcelino (1984) show that:

> An assessment of a decade of active use of Filipino in Philippine psychology has shown the adequacy and appropriateness of the native language as a tool of expression in contemporary psychology. In particular, it has shown alternative ways of developing terminology in Filipino which can be utilized in varying degrees of effectiveness. It has also shown the rich resource available for the categorization of words and concepts which give rise to significant psychological theories that comprehend better the realities of Philippine society and culture. Finally it has identified bases for the choice and planning of terminology in a Southeast Asian context towards the further growth and development of both the Filipino language and "Sikolohiyang Pilipino."

Calls for an indigenous psychology, therefore, have not been limited to rhetoric. Substantial efforts are underway especially in the formulation and utilization of various indigenous methods.

Much of this is based on the work of Santiago and Enriquez (1976). As a preliminary research model, it is organized around two scales: (1) "Iskala ng Mananaliksik" (Scale of the Researcher), and (2) "Iskala ng Pagtutunguhan ng Mananaliksik at Kalahok (Scale of the Relationship of the Researcher and Participant). The "Scale of the Researcher" represents a continuum varying from the relatively unobtrusive observational methods at the one end to the more obtrusive, researcher-participative methods at the other. This is illustrated in the following:

> pagmamasid (general scanning or looking around)
> pakikiramdam (sensing or feeling through)
> pagtatanong-tanong (unstructured, informal interactive)
> pagsubok (testing the situation)
> padalam-dalam (occasional visits made to respondents' homes)
> pakikilahok (participating with)
> pakikisangkot (deeper participation and involvement)

The "Scale of the Relationship of Researcher and Participant" is based on the Filipino view of the equality of this relationship and the fact that it passes through different levels. The top of the scale describes a relatively superficial level of researcher-participant relationship, while the bottom of the scale touches on the deepest levels of relationships. Again, this is shown in the following:

Outsider Category

> pakikitungo (level of superficial good manners)
> pakikisalamuha (level of casual socializing with)
> pakikilahok (level of actual participation)
> pakikibagay (level of adjusting one's feelings and speech for others)
> pakikisama (level of joining in for the sake of civility)

Insider Category

> pakikipagpalagayang-loob (level of trust)
> pakikisangkot (level of deeper participation and involvement)
> pakikiisa (level of deep respect where behavior feelings and speech show full love, understanding and acceptance of the other's aim as one's own)

The important point for the researcher is that the type, reliability, and genuineness of the information obtained by the researcher is a function of the level of researcher-participant relationship.

Torres (1980) defines an indigenous method called "pakapa-kapa" (literally, groping or searching) as "a suppositionless approach to social and scientific investigations characterized by groping, searching, and probing into an unsystematized mass of social and cultural data to be able to obtain order, meaning, and directions for research." Data is explored without the chains of overriding theoretical frameworks borrowed from observations outside the focus of investigation. The rationale for the method is based on the need for "Sikilohiyang Pilipino" to generate a broad data-base of concepts and behavior, free from the biases and frameworks of Western concepts and methodology. However, it may be best to view "pakapa-kapa" as a research approach or philosophy rather than a specific method in the usual sense.

The indigenous method of "pagtatanong-tanong" has also been widely discussed by many authors (e.g., Gonzales, 1982; Nicdao-Henson, 1982; Santiago, 1982; Pe-Pua, 1985). "Pagtatanong-tanong" is an unstructured, informal, and interactive form of questioning. It describes characteristics of the researcher and the respondent, suggestions for timing and location, and certain procedural steps.

Margallo (1981) concludes that while indigenous methods appear simpler and more appropriate than traditional Western approaches, they need much more skillful handling in order to uphold the scientific and ethical nature of research. She cautions the user on subjectivity that could lead to a higher probability of data contamination.

SIKOLOHIYANG PILIPINO: PRACTICAL APPLICATIONS IN THERAPY

The development of culture-relevant therapeutic techniques rely heavily on studies related to the Filipino's world view and cognition, motivation, and emotion, and contrast and changes in values and behavior. Several writers have discussed various aspects of the Filipino world view as personalistic rather than mechanistic (Lynch, 1973), with authoritarian rather than libertarian norms (Andres,

1981), more in a receptive rather than active cognitive mode (Bulatao, 1979), and more external than internal in their perceived locus-of-control (Bonifacio, 1977; Guthrie, 1968).

Other authors have sought to clarify the Filipino's world view through metalinguistic analyses, under the assumption that particular features of a language will provide clues to world view (Constantino, 1980; Enriquez & Alfonso, 1980). Similarly, Mercado (1974) drawing on some features of Philippine dialects concludes that the Filipino's thinking is intuitive, inductive, subjective, and non-dualistic.

A negative description of motivational aspects of the Filipino behavior repeatedly found in early writings on Filipino personality was the purported laziness or "indolence" of the Filipino. Rizal (1890/1957) argued that indolence was not inherent in the Filipino but the result of climactic conditions and Spanish misgovernment. He showed evidence that prior to the arrival of the Spaniards, the Filipino was not indolent. Lawless (1967), on the other hand, points out that labeling the Filipinos as lazy was an incredible value judgment and to expect Filipinos to work in pursuit of Western values is simply ethnocentric.

The Filipino's philosophy of work, according to Mercado (1974) is consistent with the non-dualistic world view. He cites examples of rural workers' and urban office workers' habit of combining work and leisure and explains this in terms of the high emphasis placed on personalism and interpersonal relations.

Many contrasts or conflicts between Filipino values or ideals and actual behavior has been noted by various authors (Nydegger & Nydegger, 1963; Bulatao, 1965) who suggest that this dichotomy may be due to inter-related urban-rural, traditional-modern distinctions and influences of social class. However, additional research is necessary to obtain firmer conclusions.

Unlike the significant efforts to develop indigenous research methods, attempts to formulate appropriate techniques in therapy suited to the Filipino personality are minimal. One of the few attempts was done by Bulatao (1978) in what he describes as "transpersonal counseling" where he made the following assumptions regarding counseling in the Philippines: (1) Filipinos are freer to be themselves when in a sympathetic group of friends than in a one-on-

one situation; (2) when supported by the group, Filipino clients prefer paternalistic counselors to non-directive ones who are perceived as detached, and non-caring; (3) the Filipino character is contemplative, patient, and accepting of things as they are; and (4) Filipino subjects readily enter into altered states of consciousness.

Another area of application is found in efforts at treatment and rehabilitation of traumatized children of political violence (e.g., detention, torture, massacre, bombing, etc.) which is being done by a group of psychologists (including this author), social workers, and medical doctors. The rehabilitation program focuses mainly on crisis intervention and psychological help while at the same time providing for basic support services (e.g., medical, nutritional, and educational).

Most of the treatment given to the children and their families applies the orientation of "Sikolohiyang Pilipino" in terms of looking at the problems of the children at two levels. The first level focuses on the specific needs and problems of the individual child to ensure proper physical, emotional and intellectual and social development. The second level is societal which focuses on the socio-economic and political roots of the problems and its consequences on the child's rights and welfare (Marcelino, 1986).

Treatment has focused mainly on group therapy rather than individual counseling because the former has been more effective. In terms of assessment and therapeutic techniques, indirect, informal, and unobtrusive measures rather than standardized testing instruments have been utilized.

There are few if any specific studies focusing on feminist treatment, but it does not mean that there is no practical work going on in this area. Using the same principles of indigenous psychology, clinical psychologists who have treated women clients espoused the acceptance of and respect for the different social and cultural factors affecting women in Philippine society. Conceptualization of culture-relevant therapies in the Philippines can draw on the initial findings of the reticence of Filipinos to go for therapy, their tendency to be family and small-group oriented, their paternalistic and authoritarian norms, and their strong need for acceptance and emotional security. Consequently, such an approach will broaden one's view of the world and could possibly lead to the identification of universal components necessary for all effective treatments whether Western or non-Western, traditional or non-traditional.

CONCLUSIONS

The arguments for, and efforts towards, an indigenous Filipino psychology continue to be vigorous. The bases for an indigenous national psychology are to be found in one's own history and culture. One can look into legends, proverbs, folklore, prayers, and other such rites and rituals; local conceptions and definitions of the human psyche; the everyday manifestation of behavior, attitudes, skills and values; concern for social issues and problems; and the role of native languages and the development of a national consciousness among the Filipino people.

Filipino psychology as a scientific discipline is a necessary and indispensable tool in the process of forging a nationalist, mass, and scientific culture borne out of a heightened sense of national identity and consciousness. For in the final analysis, the growth of "Sikolohiyang Pilipino" contributes to the just and legitimate aspirations of the Filipino people to place their cultural, linguistic, and scientific future in their own hands.

REFERENCES

Andres, T.D. (1981). *Understanding Filipino values: Management approach.* Quezon City: New Day Publishers.

Arkoff, A., Thaver, & Elkind, L. (1966). Mental health and counseling ideas of Asian and American students. *Journal of Counseling Psychology, 13,* 219-223.

Bonifacio, M.F. (1977). An exploration into some dominant features of Filipino social behavior. *Philippine Journal of Psychology, 10*(1), 29-36.

Brislin, Richard (1977). Ethical issues influencing the acceptance and rejection of cross-cultural researchers who visit various countries. In L.L. Adler (Ed.), *Issues in Cross-Cultural Research (Annals of the New York Academy of Sciences),* pp. 285, 185-202.

Bulatao, Jaime (1964). Hiya. *Philippine Studies, 12* (3), 424-438.

Bulatao, Jaime (1965). Conflict of values in home and school. *The Guidance and Personnel Journal, 1* (1), 50-53.

Bulatao, Jaime (1980). Filipino transpersonal world view. In V.G. Enriquez

(Ed.), *Philippine World Views*. Manila: Philippine Psychology Research House.

Chirino, Pedro (1604). Relacion de las Islas Filipinas. Rome: 1604; 2nd ed., Imprenta de Esteban Balbas, 1980. Cited by T.A. Agoncillo in *Introduction to Modern Filipino Literature*. Edited by E. San Juan, New York: Twayne Publishers, Inc., 3, pp. 228.

Church, Timothy (1986). *Filipino Personality: A Review of Research and Writings*. Manila: De La Salle University Press.

Constantino, Ernesto (1980). The world view of the Ilocanos as reflected in their language. In V.G. Enriquez (Ed.), *Philippine World Views*. Quezon City: Philippine Psychology Research House.

Constantino, Renato (1975). *The Philippines: A past revisited*. Quezon City: Malaya Books, Inc.

Cuizon, E.A., & Zingle, H.W. (1968). A rational approach to counseling. *The Guidance and Personnel Journal, 3*(1), 92-100.

Enriquez, Virgilio (1977). *Filipino Psychology in the Third World*. Quezon City: Philippine Psychology Research House.

Enriquez, Virgilio, & Alfonso, Amelia (1980). The world view and weltanschauung of the Filipinos as reflected in the Tagalog language. In V.G. Enriquez (Ed.) *Philippine World Views*. Quezon City: Philippine Psychology Research House.

Enriquez, Virgilio, & Marcelino, Elizabeth (1984). *Neo-colonial Politics and Language Struggle in the Philippines*. Quezon City: Philippine Psychology Research House.

Estrada, Rita (1981). An inquiry into sexism in the Tagalog language. *Philippine Social Science and Humanities Review*, Vol. XLV, Nos. 1-4.

Feliciano, Gloria (1965). The limits of Western social research methods in rural Philippines: the need for innovation. *Lipunan, 1* (1), 114-138.

Felipe, Abraham (19 —). Social desirability and endorsement on the EPPS: Preliminary findings. *Phillippine Journal of Psychology, 1*(1), 62-70.

Fox, R.B. (1956). The Filipino concept of self-esteem. In *The Philippines* (vol. 1) New Haven: Human Relations Area Files, Inc.

Galvez-Tan, Jaime (1977). Religious Elements in Samar-Leyte Folk Medicine. In L.N. Mercado (Ed.), *Filipino Religious Psychology*. Tacloban City: Divine Word University Publications.

Gonzales, Lydia (1982). Ang Pagtatanong-tanong: Dahilan at Katangian. In R. Pe-Pua (Ed.), *Sikolohiyang Pilipino: Teorya, metodo at gamit*. Quezon City: Psychology Research and Training House.

Hare, A.P. (1969). Cultural differences in performance in communication networks among Filipino, African and American students. In W.F. Bello & A. de Guzman II (Eds.), *Modernization: Its Impact in the Philippines IV* (IPC papers no. 7) Quezon City: Ateneo de Manila University Press.

Hendershot, G.E. (1968). Characteristics of the interview situation in a Manila survey. *Philippine Sociological Review, 16* (3-4), 152-161.

Kaut, C.R. (1961). Utang na loob: A system of contractual obligation among Tagalogs. *Southeastern Journal of Anthropology*, *17* (3), 256-272.

Lagmay, Alfredo (1984). Western psychology in the Philippines: Impact and Response. *International Journal of Psychology*, (19), 31-44.

Lawless, R. (1967). The foundations for culture and personality research in the Philippines. *Asian Studies*, Quezon City: University of the Philippines, Institute for Asian Studies, *5*(1), 101-136.

Lynch, Frank (1961). *Social Acceptance: Four Readings in Philippine Values*. (IPC Papers no. 2), Quezon City: Ateneo de Manila University Press.

Marcelino, Elizabeth P. (1986). Psychological help to children victims of political armed conflict. Unpublished paper read at the National Conference of the Philippine Psychiatric Association, Manila, Philippines.

Margallo, S.P. (1981). The challenge of making a scientific indigenous field research: An evaluation of studies using makapilipinong pananaliksik. In S.P. Margallo (Ed.), *Relevance and indigenization: From concepts to concrete application*. Quezon City: University of the Philippines.

Mercado, L.N. (1974). Notes on the Filipino philosophy of work and leisure. *Philippine Studies*, *22* (1-2), 71-80.

Munoz, Alfredo (1971). *The Filipino in America*. Los Angeles: Mountainview Publishers.

Navarro, Jovina (1974). The flight of newly-arrived immigrants. In J. Navarro (Ed.), *Diwang Pilipino*. California: Asian American Studies, University of California, pp. 17-44.

Nicdao-Henson, Erlinda (1982). Pakikipanuluyan: Tungo sa pag-unawa sa kahulugan ng panahon. In R. Pe-Pua (Ed.), *Sikolohiyang Pilipino: Teorya, metodo at gamit*. Quezon City: Philippine Psychology Research House.

Nydegger, W.F., & Nydegger, C. (1963). Tarong: An Ilocos barrio in the Philippines. In B.B. Whiting (Ed.), *Six cultures: Studies in child-rearing*. New York: John Wiley and Sons.

Pe-Pua, Rogelia (1985). Ang Pagtatanong-tanong: katutubong metodo ng pananaliksik. In Aganon, A. and David, A. (Eds.), *Sikolohiyang Pilipino: Isyu, Pananam at Kaalaman*. Quezon City: National Bookstore, pp. 416-432.

Rizal, Jose (1890/1957). The indolence of the Filipino. In G.F. Zaide (Ed.), *Jose Rizal: Life, works and writings*. Manila: Villanueva Bookstore.

Salazar, Zeus (1976). Ilang batayan para sa isang Sikolohiyang Pilipino. In Pe-Pua, Rogelia (Ed.), *Sikolohiyang Pilipino: Teorya, metoda at gamit*. Quezon City: Philippine Psychology Research House.

Samonte, Elena (1973). Kabuuan ng mga kahulugan ng mga salita sa larangang leksikal ng loob. Unpublished paper. Quezon City: University of the Philippines.

Santiago, Carmen (1982). Pakapa-kapa: Paglilinaw ng isang konsepto sa nayon. In Pe-Pua, Rogelia (Ed.), *Sikolohiyang Pilipino: Teorya, metodo at gamit*. Quezon City: Philippine Psychology Research House.

Santiago, Carmen, & Enriquez, V. (1976). Tungo sa makapilipinong pananaliksik. *Sikolohiyang Pilipino: Mga ulat at balita*, *1* (4), 3-10.

Sechrest, Lee, & Guthrie, G. (1974). Psychology of, by and for Filipinos. *Philippine Studies: Geography, archaeology, psychology and literature*. Center for Southeast Asian Studies, Northern Illinois University, pp. 44-70.

Sevilla, Judy (1982). Indigenous research methods: Evaluating first returns. In R. Pe-Pua (Ed.), *Sikolohiyang Pilipino; Teorya, metodo at gamit*. Quezon City: Philippine Psychology Research House.

Sibley, W. (1965). *Area handbook on the Philippines*. Human Relations Area Files, Inc. University of Chicago.

Sue, D.W. (1978). World views and counseling, *Personnel and Guidance Journal, 56*, 458-462.

Torres, Amarylis (1980). Pakapa-kapa as a method in Philippine Psychology. In R. Pe-Pua (Ed.), *Sikolohiyang Pilipino: Teorya, Metodo at Gamit*. Quezon City: Philippine Psychology Research and Training House.

Valencia, L.B., & Palo, E.M. (1979). Community responses to mental illness and utilization of traditional system of medicine in three selected study sites in Metro-Manila: Some implications for mental health planning. *Philippine Sociological Review, 27* (2), 103-115.

Varias, R.R. (1963). Psychiatry and the Filipino Personality. *Philippine Sociological Review, 11* (3-4), 179-184.

Weightman, G. (1964). A study of prejudice in a personalistic society. *Asian Studies*, University of the Philippines Institute for Asian Studies, 2 (1), 87-101.

Whorf, Benjamin L. (1940). Science and Linguistics. *Technological Review, 42*(6), 229-231.

An Analysis of Domestic Violence in Asian American Communities: A Multicultural Approach to Counseling

Christine K. Ho, PhD

SUMMARY. This article presents a preliminary analysis of domestic violence in Asian American communities, and reports results from a focus group study on domestic violence in Southeast Asians (Laotians, Khmer, Vietnamese, and Chinese). It examines the influence of traditional Asian values, the assimilation process into American cultures, and the impact of sexism and racism on the oppression of Asian women. It is suggested that traditional Asian values of close family ties, harmony, and order may not discourage physical and verbal abuse in the privacy of one's home; these values may only support the minimization and hiding of such problems. The role of the cultural values of fatalism, perserverance, and self-restraint reduce the incentive of Asian American women to change their oppressive situations. The results from the focus group study have implications for clinical and community intervention.

Christine K. Ho is a Chinese American born in Bangkok, Thailand. She grew up in Hong Kong and moved to the United States when she was twelve years old. She is bilingual, speaking Cantonese, a Chinese dialect, and English. She received her BS from Brown University in 1977 and PhD in Clinical Psychology from University of Washington in 1985. She currently is a psychologist in private practice in Seattle, WA, specializing in post-traumatic stress disorder resulting from domestic violence and sexual abuse.

The author would like to acknowledge the funding from the Women of Color Committee of the Washington State Shelter Network, and the support of the Asian Family Violence project in Seattle, WA, which made the focus group research project possible. Special thanks are extended to Maria Root, PhD, and Laura Brown, PhD, for their editorial comments, and to Anne Ganley, PhD, for her support and feedback.

Correspondence may be addressed to the author at: 1728 East Madison, Seattle, WA 98122.

INTRODUCTION

Violence against women is oppressive and intolerable regardless of a woman's cultural and social background. Nevertheless, cultural distinctions have been overlooked. The current domestic violence literature mainly examines Western cultures, families, and individuals (Gelles, 1972; Schecter, 1982; Martin, 1976; Walker, 1979); it does not take into account cultural and social factors which differ from those of Western culture. Although some attention is being given to cultural issues of domestic violence among Black Americans (Hampton, 1987), this analysis is essentially from a Western perspective. Thus, the domestic violence problem in Asian American communities has been neglected.

Domestic violence within Asian American communities has generally been ignored because it rarely comes to the attention of authorities. Although reported cases of domestic violence in Asian American communities may be low (Eng, 1986), it is unclear whether this low reported frequency reflects an actual lower rate of Asian American domestic violence, Asian Americans' lack of utilization of public assistance (Eng, 1986; Root, Ho, & Sue, 1986; Sue & Mckinney, 1975), inadequate mental health services available to Asian Americans (Root et al., 1986; Sue & Morishima, 1982), or other factors. What is clear is that the current model of domestic violence, which is based on analyses of Western society, may be inadequate in addressing the domestic violence problem in Asian American communities.

The current analysis of domestic violence grew out of the women's movement. The women's movement has brought domestic violence out of the closet of the home into the limelight of the public. It has changed our understanding of domestic violence from an individualistic and family problem to a socio-political phenomenon. Specifically, the socio-political approach focuses on the influence of culture, history, sex-roles, socialization, politics, and available resources on the flight of women from domestic violence (Martin, 1976).

The feminist analysis of domestic violence places the roots of domestic violence in the unequal power relationship between men and women in a patriarchal society (Dobash & Dobash, 1979;

Schecter, 1982). Women, historically in Western society have had few rights and minimal power. They have been considered the property of men. They belonged to their father before marriage, and to their husband after marriage.

Violence against and domination over women has also been publicly sanctioned through the media. Degradation of women can be seen daily on television, and in movies, books, and magazines. The legal system and society have given men permission to dominate and control women. Courts tended to advocate for battered women to stay in their home and solve the problem within the family. Police have been hesitant to be involved in domestic disputes. Violence in the home was therefore considered to be a family problem and not a societal concern. Only recently has such violence been considered unacceptable and illegal, and the laws prohibiting it enforceable.

The societal attitude toward domestic violence is also reflected in the community resources available to battered women. Not only did the legal profession ignore battered women, but mental health and social services were also inadequately staffed, and their staffs inadequately trained to deal with domestic violence. There were no shelters or financial resources available for women and their children to escape from violent men. Mental health professionals tended to advocate that the couple stay together; therapy tended to focus on the couple's interaction, and would usually blame the victim, rather than placing the responsibility for the abuse on the abuser and the social system (Ganley, 1981; Martin, 1976; Schecter, 1982; Walker, 1979).

The feminist analysis, which uses a socio-political approach, has emphasized the influence of historical, cultural, and social factors in the understanding of domestic violence. Although this approach has expanded our analysis of domestic violence to such factors, it offers only a monocultural analysis of domestic violence. An analysis predicated on a Western cultural context offers a limited view of domestic violence for people from non-Western cultural backgrounds. Since the socio-political approach emphasizes cultural, historical, and social factors, it is therefore important to examine how domestic violence is manifested in people from non-Western cultures.

The purpose of this paper is to present an analysis of domestic violence in Asian American cultures and to provide a framework to understand and work with domestic violence in Asian Americans. It is important to understand the cultural context of domestic violence and specific treatment needs of Asian Americans in order to provide culturally sensitive interventions. This paper will provide a general analysis of Asian American cultures and illustrate cultural similarities and differences among Asian Americans. It will also present results from a community research project on domestic violence in Southeast Asian refugees (Ho, Thornton, Wong, & Kultangwatana, 1987) and offer an analysis of the family, sex-roles, the role of physical violence, and the availability of resources for coping with domestic violence in these cultures.

ASIAN AMERICANS' CULTURAL AND SOCIAL BACKGROUNDS

It is beyond the scope of this paper to illustrate all the separate cultural issues which may be related to domestic violence in Asian Americans. Rather, this paper will highlight the most significant cultural and social contributions to domestic violence and illustrate similarities as well as differences within some of these separate Asian American cultures.

Asian Americans are a diverse group of Asians who live in the United States. We are Chinese, Japanese, Koreans, Filipinos, Vietnamese, Laotians, Khmers, Pacific Islanders, and more. We differ from each other not only in our country of origin, language, history, and religions, but also in assimilation and acculturation to the Western culture, in reasons for immigration, and in experiences of acceptance in the United States. Asian Americans' experiences are therefore influenced both by their country of origin as well as their assimilation to the American society.

Status of immigration (e.g., refugee or immigrant), generation from immigration, and years of residence in the United States all affect an Asian American's ability to assimilate and acculturate (Fong, 1965, 1973; Fujitomi & Wong, 1973; Yao, 1979), and her or his ability to utilize community resources. A voluntary immigrant is usually more prepared for immigration, and has more financial and social resources than a refugee from the same country (Aylesworth, Ossorio, & Osaki, 1980). She/he also may be more assimilated to the Western culture and more able to use community resources. A second generation Asian American may differ from a third generation Asian American in her/his native language fluency, attitudes, beliefs, ways of coping, network of friends, and the place of residence (Kitano & Kikumura, 1976). Fong (1965) reported that Chinese Americans showed an increased internalization of American perceptual norms as they became progressively removed from their ancestral culture. Fujitomi and Wong (1973) reported that interracial marriage and divorce rates among Sansei (third generation Japanese Americans) were higher than among Nisei (second generation Japanese Americans). Asian Americans' values, beliefs, and ways of coping are therefore evolving with assimilation and acculturation.

The Influence of Close Family Ties

Attitudes toward domestic violence are rooted in Asian Americans' traditional values toward the family, marriage and sex-roles. Asian Americans share fundamental values and attitudes different from Western orientation even though these orientations are evolving. This similarity is due to the socio-political exchange among Asian countries throughout the centuries (Shon & Ja, 1982) as well as the Chinese imperialist influences in Asia. These fundamental orientations reflect more on recent immigrants than people whose families have lived in the West for a longer time, such as third and fourth generation Asian Americans.

One major fundamental difference between East and West is the orientation toward the family and the group rather than the individual (Hsu, 1970; Kitano & Kikumura, 1976; Root et al., 1986; Shon & Ja, 1982). This stems from the strong influence of Confucian teaching throughout Asia. The Confucian philosophy emphasizes *close family ties, hierarchy, and order* and does not stress independence and autonomy of the individual (Hsu, 1970; Shon & Ja, 1982). The individual is a representative of the family. The family is viewed as more important than the individual: its needs take precedence over the individual's needs. Each member of the family is expected to keep harmony, adhere to a specified hierarchical role, and comply with familial and social authority to the point of sacrificing his/her own desires and ambitions.

The emphasis on close family ties is rooted in the fundamental Confucian concept of *filial piety*. It essentially means unquestioning respect for parents, grandparents, and other meaningful elders. The family is viewed as continuous and interdependent. An individual is the product of all the generations from the beginning of time. A person's behavior therefore reflects on not only the individual, and the nuclear and extended family, but also on all preceding and proceeding generations (Shon & Ja, 1982). The significance of this value orientation is that it maintains group orientation, interdependency among the family, and a specified hierarchy in relationships (Kim, Okmur, Oza, & Forrest, 1981).

In a family and group oriented society where the individual represents the family, *guilt and shame* assume a different meaning. The Asian concept of "loss of face" implies that the entire family clan looses respect and status in the community when an individual is shamed (Hsu, 1970). This places a severe burden on the individual to keep harmony and order, and to minimize any conflicts and problems which could bring guilt and shame to the family.

The minimization of conflict is also reflected in the emphasis on *self-restraint* in behavior and expression among many Asian Americans. Communication is often indirect and non-verbal; direct confrontation is avoided if possible (Sue, 1981; Kitano & Kikumura, 1976; Root et al., 1986). Self-restraint, on one hand, can serve to restrain physical violence in the home. On the other hand, when a person keeps feelings and expressions tightly checked, he or she may at points become explosive and lethal. For example, Kitano and Kikumura (1974) pointed out that Japanese families tend to have a high initial tolerance for misbehavior for children, but once the limits are surpassed, Japanese discipline may be quite severe.

On the surface, domestic violence in Asian American communities may be restrained by the pressure to prevent "loss of face," and the emphasis on self-restraint. However, as with discipline of children, physical violence toward a spouse can become extreme when restraints are removed, such as inside one's bedroom. Indeed, Yi, Zane and Sue (1986) reported that Asian Americans' behaviors as compared to Caucasian Americans' behaviors are more situation specific. They found differences in assertive behavior between Asian Americans (Chinese and Japanese) and Caucasian Americans only in public situations, but not in private situations. Expression of physical violence in the home therefore may be quite different than behaviors and attitudes exhibited in public. In fact, wife beating was reported to be common and sanctioned in China before the Chinese revolution (Walstedt, 1978). Furthermore, due to the pressure to prevent "loss of face," Asian Americans tend to hide domestic violence problems within the family and avoid outside intervention.

The Influence of Sex-Roles

The domestic violence problem is also rooted in the oppression of women in Asian cultures. The relationship hierarchy in the Asian cultures specifies a defined role expectation, from elder to younger, and man to woman (Hsu, 1970). Members of the family are expected to conform to their specified role in the family. Males are highly valued in Asian cultures. They are expected to financially support and govern the family. Women, with their secondary status in Asian cultures, are expected to be subserviant, obedient, and quiet. They are responsible for taking care of the children, husband, and parents.

The status of women in Asia is lower than that of men from birth and determines rights and privileges from birth until after death. This is exemplified in a Confucian saying about the three pathways of a woman. "In her youth, she must follow her father. In her adulthood, she must follow her husband. In her later years, she must follow her oldest son" (Shon & Ja, 1982, p. 211-212). A male child is viewed as someone who can assure the continuation of the family name and ancestor worship (Shon & Ja, 1982; Walstedt, 1978). Females are considered to be a liability. In time of famine and poverty, female infants were sold, abandoned or even drowned in China (Fujitomi & Wong, 1973; Hsu, 1970; Shon & Ja, 1982; Walstedt, 1978). Formal education is reserved for males. Females were discouraged from gaining abilities and talents which might be useful for a career outside the home. Sue and Morishima (1982) pointed out that the traditional "foot binding" (feet of Chinese women were bound so tightly that they could not grow) in the Chinese upper class is a symbolic means of fostering dependence, helplessness, and immobility in women. The degraded status of women is further echoed by the poet, Fu Hsuan's description of women in China, "How sad it is to be a woman! Nothing on earth is held so cheap" (Walstedt, 1978).

Suffering and persevering are valued virtues for women in many Asian cultures. The ability to persevere and suffer is fundamental to building a strong character. In Japanese, to "gaman," to carry on without complaints, is a measure of one's dignity. In Vietnamese, to complain is to show "ki ga chiisai," which means your spirit is small (Kim et al., 1981). This emphasis on suffering and persevering has been adaptive in Asian culture in that it serves to preserve harmony and order in the family. Women are given support and recognition for enduring hardship and are discouraged from speaking up. Thus, they are taught to accept their suffering rather than change an intolerable situation.

The concept of enduring suffering and persevering is also consistent with Buddhism's belief in the *acceptance of fate*. In Asian philosophy and religion, fate is considered to be positive rather than negative. In Eastern philosophy, it is important to accept that a situation is as fate intended, and not to challenge it (Kim et al., 1981; Kitano & Kikumura, 1974). This concept, therefore, further supports the maintenance of tradition and order, and discourages attempts to change problematic situations such as violence in the family.

The Influence of Traditional Attitudes Toward Marriages

Traditional attitudes toward marriages limit rights and resources of women to cope with domestic violence. Marriages traditionally in many Asian countries were prearranged; women had little say about the choice of their mates (Fujitomi & Wong, 1973; Walstedt, 1978). Some marriages (e.g., among Laotions and Hmong) involved an exchange of money from the man's family to the woman's family (Dao, 1988). A wife is therefore considered to be a property paid for by the husband. She is expected to be submissive, uncomplaining and devoted to her husband, husband's parents and extended family (Fujitomi & Wong, 1973). A wife is to be pure and chaste; a husband is allowed to be promiscuous, have additional wives and visit prostitutes.

Many Asian American wives feel that they have no right to ask for a divorce, to have custody of their children, to own property, or to possess other means of supports. Marriages are considered permanent; divorce rates are low among Asian Americans (Tien, 1976). They remarried only under severe social sanctions (Sue & Morishima, 1982). This loyalty to the husband is exemplified in China, where even betrothed "widows" were expected to commit suicide or to remain chaste and unmarried out of loyalty to their fiances (Walstedt, 1978).

The understanding of cultural values and philosophies is fundamental to our understanding of domestic violence in Asian American communities. The power differential between the sexes sets the foundation for maintaining domestic violence. It gives power and permission to Asian American men to dominate and control Asian American women. Asian American women, who feel they have no rights to property or to ask for a divorce, have few resources to cope with domestic violence. Although the high value placed on close family ties, harmony, and order discourages overt physical and verbal abuse, these values do not necessarily affect behavior in private. They may only support the minimization and hiding of such problems. In addition, the roles of fatalism, perseverance, and self-restraint further reduce incentives for Asian American women to alter and change their inferior and oppressive positions. Thus, external harmony and order in Asian American communities are accomplished at the expense of Asian American women.

ASIAN WOMEN'S IMMIGRATION HISTORY IN THE UNITED STATES

The exploitation of Asian women is also evident in the immigration history in the United States. Many early Japanese immigrant women were lured over as "picture brides" in arranged marriages, under the pretense of an easy life in the United States with Japanese sojourners (Fujitomi & Wong, 1973). Many early Chinese women immigrants were abducted from their homeland and forced into prostitution in the United States. There was a disproportionate number of Chinese males to females among immigrants from China due to the Chinese Exclusion Act which prohibited the entry of Chinese women who were included in the Chinese Exclusion Act. The majority of the Chinese immigrants' wives were denied entry into the United States by the Exclusion Act since their husbands were laborers (Fujitomi & Wong, 1973). These early immigrant women were survivors of racism and sexism.

The exploitation of Asian women continues even to present day immigrant groups. Asian women from families in Malaysia and Philippines have been advertised through mail-order firms as the ideal subservient wives who will cater to every wish of their husband (Lai, 1986). These paid-for-brides, with few financial and social supports are particularly vulnerable to abuse since they are completely dependent on their husband. They often speak little English, have minimal family support, and lack familiarity with the American culture.

Asian women married to American military men have also been identified as a group who are more vulnerable to domestic violence (Kim et al., 1981; Lai, 1986). Many of these Asian women, like the mail-order brides have few financial and social resources after they move to the United States with their husbands. They suffer from prejudice against interracial marriages from people from their native country as well as from their U.S. neighbors. Because of their isolation and lack of financial and social resources, they are more vulnerable to domestic violence.

EXPERIENCE OF RACISM

The problems associated with domestic violence for Asian Americans are also related to experiences of racism. Experiences of racism pressure Asian Americans to stay invisible (Kitano & Kikumura, 1976) to avoid further racial attack and discrimination. Regardless of assimilation, acculturation, and generations in the United States, Asian Americans are considered to be foreign and different in our own country, the United States. This is because the color of our skin and hair, and the features of our face look different from European Americans. As a result, Asian Americans are reluctant to report our own people to law officers, or to seek help from the social services.

Many Asian Americans distrust and dislike the American legal and social systems due to our experience of racism. Historically in the United States, Asian Americans have experienced adversity and received minimal protection from the legal system. When the Chinese became financially successful, the Chinese Exclusion Act was enacted in 1882 to prohibit early Chinese immigrants from voting, sending for their wives in China, owning property, and testifying in court on their own behalf. Japanese Americans were forced to sell their property, and were imprisoned in concentration camps as if they were war criminals, while their sons fought in Europe during World War II. As recently as in June 1982, Vincent Chin, a 27-year-old Chinese American was beaten to death in Detroit when his attackers thought he was Japanese, and blamed him for autoworker unemployment (cf. Lai, 1986). In a study of the admission process of Ivy League universities, Hsia (1986) reported that even though Asian Americans' grades were above average, they received lower than average ratings on subjective non-academic portions of the admission process, and were accepted in a smaller proportion than white applicants in some Ivy League universities. Although these overt racism events are oppressive, covert racism has even more damaging impact since it is more difficult to confront.

The lack of culturally sensitive interventions is a form of covert racism. It is manifested in the lack of appreciation of the different and diverse needs of Asian Americans. This leads to erroneous assumptions which suggest that Western approaches are appropriate for people with a different cultural background or that one treatment style is appropriate for all Asian Americans.

THE FOCUS GROUP RESEARCH PROJECT

Because the problem of domestic violence within Asian American communities is poorly understood, a community research project was initiated in Seattle to investigate attitudes towards domestic violence among Southeast Asian refugees (Ho et al., 1987). The community research project drew data from eight focus groups in four Southeast Asian groups: Laotians, Khmers, Vietnamese, and Southeast Asian Chinese. Each ethnic group was divided into two groups by sex.

Participants were recruited by facilitators of the groups who are members of the ethnic community, and have some training in facilitation. Participants need not have experienced domestic violence or sexual abuse to have been eligible for participation. The age of the participants ranged from 18 to 70. Each group consisted of 6 to 10 participants and was run by a facilitator using structured guidelines in the native language. Each group was recorded by a tape machine and a human recorder, and was translated to English by the recorder. Recorders and facilitators participated in a half-day training on issues related to facilitation, recording, and sexual and domestic violence problems prior to running the focus groups.

The focus group approach was chosen as a research method in this population because it allowed participants to freely explore issues within their cultural context in their native language without the artificial restraints of structured interviews and questionnaires. This method is an effective means of gathering cultural ideals, myths and realities in non-Western and less literate populations (Wong, 1987). This method, however, is highly subjective: interpretations of the results are easily influenced by personal bias.

Three major questions regarding domestic violence were examined in the focus groups: (1) What are the power differentials between the sexes? (2) What is the role of physical violence? and (3) What are factors and resources which impact women's ability to leave the battering relationship?

The Power Differentials Between Sexes

The results illustrated that the degree of male domination and control over females varied among the Southeast Asians in the focus groups even though males hold more powerful positions in all these groups. The Chinese reported a subtle and indirect means of control in their families: order and hierarchy are assumed and expressed mostly by nonverbal means. Chinese men reported that they give an illusion of power to their spouse by agreeing with them although they hold the final decisions and power.

The domination of women was reported to be more openly accepted in the Vietnamese community by the Vietnamese focus groups. The Vietnamese men described a sense of ownership over their wives. They considered their wife to be their property after marriage. The Vietnamese women exemplified this dynamic when they reported that a wife cannot reject sex with her husband without a good excuse. They also felt that they had to tolerate their husbands' extramarital affairs.

Laotian and Khmer women were described as even more subservient than the Chinese and Vietnamese women in the focus groups. They reportedly are expected to stay at home while their husbands work in their countries of origin. Khmer women gave an example of a word in Khmer that means that women should stay in shadows and in the home. Laotian women reported that they are expected to care for their husbands' needs and feelings. They felt that they could not say "no" to sex with their husbands for fear that their husbands would suspect that they were having an extramarital affair.

Child rearing practices also illustrated the power differentials between the sexes. In all four Southeast Asian groups, girls reportedly were raised more strictly than boys. Girls are taught to obey orders and keep in line while boys are allowed to do as they wish. For example, the Laotian women reported that they need to be stricter with girls than boys since girls need to learn to suffer in order to survive in their society. This would also prepare girls to become obedient and subservient wives.

The Role of Physical Violence

We first examined the cultural perception of physical violence through studying the attitude toward the use of physical discipline toward children. This is to assess the readiness to use physical violence toward people as well as to investigate the socialization of physical violence.

Physical discipline was reported to be a common way to discipline children in the four Southeast Asian focus groups. The Khmer and Laotian groups reported that the use of small sticks to discipline children is common, although they emphasized that they are careful where they hit their children. Physical punishment was aimed at children's legs, arms, buttocks; the head, back or ribs were avoided. Vietnamese also reported that hitting is a common type of discipline. They emphasized that hitting should be done by hands and not with sticks, and should be done with love rather than anger. The Chinese, on the other hand, gave mixed reports about hitting as a means of discipline. Some said it is acceptable, while others insisted that it is not. Most, however, reported that hitting is used as a last resort. They also blamed the practice of hitting mainly on the poor, uneducated, and rural members of their community. Physically punishing children, therefore, may be less acceptable for the Chinese because they publicly deemphasized its use. This report certainly does not indicate that physical punishment is not a common practice among the Chinese; it merely suggests that physical punishment is less openly accepted in that group than in other Southeast Asians studied.

The attitude toward physical violence toward spouses also varied among the four Southeast Asian focus groups. The Chinese men emphasized indirect and nonviolent means of dominating and controlling their spouses. Physical violence toward women reportedly was unacceptable in the Chinese community. They again blamed the practice on the less educated, rural, poor, and ethnic subgroups. The Chinese women in the focus group were very clear about their feelings toward domestic violence. They reported that they were not willing to accept beating as a way of life. They said that "once you are hit by your husband, you will be hit again." They, however, estimated that 20% to 30% of Chinese husbands hit their wives.

The Vietnamese women appeared to be more tolerant of physical violence in their home. They reported that "physical abuse of a wife once in a while is okay." The Vietnamese men also reported that they hit their wives when they are angry and out-of-control.

Both the Khmer and Laotian groups also reported that physical violence in a spousal relationship is common and tolerated. The Laotian men reported that a man can hit his wife if he has a "good reason."

Although the actual frequency and intensity of physical violence cannot be estimated based on the above data, the reports of physical violence among the Vietnamese, Khmer, and Laotians indicated a degree of personal and social acceptance of physical violence. Domestic violence may therefore be more prevalent among these groups than among the Chinese refugees since there would be less inhibition against violence.

Factors and Resources Which Affect Women's Ability to Leave a Battering Relationship

Southeast Asians' options for coping with domestic violence by leaving home and seeking outside help are influenced by their cultural beliefs, limited financial resources, and racism experiences. Seeking outside help and leaving home would not only cause Asian women to break away from their traditional expectation to persevere, keep peace, and care for the home and husband under any circumstances, it also would cause shame and loss of face for the entire family.

The Vietnamese women in our focus group indicated that their ability to leave home is hampered by having to separate from their children. They felt that their children belong with their father, therefore, they cannot leave with their children. Laotian and Khmer women also reported that the traditional role of women to stay home and keep quiet interferes with their ability to leave home. The Chinese women were the only group who felt that it was appropriate for women to temporarily leave the home. They, however, emphasized that it was important not to get help outside of the family since it could bring shame to the family.

Limited financial resources are also factors which influence women's ability to deal with domestic violence. Financial resources tended to be limited for many refugees and immigrants. Language, cultural and employment inexperience, and racial prejudice limit many job options. This is especially true for Laotian and Khmer women whose backgrounds were rural and less literate.

In addition to cultural attitudes and limited financial resources, the problem of domestic violence in Southeast Asians is also associated with the lack of appropriate community resources, social-economic difficulties, and the degree of assimilation to Western society. Many refugees are ill prepared for resettlement in the United States. Resettlement causes massive change and stress in their social and family structure. Many Southeast Asian men have trouble finding employment in the United States, especially, an employment situation similar to their previous status. Women also are forced to venture out of their home to seek outside employment for the first time. This change in family structure was reported by the Laotian women to cause more domestic problems. Women feel more empowered by their ability to earn income and are less willing to be dominated and controlled by their husband. Laotian husbands were reportedly more threatened, and became more suspicious of sexual inpropriety in their wives.

Changes in the social and family structure of Southeast Asian refugees also alter traditional Asian resources available to cope with all family problems, including domestic violence. Traditionally, elders and other extended family members intervened in family violence. Separation from the extended family in the United States removes one resource for traditional intervention; unfamiliarity and discomfort with community resources limit women's ability to deal with domestic violence. Shelters and social programs are unprepared to deal with the cultural and language needs of Asian battered women. The Vietnamese women in the focus group reported that Vietnamese family members and neighbors are less likely to intervene in the United States since they feel the woman can call the emergency number for such assistance. However, many refugees and immigrants are afraid of the police and legal system. Thus, many Southeast Asians are left with minimal resources in dealing with domestic violence in the United States: they have fewer opportunities for family intervention and fewer community resources.

SUMMARY OF RESEARCH FINDINGS

Domestic violence in Asian American cultures is rooted in sexism and racism. Traditional Asian cultures favor males over females. Men by virtue of their sex are given power to control and dominate women. Women are taught to accept their secondary roles through cultural values and customs. This power differential sets the conditions which foster the abuse of power since women have little recourse when the power is abused.

The responses from the community focus group study illustrated the cultural context of domestic violence in the four Southeast

Asian groups. Although all four groups described men's domination and control over women, the overt power differential between the sexes appeared to be greater among the Laotian and Khmer groups than the Chinese and Vietnamese groups. The Laotians, Khmer, and Vietnamese groups were more willing to acknowledge and accept physical violence than the Chinese. Laotian and Khmer women also appeared to have less economic and social resources to cope with domestic violence due to the dissimilarity between their cultures and Western cultures.

The problem of domestic violence among refugees and immigrants is more complex than among second and third generation Asian Americans. Immigrants lack traditional resources, speak little English, and are unfamiliar and unable to use resources in the United States. Second and third generation Asian Americans continue to face culturally insensitive and inappropriate intervention and racism. They may still share some traditional values which discourage them to seek outside help. Although they were born and raised in the United States, the color of their skin and hair set them apart from Caucasian Americans. The lack of understanding regarding their needs perpetuates their separation from the mainstream and denies them adequate services.

The focus group study provides a preliminary examination of the domestic violence problem only among Southeast Asians. It should not be generalized to second and third generation Asian Americans. The generalization of these results to other Southeast Asian refugees also should be made with caution since the focus group method is subject to interpretation and sampling bias. This research method, however, is effective in breaking through cultural barriers and providing preliminary information about working with Asian Americans.

IMPLICATIONS FOR CLINICAL INTERVENTIONS

Clinical intervention in domestic violence problems in Asian Americans is complex. We need to be sensitive to cultural values as well as advocate for women's safety. Clinical interventions should be focused on cultural values that empower women and utilize cultural resources which enable them. For example, the values of close family ties and hierarchy can make elders in the community an asset for dealing with domestic violence. Elders who are supportive of the woman's well being can be solicited to help intervene with domestic violence.

Guilt and shame caused by public exposure of the abuse can help inhibit future abuse. Dao (1987) reported that physical violence is reduced with Asian Americans when police intervene. She also pointed out that cultural naivete caused judges to sentence Asian American abusers to lighter sentences. Since Asian Americans value authority and hierarchy, the use of court ordered treatment and psychoeducation is culturally consistent in the work with abusers. Emphasis can be placed on the law against domestic violence in the United States and Asian Americans' respect for law and order. Similar to treatment for Caucasian Americans, treatment for Asian American abusers needs to focus on self-restraint and anger management. Asian Americans should not be allowed to use their cultural background as an excuse for their abusive behavior.

Community and family elders are also useful in aiding battered women. They can help bypass Asian American women's loyalty to their husbands by giving them permission to escape dangerous situations. Therapeutic processes need to be sensitive to individual differences. For example, some Asian American battered women require support from people from their ethnic group while others prefer help from outside of their ethnic group. As in work with Caucasian battered women, patience is required to deal with Asian American battered women. Separation from violent relationships is difficult for many Asian Americans because of their cultural values and limited resources. Intervention with immigrants and refugees needs to give special attention to the use of translators. Several community workers have reported experiences with translators who offered their own opinions about domestic violence rather than translating the interviewer's questions (Dao, 1988; Sojodin, Richards, & Eng, 1988).

Asian Americans are diverse because of their different ethnic background and different assimilation and acculturation patterns. These differences are more apparent when refugees and immigrants are compared with second and third generation Asian Americans who are more assimilated to Western ideas and ways of coping. In their study of mental health treatment modalities of Pacific/Asian

American practitioners, Matsushima and Tashima (1982) reported that more interpretative methods were used with Western oriented clients and more directive methods were used with traditional Asian oriented clients. Clinical intervention therefore needs to be flexible in response to the individual's cultural orientation and ways of coping. Therapists need to carefully assess Asian Americans' background including at least ethnicity, language, the place of origin, and the generation in the United States. Since Asian Americans experience Western influence differently, attention to matching and fitting between clinical modalities and the individual is critical in working with Asian Americans (Sue & Zane, 1987).

IMPLICATIONS FOR COMMUNITY INTERVENTION

Clinical intervention only provides a band-aid approach to the problem of domestic violence. In order to challenge the roots of domestic violence, Asian American women need to examine the inequality between the sexes within our cultures. Even though physical violence might have been acceptable in some Asian cultures, it does not make it less painful for the victims. Violence hurts victims physically regardless of cultural heritage and customs. The Western domestic violence movement has demonstrated that challenging the traditional status of women and confronting the unequal domination of men are necessary since the roots of domestic violence problems lie in the unequal power between men and women. It is only through equality that women can gain rights not to be physically harmed.

The problem of domestic violence therefore needs to be addressed within Asian American communities. There needs to be grassroots consciousness raising/discussion groups to examine the problems within Asian American cultures. We can begin this process through the use of focus groups with different ethnic groups to determine culturally appropriate means to educate ourselves about Asian American women's safety and our rights to safety. Child rearing practices needed to be examined regarding our messages to our children about violence and safety, and also about the value of males and females. The focus group approach has already been successfully applied to help develop educational materials for preventing sexual and physical abuse of children in Southeast Asian communities (Wong, 1987). Furthermore, we need to develop *realistic* options for Asian women to avoid violence. For example, we need to develop culturally sensitive shelters, and staff them with bilingual Asian Americans. Currently, few such shelters are available (Eng, 1986).

My recommendations may bear similarities to messages from the Western women's movement. I feel that we can learn from Western feminists in their challenge for equality. Our cultures need to be challenged in order for us to gain safety and equality for women. The means we use to establish equality, however, need to be developed within Asian American communities. Changes in inequality between the sexes have already been initiated in our countries of origin. The Chinese revolution has made equality between men and women a priority (Walstedt, 1978). The Philippines has made public denegration of women illegal. Korea has passed a law to prohibit couples from either prenatally manipulating the sex of a child or getting rid of female children. Our countries of origin have begun to change our old customs. It is up to us to secure safety for ourselves in the United States.

CONCLUSION

The Asian cultures are complex and rich in traditions; Asian Americans' experiences are diverse and different. This article presents a preliminary analysis of domestic violence in these complex and diverse communities. The purpose of this analysis is to present a cultural context for working with domestic violence in Asian American communities; it is important not to use the information as a means to stereotype an individual.

REFERENCES

Aylesworth, Laurence S., Ossorio, Peter G., & Osaki, Larry T. (1980). Stress and mental health among Vietnamese in the United States. In Russell Endo, Stanley Sue and Nathanial N. Wagner (Eds.), *Asian-Americans: Social and psychological perspectives: Vol II* (pp. 64-80). Palo Alto, CA: Science and Behavior Books.
Dobash, Rebecca E., & Dobash, Russell P. (1979). *Violence against wives: A case against the patriarchy.* New York: Free Press.
Dao, Ha (1988, July). *The battered Southeast Asian woman — Who is she?* Paper

presented at National Coalition Against Domestic Violence Fourth National Conference and Membership Meeting, Seattle, WA.

Eng (1986, Oct 10). Shelter: Offers help to battered Asian wives. *The Los Angeles Times*, pp. 2,30,31.

Fujitomi, Irene, & Wong, Diane (1973). "The new Asian-American woman." In Stanley Sue and Nathaniel N. Wagner (Eds.), *Asian-Americans: Psychological perspectives* (pp. 252-263). Palo Alto, CA: Science and Behavior Books.

Ganley, Anne (1981). *Court-mandated counseling for men who batter: A three-day workshop for mental health professionals.* Washington DC: Center for Women Policy Studies.

Gelles, Richard J. (1972). *The violent home: A study of physical aggression between husbands and wives.* Beverly Hills, CA: Sage Publications.

Fong, Stanley, M. (1965). Assimilation and Chinese in America: Changes in orientation & social perception. *American Journal of Sociology, 71*, 265-273.

Fong, Stanley, M. (1973). Assimilation & changing roles of Chinese Americans. *Journal of Social Issues, 29*, 115-127.

Hampton, Robert L. (1987). *Violence in the Black family.* Lexington: Lexington Books.

Ho, Christine, K., Thornton, Sharyne S., Wong, Debbie, & Kultangwatana, Vivian (1987, May). *Cultural meaning of domestic violence in Southeast Asian refugees.* Paper presented at The Second Asian Family Violence Conference, Seattle, WA.

Hsia, Jayjia (1986). The new racism, affirmative discrimination and Asian Americans. *Asian American Psychological Association Journal*, 19-21.

Hsu, Francis L.K. (1970). *Americans and Chinese.* New York: Doubleday.

Hsu, Francis L.K. (1971). Psychosocial homeostasis and jen: Conceptual tools for advancing psychological anthropology. *American Anthropologist, 73*, 23-44.

Kim, Bok-Lim. C. (1977). Asian wives of U.S. servicemen: Women in shadows. *Amerasia Journal, 4*, 91-115.

Kim, Bok-Lim C., Okamura, Amy I., Ozawa, Naomi, & Forrest, Virginia (1981). *Women in shadows.* LaJolla, CA: National Committee Concerned with Asian Wives of U.S. Servicemen.

Kitano, Harry, & Kikumura, Akemi (1976). The Japanese American family. In C.H. Mindel and R.W. Havenstein (Eds.), *Ethnic families in America.* New York: Elsevier.

Lai, Tracy A. (1986). Asian Women: Resisting the violence. In Maryviolet C. Burns (Ed.), *The speaking profits us: Violence in lives of women of color* (pp. 8-11). Seattle, WA: Center for the Prevention of Sexual and Domestic Violence.

Martin, Del (1976). *Battered wives.* San Francisco, CA: Glide Publications.

Matsushima, Noreen M., & Tashima, Nathaiel (1982). *Mental health modalities of Pacific/Asian American practitioners* (Report number 1-R01-MH32148). Washinton, DC: National Institute of Mental Health.

Root, Maria P.P., Ho, Christine K., & Sue, Stanley (1986). Issues in the training of counselors for Asian Americans. In Harriet P. Letley & Paul B. Pedersen

(Eds.), *Cross-Cultural Training for Mental Health Professionals* (pp. 199-209). Springfield, IL: Charles Thomas.

Schecter, Susan (1982). *Women and male violence: The visions and struggles of the battered women's movement.* Boston: South End Press.

Shon, Steven P., & Ja, Davis Y. (1982). Asian Families. In Monica McGoldrick, John K. Pearce, and Joseph Giordano (Eds.), *Ethnicity and family therapy* (pp. 208-229). New York: Guilford Press.

Sojodin, Larie, Richard, Liz, & Eng, Denise (1988, July). *Working with Southeast Asian Women — Strategies for Successful Outreach.* Paper presented at National Coalition Against Domestic Violence Forth National Conference and Membership Meeting, Seattle, WA.

Sue, Derald W. (1981). *Counseling the culturally different: Theory and practice.* New York: Willey.

Sue, Stanley, & McKinney, H. (1975). Asian-Americans in the community mental health care system. *American Journal of Orthopsychiatry, 45,* 111-118.

Sue, Stanley, & Morishima, James K. (1982). *The mental health of Asian Americans.* San Francisco, CA: Jossey-Bass Inc.

Sue, Stanley, & Zane, Nolan (1987). The role of culture and cultural techniques in psychotherapy: A critique and reformulation. *American Psychologist, 42,* 37-45.

Tien, Juliet (1986). Attitudes toward divorce across three cultures. *Asian American Psychological Association Journal,* 55-58.

Walker, Lenore E. (1979). *The battered woman.* New York: Harper & Row Publishers.

Walstedt, Joyce (1978). Reform of women's roles and family structure in the recent history of China. *Journal of Marriage and the Family,* 379-392.

Wong, Debbie (1987). *Southeast Asian child sexual assualt prevention project* (Report No 90-CA 1147/01) Washington, DC: Department of Health and Human Services.

Yao, Esther L. (1979). The assimilation of contemporary Chinese Immigrants. *Journal of Psychology, 101,* 107-113.

Yi, Kris, Zane, Nolan, & Sue, Stanley (1986). Cognitive appraisal of assertion responses among Asian and Caucasian Americans. *Asian American Psychological Association Journal,* 65-68.

Ethnic and Cultural Diversity: Keys to Power

Julia A. Boyd, MEd

SUMMARY. Within the past decade, feminist therapists have successfully taken a leadership role in challenging the traditional and inherent prejudice and discrimination concerning women in psychotherapeutic counseling theory and practice. As progress is made in research, theory, and practice affecting the mental health of women in therapy, more complex issues emerge. This paper will focus on the issues of ethnic and cultural diversity, as it applies to women of color seeking therapy.

WHAT IS PERSONAL IS ALSO POLITICAL

Difference is that raw and powerful connection from which our personal power is forged. (Lorde, 1984, pg. 112)

The woman of color's self-image, her confidence (or lack of it), as well as her perceptions of the world around her have evolved out of her personal experiences. Many of these experiences are rooted in myths and stereotypes surrounding her ethnic and cultural heritage and gender. Copeland (1981) states that negative feelings brought about because of these experiences are not always measurable, but assumptions can be made that these experiences do little to enhance a positive self-concept. From early adolescence to adulthood, women of color are inundated by media and social contacts

Julia A. Boyd is a practicing psychotherapist for Group Health Cooperative Seattle, WA, and Mental Health Connections, a private practice in Federal Way, WA. She has written and published a number of articles focusing on the perspectives of feminism and women of color.

Correspondence may be addressed to the author at: 2005 South 308th St., Federal Way, WA 98003.

151

that serve to instill the belief that to be different is societally unacceptable. It is obvious that commercial media presents images of women with flowing hair and strong European features as ideals of Western beauty. Even when women of color are used within the commercial context they are chosen to reflect characteristics, i.e., long straight hair, light coloring, thin lips, and noses, that often make them indistinguishable from women of non-color. From early childhood, children in our society hear and read stories and fairytales that are dominated by beautiful blond princesses and heroines who are often being rescued, fought for, and overall cherished. The message that our children receive is that attractiveness, success, and popularity are basically unattainable for females of color.

As Pratt (1984) states,

> The values that I have at my core, or my culture, will only be those of negativity, exclusion, fear, and death, and my feelings based in the reality that the group identity of my culture have been defined, often not by positive qualities, but by negative characteristics. (pg. 39)

Women of color continue to suffer the psychological damage of negative self-image, even today, twenty years after the onset of the Civil Rights movement, which served to enlighten the dominant culture to the plight of people of color. Slogans such as "Black Pride" and "Black Is Beautiful," among others, have not totally erased the psychological damage engendered in many Black women (Copeland, 1981, pg. 397).

ETHNICALLY DIFFERENT, YET CULTURALLY THE SAME

> Our strategy is how we cope, how we measure and weigh what is to be said and when, what is to be done, and how, and to whom daily, deciding who it is we can call an ally, call a friend. We are women without a line. (Moraga, 1981, pg. 12)

How does the woman of color know she can trust her feminist therapist to be a friend and ally? Her reality is based in the constant struggle for survival, which demands that she be cautious. Generational teachings regarding trusting others outside the ethnic and cultural community have been strongly enforced by family and respected community members (Richie, 1983, pg. 20). From early childhood, women of color have been taught that personal disclosure outside the ethnic and cultural community is synonymous with treason. This strong devotion to non-disclosure has for many years silenced women of color in personal crisis. In order for the feminist therapist to effectively help women of color in therapy, the therapist must first understand the ethnic and cultural framework that supports the women of color's world. In order to illustrate this concept in concrete terms, I have chosen to include the following story I wrote as a miniature portrait of what this paper represents (Boyd, 1987).

THE GOSPEL ACCORDING TO ME

Yesterday during lunch Beth told me that I was her best friend. Now, I'll never understand why it is that this woman always chooses to get relevant when I'm trying to do justice to my stomach. Knowing Beth as well as I do, I knew she was expecting some tactful response on my part. But it's tough being polite when you're hungry, and my stomach had been throwing some large hints to my brain and everybody else's within earshot all day about its empty state of affairs. So as I bit into my grilled cheese sandwich, I told Beth that I'd have to give the matter of her being my best friend a lot of thought, because having a best friend, someone who was really ace, numero uno in your life, deserved some heavy contemplation.

Thinking back on it, I guess I could have given Beth an answer during lunch. But how do you tell a white woman that it's still politically dangerous to have white folks for best friends, even if it is 198 — . I mean now really! Mama always taught me that a dollar bill was a Black person's best friend, and so far as I know, Mama ain't lied to me yet. The gospel according to Mama states that a dollar bill don't give you no lip, it keeps food in your stomach, clothes on your back and a roof over your head. If you treat it right it multiplies and if you don't it disappears, but the bottom line is if you've got a dollar you've got a friend for life. I know Beth wouldn't understand Mama's logic because we come from two different worlds. It's not that I'm trying to discourage Beth, I really do like her. But having an ace partner means more to me than just sharing office space and having lunch together a couple times a week. I know that Beth made her comment sincerely. She wants me to notice that she's trying to bridge the gap, but what she doesn't understand is that it may take me longer to come over the water, because bridges have a way of not being stable when the winds blow too strong. As it is I've already got the neighbors talking because I've invited Beth to my apartment a couple of times. Wilda, my neighbor downstairs, almost broke her neck running up three flights of stairs to my place after Beth's first visit. It's not that Wilda's nosey you understand, it's just that she was concerned. Wilda knows that white folks driving 280Z's and wearing Klein jeans don't come around the projects very often and they never come in the building unless they're after something or somebody. I had one tough job on my hands explaining to Wilda that Beth really was "okay" and through Beth's volunteer work at the Women's Center she and I had gotten to be friends. Now Wilda, who is a whole like Mama in her logical thinking, feels it's her sworn duty to look out for me. And she will generally tell anyone within earshot, including me, that she thinks I'm a little strange but likable in my own fashion. But the look she gave me out of the corner of her eye let me know that now she really thinks I've lost all my street school'n. But like I said before Wilda preaches from Mama's gospel and Mama's Word states that you don't trust nobody two shades lighter than Black.

When I think about the pro's and con's of my friendship with Beth, both sides of the scale don't always equal out. Seventy-five percent of the time we get along pretty good: we believe in the same political causes even if our personal reasons are miles apart; we share similar interest in books, movies, and music; and we share the belief that going after what you want in life "is the name of the game." However, the other twenty-five percent of the time is what divides us. Beth would like to believe that as women and activists we are equals. She professes confusion when I speak about my Blackness being more than just skin color and hairstyle but a generational lifestyle that is rich in culture and value. Beth wants to form a friendship and bond with my womenness, the part of me which she can relate to as white woman that bears a striking resemblance to her feminist ideals. What she fails to understand is that in only identifying with that part of me she denies my existence as a whole person. I don't know about Beth, but I'm greedy. I want a whole friendship or none at all. Beth has the privilege to forget that she's white and middle-class and I have the right to remember that I'm Black folk ethnic. Our relationship as friends may never equal best, but at least it's a start to something better, and that's the Gospel according to Me.

* * *

This story, points out some very real issues acted out in the therapy between women of color and white feminist therapists. While it was painful, I understood Beth's concept of me as a Black woman/ feminist. Her assumptions were based on the limited interactions and information she had with people of color prior to our friendship. I could see the parallels in our shared cause, and the contradictions based in our realities of Black and White. Beth assumed that our parallel interest, feminism, would be enough to bridge the gap between our worlds. However, my assumptions about Beth, as a white woman/feminist were based on my reality (read survival) as a woman of color living in this society. Beverly Smith (1984, pg. 32) states, "It's impossible, I think to be a Black person in this country and not be deeply aware of white people. Part of our awareness is knowledge we need to survive." Joining the ranks of feminist leadership, did not/could not erase the historical legacies that Beth and I brought to our relationship as friends. All too often therapists have entered the counseling relationship unmindful of the intrusion of their excessive, white, middle-class, cultural baggage (Smith, 1981, pg. 180). Therapeutically, the unaware feminist therapist will choose to believe that the struggles and values of the woman of color client should and will equal her struggles. *Often the values of the white feminist therapist overshadows the commitment and values of the woman of color, which would cloud the constructive nature of the therapy relationship.* An example taken from a woman participating in a Black women's support group illustrates this point.

When I heard about this group I asked my therapist (a white woman) if I could attend. It seemed like all she was concerned about was the fact that I got raped. Hell! I know that was important, but that bastard got my last twenty-five dollars. That was all the money I had, till payday. I can deal with the rape later, but I won't have a job if I can't get back and forth to work. (Black rape victim, 1985)

In not recognizing the economic crisis as a major part of the client's concern, the white therapist alienated the client, thus making her value (the rape), the client's value. Elsie Smith (1981) reports that "white therapists hide behind the liberal facade of counseling, in trying to impose their values on their client" (pg. 141). Their racial and cultural perspectives are assumed to be those of their clients. In ignoring the ethnic and cultural differences, the white feminist therapist also ignores the realities. Those differences cannot be ignored in a therapeutic setting without diminishing the chance for effective healing.

ETHNIC AND CULTURAL SOURCES OF STRENGTH

As women, we have been taught either to ignore our differences or to view them as causes for separation and suspicion, rather than as forces for change. (Lorde, 1984, pg. 112)

Denial of differences and lack of educational awareness on the part of the therapist are two major reasons that women of color give for avoiding psychotherapy (Shipp, 1983). There is a very real fear that therapists will view ethnic and cultural behaviors and beliefs as pathologic, as opposed to legitimate survival responses. Women of color are acutely aware that much of the social research involving them has only served to perpetuate myths and stereotypes concerning ethnic groups. A prime example of distorted research that has caused a continuous backlash for Black women is the Moynihan Report (1965) in which the Black family was viewed as disintegrating due to the "matriarchal" family structure. Bell Hooks (1981) points out quite eloquently in her book *Ain't I A Woman* that labeling Black women as matriarchs is analogous to labeling female children who are playing house and acting out the role of mother as matriarchs. In both instances *no real effective power exists that allows the females in question to control their destiny.*

Thus, Moynihan's report only serves to heighten the racist, socially accepted myth that Black females are unable to sustain interpersonal relationships. The so-called "Black matriarch" is a kind of folk character largely fashioned by whites out of half truths and lies about the involuntary conditions of Black women (Bond & Perry, 1975).

Women of color are not unaware of the socially accepted forms of labeling that are used to define their person and environment, and this awareness legitimizes their caution in seeking professional therapy. Feminist therapists are not exempt from bias in their attitudes and beliefs concerning women of color especially when their professional training has been designed to exclude ethnic and cultural normative values. The following case example helps to illustrate my point.

A young Southeast Asian woman was court ordered to therapy for repeatedly shoplifting merchandise from a neighborhood grocery store. The young woman had been in this country less than a year and spoke minimal English. She was assigned to a white therapist who after several failed attempts to get the young woman to communicate her reasons for shoplifting informed the court that the client was withdrawn, uncommunicative, and appeared depressed. A young Asian paralegal working in the office at the time read the case and was able to shed some light on the problem. The Asian paralegal related that the item, repeatedly stolen from the store, sanitary napkins, was not openly displayed, or sold in public markets in the country of the Southeast Asian woman. The paralegal explained that in this woman's country, it was considered highly improper for women to publicly acknowledge their monthly menses. Purchasing the pads outright or explaining her reasons for taking this product would have caused this woman great embarrassment and public shame, not to mention a breach of her ethnic and cultural values on proper conduct.

The assigned therapist in this case overlooked critical information in her written assessment of this case. Thus, this Southeast Asian woman became an ethnic and cultural victim. The therapist's unwillingness to go beyond her training to gather necessary ethnic and cultural information led her to be ignorant of and thus insensitive to her client's value system.

CRISIS

In times of crisis or conflict, women of color will often cloak themselves in their ethnic and cultural traditions, looking to these traditions as a source of reawakening personal strength. By calling on the teachings and traditions of the ethnic culture, women of color gain a unique sense of personal power that is limitless. Every ethnic culture holds a key linked to the power of survival for the women of color. For the Latina woman it may be speaking only in her native tongue; the American Indian woman may turn to purification rituals; and the Black woman may take solace in religion (Bush & Babich, 1984). Another case example is used to understand this point.

Recently a Native American woman who was brutally raped completed her healing and recovery process by retreating to her aunt's reservation and purifying her mind, body, and soul through a ritual meditation and sweat ceremony. This woman also sent her therapist (a white woman) a letter and a small bundle of sweet smelling sage to thank her.

For many women of color defining a sense of identity through rituals and traditional customs is paramount in developing a stronger sense of self individually and collectively.

DIVERSITY

Characterizing women of color into neatly packaged groups defined by customs and traditions might be an easy task, if the groups were not made up of individuals. Joyce Ladner (1971) in *Tomorrow's Tomorrow: The Black Woman*, points out that there is no monolithic concept of the Black woman, but there are many models of Black womanhood. This concept applies to all women of color. As women, women of color are distinct individuals who make choices as to the many ways in which they gain their strength. There are women of color who may not look to their ethnic and cultural traditions for subsistence. However, it is very likely that on some level such a woman will look to a source of comfort and/or nurturing that only her community or family of origin can offer. This attention to both group and individual needs may sound complex to a white feminist therapist. However being of one body yet sharing many voices is the daily life and strength of women of color.

BICULTURALISM AS SURVIVAL

In order to survive women of color have become masters in the art of being bicultural. Beverly Smith (1983), in her article *Some Thoughts on Racism* writes, "There is a lot of propaganda in this culture for the normality of the rightness of whiteness" (pg. 27). Generations of exposure to the socially accepted norms of whiteness have made it virtually impossible for women of color not to adopt specific behaviors, i.e., standards of beauty, language and mannerisms associated with white culture that would allow them to survive. In order to survive, Audre Lorde (1984) states,

> those of us for whom oppression is as American as apple pie have always had to be watchers, to become familiar with the language and manners of the oppressor, even sometimes adopting them for some illusion of protection. (pg. 114)

From an early age women of color learn the rudiments of ethnic culture at home and the crazy making double standards of social acceptance outside the home. Beginning in school young girls of color are introduced to *White Fairy Princess* or *Snow White* (Copeland, 1981). As these young girls grow into adolescence and adulthood they are repeatedly deprived of consistent models of women of color on which they can build solid images that reflect their ethnic heritage. For women of color learning to comply publicly with white standards has not been as much a choice as a dictate necessary for survival.

> "Sometimes you can hear them thinking in your bones."
> "They don't know this is my life they're playing with and I was born, knowing the rules."
> "Why do they play these silly head trip games, I don't trust any of them."
> "I'm afraid of God, dogs and the dark, in that order anybody else I'll fight." (Women of Color Support Group, 1987)

These quotes were taken from a women of color support group meeting. The subject was racial harassment on the job. Many of the women present had been seen individually by a white therapist who had referred them to the group after the women of color had started expressing pent up feelings of anger and rage at white employers. The continued challenge of being caught in a system that values only one set of standards is a constant burden for women of color. For the woman of color to openly fight back is an invitation to become a target of institutionalized racism designed in the form of rules and regulations to keep one in the proper place. The following example illustrates the sort of institutionalized racism that confronts women of color in daily work life.

A Black city worker was disqualified from a higher paying non-traditional position, after she began taking the physical exercise portion of the test and noticed that the equipment was faulty. She pointed out to the test facilitator a white female, the dangers of the equipment. The facilitator ignored her complaint and told her to quit complaining and complete the course like everybody else. When the Black woman refused due to the safety hazards involved she was disqualified. The Black woman filed a grievance and returned to her regular position. Due to the fact that her grievance was filed against her current employer she believed and rightly so, that she was singled out for continual covert harassment, that caused her to lose time from work, and eventually led her to seek therapy. In group the woman explained her situation and added that a white feminist group had offered her support which she refused. "After all," she explained, "just because they say they're feminist, that's no guarantee they'll understand my problem. They're white too."

This woman's sentiments are reflective of the feelings that many women of color share regarding white feminists. Women of color have been raised to see women of the dominant society as the standard by which they are measured. However, women of color are aware that the standards of measure are unequally balanced historically with the higher premium favoring whiteness. The term feminist, for many women of color has very little meaning, because as Barbara Smith (1984), points out, "people of color have profound skepticism that white people can actually be oppressed" (pg. 30).

FEMINISM THROUGH EYES OF COLOR

The master's tools will never dismantle the master's house. (Lorde, 1984)

Feminist theory and philosophy defined and written by white middle-class, college educated women in the '70s basically ignored the primary concerns of women of color. Bell Hooks (1984) states, "White women who dominate feminist discourses today rarely question whether or not their perspective on women's reality is true to the lived experiences of women as a collective group" (pg. 65). By generalizing the need to end sexist oppression, feminist theoreticians assumed their experiences as women should/would cover the needs of all women. However, their perspectives did not reflect the experiences or history associated with women of color, who were bound by race and class (Giddings, 1984). Black women took personal affront to much of the feminist philosophy on the grounds that it equated white women's problems to the struggles of the Black experience (Smith, 1982). White feminists drew analogies between women and Blacks, making the assumption that Black women's experiences were unlike those of Black men (Hooks, 1981). It became exceedingly clear, to Black women, throughout the initial stages of the women's movement that the daily and historical contributions made by women of color were being downplayed or ignored. Black women and their sisters of color saw white feminists vying for the same (not equal) institutionalized racist oppressive power held by white males in this country. White feminists failed to recognize that feminism was not synonymous with freedom or fairness for women of color. Understandably, women of color felt cheated, thus victimized by a political move that was supposed to liberate and validate their reality. Akemi Kikumura (1981), in her book *Through Harsh Winters, The Life of a Japanese Immigrant Woman*, recalls the wisdom of her mother in saying,

> During my lifetime I hope that I can convince you that as long as you look Japanese, you are going to be Japanese. No one is ever going to say, Oh, look there goes an American. And you may never see Japan, but everyone is going to say, There's that Japanese girl. (pg. 93)

Women of color view feminism as yet another system in which they have to define and justify their reality, which makes it (feminism) just as oppressive as the traditional sexist patriarchal system.

Psychotherapy and counseling are primarily Western concepts based on the philosophical assumptions of life, liberty, and happiness for all members of this society (Sue, 1981). While these ideals are recognized as individual rights guaranteed by the Declaration of Independence, the Civil Rights movement of the 1960s gives clear evidence that this country, in reality, supports a monolithic set of values rooted in the traditional, white, middle-class, Puritan work ethic (Sue, 1983; Bush & Babich, 1983). These traditional values give little support or acknowledgment to those who are ethnically or culturally different. The Civil Rights movement provided the impetus for change, and raised the consciousness of the dominant society.

As the country began developing a new conscience towards ethnically and culturally different individuals, professionals in the field of psychotherapy began re-examining traditional concepts of therapy (Sue, 1983; Copeland, 1981). However, these attempts were hampered by the ethnocentric belief found in the white-dominated helping professions that ethnic and cultural should aspire to the Western dominant cultural standards of sameness. For therapy, as in the culture at large, ethnic and cultural diversity were sacrificed to the belief that assimilation into the dominant culture would solve the problems of people of color. Much of the literature written and taught by mental health professionals during the sixties and seventies reflected the bias in favor of assimilation by highlighting the negative aspect of non-white, non-middle class lifestyle. So while the social milieu was appearing to change, very little change was taking place within the traditional field of psychotherapy. In order for psychotherapy to meet the needs of women of color, the traditional models of treatment must be expanded to match or fit the ethnic and cultural lifestyle or experiences of the client. The woman of color who comes in to receive services should not be expected to defend or justify her lifestyle due to lack of knowledge or ethnocentricity on the part of the therapist.

THE REALITY OF FEMINISM IN TREATMENT WITH WOMEN OF COLOR

Feminism that denies the freedom of ethnic and cultural differences is not feminism; therapy that covertly denies the validity of a woman's ethnic and cultural experiences is not therapy. Innocence does not alter the reality (Hooks, 1981) for the large number of white feminist therapists who remain in a passive state of denial concerning the therapeutic needs of women of color. Many white feminist therapists forget that they were white long before they chose to become feminists or therapists. Being a feminist therapist does not negate the societal privilege that is inherent in being born white. In America, racist oppression runs deep and dies hard. It is nurtured by generations of "hand me down" hatreds (Smith, 1981). White feminists who exercise race privilege on a daily basis often lack awareness that they are doing so (Hooks, 1984). Unconscious cultural awareness or race privilege by the white feminist therapist is for the most part accepted and validated as being the norm in a society that promotes difference as being other or alien. Beverly Smith (1983), explains the common experiences of women of color by stating "I have the feeling that no one white understands our daily experiences" (pg. 27).

To understand is to obtain knowledge, and for white feminist therapists that understanding/knowledge must begin by recognizing that their personal relationship with the woman of color client is reflective of the larger world in which they both live. As a feminist, the therapist must recognize the balance of power between herself and her client are unequal. Her role as a therapist coupled with her politics as a feminist will place her in the responsible position of equalizing the division of power by becoming knowledgeable about her world and the world of women of color. The following example illustrates how I have attempted to go about this process in my own way.

Recently I had the experience of treating a young Southeast Asian woman for depression. She told me that she had been in treatment in the past, only to find that it had not been helpful. She explained that she had little hope that therapy would be helpful this time, but she had promised her physician that she would try once more. During our first interview, I obtained a full family history which included a detailed history of her family life prior to coming to the United States. In taking the history, I encouraged the woman to elaborate, which allowed me to gain some insight regarding her world as she experienced it. After the first interview, I began doing my homework, which was to network with other Southeast Asian women and to research material that would help me to know my client as a bicultural person. During subsequent sessions, as she related information concerning her depression, I was able to shape the therapy into a context that included some of her traditional ethnic values, such as family loyalty, and a circular mode of thinking concept of harmony between self and nature. In listening to this Southeast Asian woman, I was able to glean information regarding her lifestyle, her needs, her wants, and her disappointments, which were not the same as a Black therapist. However, I was able to recognize that her depression was in some part linked to an ethnic and cultural deprivation in living in the United States. By doing prior investigating and incorporating some of the above mentioned ethnic and cultural values into the therapy, effective, culturally literate treatment could take place for this woman.

In doing therapy with women of color, feminist therapists must recognize that they will again become students. The feminist therapist will have to learn about her client's world through the client's history, networking with agencies and individuals in the client's community and through researching relevant ethnic and cultural literature. Patricia Brown (1974) states that recognition of the client's ethnic identity strengthens the relationship between therapist and client. To ignore the meaning of the client's identity is to ignore the person; if that occurs treatment cannot take place. Only through recognizing that this person has a history and an identity that is completely different from one's own can one take an effective look at the symptoms presented. As therapists, many feminists have been quick to rely on the tools and tricks of the trade. The lessons of formal education have served their purpose well. They have seduced the therapist into the model of a monolithic value system regarding the correct approach to the psychotherapeutic process. Feminist therapists must stretch themselves beyond these limits in order to explore and shape treatment that will be more effective in the long run, as opposed to short-term solutions. Making the assumption that prior mental health training or feminist politics will transcend the necessity to comprehend the ethnic and cultural lines of survival for women of color will place both the client and effective treatment in serious jeopardy.

CHANGING DIRECTION

Now is the time for our women to lift up their heads and plant the roots of progress under the hearth-stone. (Harper, 1870, pg, 97)

Feminist therapists have become pioneers in establishing previously uncharted courses in therapy. This practice must be continued in order for women of color to receive meaningful treatment. Initially, one of the most important dimensions of the counseling process is the ability to facilitate self-exploration and trust. Carkhuff (1969) refers to these facilitative dimensions as empathy, genuineness, positive regard, and concreteness. Along with Carkhuff's facilitative dimensions for providing effective treatment, the feminist therapist must be willing to examine her own beliefs regarding women of color in this society. She must be willing to analyze the myths, stereotypes, and misinformation that she has received in previous training and look at which of these have been erroneously applied to women of color. She must examine her biases in favor of the treatment modalities she has chosen to use. She must be willing to examine whether or not the framework and the concepts that she is currently using in the therapy process encourage ethnic and cultural sensitivity in the therapeutic setting. Feminist therapists must challenge and continue to challenge others in the field of psychotherapy regarding the treatment of women of color, as well as all women in the context of healing both emotionally and psychologically. As a feminist, the therapist will need to broaden her range of awareness in depth through reading, networking, and researching the lifestyles of women of color. She must teach others (feminists), and relearn the art of being a student in terms of ethnic diversity. In this way feminist therapists working with women of color will help their clients to receive effective professional mental health care.

CONCLUSION

Ideally therapy is the art of self-healing, which enables the client to draw on personal resources to empower and enrich her life. The traditional therapeutic process has denied women of color the value of self-empowerment by devaluing their ethnic and cultural identity. Women of color have the right to accurate, safe, and effective mental health treatment by feminist professionals who are ethnically and culturally literate. Ethnic and cultural literacy can only be accomplished if the feminist therapist is open to exploring ways in which traditional therapy can be ethnically and culturally sensitive, and thus, more diverse. Feminist therapists must be willing to broaden their perspective concerning the life-styles of women of color, and challenge traditional mental health modes of treatment. Feminist therapists can enable women of color to obtain the keys of personal empowerment, through sensitive ethnically and culturally diverse treatment.

REFERENCES

Babich, Karen S., & Bush, Mary T. (1983). *Cultural variations in psychosocial nursing*, Washington: University of Washington Press.

Boyd, Julia A. (1987). The gospel according to me. *Backbone: Journal of Women's Literature, 4*, 59-61.

Bulkin, Elly, Pratt, Minnie, & Smith, Barbara. (1984). *Your's in struggle*. New York: Long Haul Press.

Copeland, Elaine J. (1981). Counseling black women with negative self concepts. *Journal of Non-White Concerns, 2* (9), 397-399.

Giddings, Paula. (1984). *When and where I enter: The impact of black women on race and sex in America*. New York: Bantam Books.

Hooks, Bell (1981). *Ain't I a woman: Black women and feminism*. Boston: South End Press.

Hooks, Bell (1984). *Feminist theory: From margin to center*. Boston: South End Press.

Kikumura, Akemi (1981). *Through harsh winters: The life of a Japanese immigrant woman*. California: Chandler & Sharp.

Ladner, Joyce A. (1971). *Tomorrow's tomorrow: The black woman*. New York: Doubleday & Company.

Lorde, Audre. (1984). *Sister Outsider: Essays and speeches*. New York: The Crossing Press.

Moraga, Cherrie, & Anzaldua, Gloria (Eds.). (1981). *This bridge called me back: Writings by radical women of color*. Massachusetts: Persephone Press.

Shipp, Pamela L. (1983). Counseling blacks: A group approach. *Journal of Personnel and Guidance, 8* (2), 108-111.

Smith, Beverly (1983). Some thoughts on racism. *Aegis, 27,* 34-36.

Smith, Elsie (1981). Counseling the culturally different individual. *Journal of Non-White Concerns, 2,* (9), 141-147.

Sue, D. W., & Sue, D. (1977). Barriers to effective cross-cultural counseling. *Journal of Counseling Psychology, 24,* (5), 420-429.

Sue, S. (1983). Ethnic minority issues in psychology. *Journal of American Psychologist,* 583-592.

Compounding the Triple Jeopardy: Battering in Lesbian of Color Relationships

Valli Kanuha, MSW

SUMMARY. Over the last 15 years, societal awareness of spouse abuse has resulted in an extensive network of services, legislative reform, and research initiatives focused on increasing the public response to this serious social problem. More recently, battering in intimate lesbian relationships has gained the attention of women's and gay/lesbian organizations that deal with domestic violence issues. Lesbians in violent relationships differ significantly from heterosexual couples where battering occurs due to the powerful effect of societal homophobia that silences them from seeking help. This article will address the unique challenges faced by lesbians of color in violent relationships due to the interface not only between violence and homophobia, but racism as well. Analysis of community response to lesbians of color, and clinical issues presented in therapy by lesbians of color who are battered will also be discussed.

While it was once assumed that battered women represented a small segment of society, it is now conservatively estimated that almost two million women in the United States are abused by their male partners every year (Walker, 1979). Due to the courage of many battered women and the support of women's advocates who together have worked to end violence in the lives of men, women,

---

Valli Kanuha is Clinical Supervisor in Crisis Intervention Services at Gay Men's Health Crisis in New York City. She has worked in feminist and community-based organizations as a therapist, consultant, and trainer. Born and raised in Hawaii, Val's parents are of Japanese and Hawaiian-Chinese descent.

Correspondence may be addressed to the author at: 540 Ft. Washington Avenue #4B, New York, NY 10033.

169

and children, a growing network of shelter and non-shelter services as well as extensive legislative and judicial reform have begun to address this longstanding social problem (Schecter, 1982).

One aspect of domestic abuse that has been receiving more attention in women's communities and in programs that serve women and lesbians, is violence in lesbian relationships. Due to societal heterosexism and its effect in closeting lesbians who are experiencing violence, research and analysis on this very complex issue are still in the formative stages (Paisley & Krulewitz, 1983). Most literature on lesbian battering has been available through women's and gay/lesbian publications, and is primarily anecdotal in nature (Irvine, 1984; Kaye, 1984; Klauda, 1984; Western Center on Domestic Violence, 1984). Meyer and Hunter (1983), Chapman and Karcher (1983) and Livingstone (1982) have conducted the only available surveys of lesbians who have been abused by their partners. These reports indicate some similarities between battered lesbians and their heterosexual counterparts, such as the range of violent behaviors exhibited by batterers and possible correlations between violence and chemical abuse. Kerry Lobel (1986) has edited the only anthology on lesbian battering in which a number of lesbians describe their experiences of being battered, and workers in the battered women's movement offer theoretical analyses of violence in lesbian relationships.

Most of the discussion on lesbian battering cited above have been limited to perspectives by and of White lesbians. While battered lesbians share many of the same experiences that all battered women face, it is the *combination* of being women, battered, lesbians, and people of color that create significant barriers for lesbians of color in the writing and telling of their battering experiences. Because battered lesbians of color are women, they are the victims of societal sexism that pervades all women's lives. Because they are battered, they struggle to maintain a sense of their physical, emotional, and spiritual selves in the midst of daily terrorization. Because they are lesbians, they are a stigmatized, invisible group that is often silenced due to the powerful influence of homophobia. And finally, because they are women of color, they have survived a centuries-old legacy that oppresses them based solely on the color of their skin.

The following article is based on extensive clinical experience with lesbian abusers and battered lesbians, but with more limited experience specifically with lesbians of color in battering relationships. This article will begin with an exploration of lesbians of color, and the combined effect of racism in feminist and lesbian communities, and sexism and internalized oppression in communities of color in silencing these women. It will also discuss the implications these issues have for the ways communities and lesbians of color address violence in their intimate relationships.

THE ROLE OF RACISM IN LESBIAN AND FEMINIST COMMUNITIES IN SILENCING LESBIANS OF COLOR

In the United States, the liberation movements of the '60s and '70s began a process whereby many oppressed classes of people including lesbians and their communities were empowered to live with strength and pride. Despite the continued and growing prevalence of societal homophobia in the 1980s, lesbians have maintained their visibility through active participation in all aspects of society including childbearing and childrearing, social and professional associations, political work, and the full range of activities that were once solely the public domain of heterosexuals.

While the development of a distinct lesbian culture is evidenced by music, art, literature, and research that is reflective of lesbian lifestyles, most of the cultural artifacts that supposedly represent "the" lesbian community have been White (Roberts, 1981; Vida, 1978). This predominantly White lesbian perspective has been broadened in the last few years through the articulate voices of many lesbians of color and others who have written and spoken about their experiences (Allen, 1981; Moraga & Anzaldua, 1983; Noda, Tsui, & Wong, 1979; Smith, 1983; Walker, 1982).

The relative absence of lesbian of color perspectives in the definition of lesbian culture can be attributed primarily to racism which manifests itself in a variety of ways. First, lesbian communities are not immune from the pervasive effects of societal racism which results in the exclusion of lesbian of color perspectives in social, political, economic, and academic institutions. This is not to imply that lesbians of color are not present in those institutions; rather, lesbians of color and their experiences are not actively and publicly included with the same frequency as White lesbians.

Another effect of racism is evidenced by the social-political analysis of many White lesbian-feminists that heterosexism is the primary or even sole oppression that lesbians must face. This assumption commonly manifests itself by either White lesbians' insistence that homophobia overrides racism as a system of oppression, or by their completely overlooking the interface of racism with heterosexism (Combahee River Collective, 1983; Smith & Smith, 1983). While affirming the premise that discrimination against lesbians and gay men is based on heterosexism, the assumption that *all* lesbians suffer equally from homophobia denies the very existence of lesbians of color and other groups of lesbians that are affected by other forms of oppression, such as ageism, classism, anti-Semitism, and ableism.

Related to the above is the fact that the racial solidarity and privilege among White people which maintains the institution of racism allows most White lesbians the free choice to dissociate themselves on the basis of lesbian and gender identity from men (White and non-White), whether or not those lesbians define themselves as separatists. *Due to racism and the concomitant need for people of color to bond together against it, however, lesbians of color are inextricably bound to their racial-ethnic communities and therefore to men of color.* While such an alliance does not preclude many lesbians of color from strongly identifying with lesbian culture and White lesbians, the threat that accompanies this association cannot be overstated. For lesbians of color, embracing a lesbian lifestyle makes them vulnerable not only to homophobic attacks (which they share with White lesbians), but to *homophobic and racist* attacks (which they do not share with White lesbians).

Throughout the history of the women's movement nationally and internationally, male-dominated institutions have viewed the development of feminism and feminists as threats to well-entrenched patriarchal systems. As a defensive tool of heterosexism, "lesbian baiting" has been devised to intimidate anyone who is committed to the elimination of sexism by the suggestion and/or accusation that feminism = lesbianism. The use of homophobia as a mechanism to maintain sexism is critical in our analysis of women's oppression (Clarke, 1983; Pharr, 1988). However, the power of the patriarchy is witnessed by the fact that the mainstream women's movement has, until recently, been remiss in its active support of lesbians and their contributions to feminism (Steinem, 1978).

What I would suggest, however, is that the fear and hatred manifested against lesbians by the patriarchy is of *White* lesbians, and not a fear of lesbians of color. If racism functions to oppress non-White people, it interacts with sexism to deny the mere existence of lesbians of color. On a "hierarchy of oppression," lesbians of color are not deemed a threat to the White, male, heterosexual system because by their identity as *non-White, female, and homosexual*, they hold very little power and status in society. As a result, heterosexism relegates lesbians of color to a much lower status than that of White lesbians, and works effectively to silence them not only in the larger society but in lesbian and feminist communities as well.

Many women of color have confronted White feminists about the subtle and direct manifestations of racism within feminist scholarship, analysis, and political organizing (Giddings, 1984; Hull, Scott, & Smith, 1982; Smith, 1983; Yamada, 1983). Still, there has been little acknowledgment of the contributions that lesbians of color have made to both the suffrage period and modern day women's movement. While Lorde (1983), Smith (1985), and other lesbian-feminists have affirmed the role of lesbians of color in the development and actualization of feminism, few White feminists have spoken with the same fervor on behalf of lesbians of color in the women's movement.

However, while lesbians of color in the early years of the movement almost came to expect that White feminists — lesbians or straight — would not acknowledge them, there had always been the hope that feminist women of color — many straight — would do so. Unfortunately, even as many feminist women of color began to advocate for a separate and distinct identity from the class of "all women," the celebration that has accompanied the affirmation of women of color has not always included their lesbian sisters (Clarke, 1983). Because the gains made by women of color on behalf of women *and* men of color have been hard sought against a racist, sexist society, the figurative (and literal) embracing of lesbians of color has been perceived as compromising those accomplishments due to the fear of homophobic retaliation upon already-vulnerable women of color. This is not an indictment of the politics of women of color, as we are well aware that some of our most articulate non-White feminists are open lesbians such as Audre Lorde, Barbara Smith, and Merle Woo. For these women and other lesbian-feminists of color, however, their analysis of racist oppression has *always* included its effect on both gay and straight, men and women of color, which has not been true with other people of color who call themselves feminist.

The preceding analysis demonstrates the power of racism, sexism, and all other forms of oppression to undermine what should be natural alliances among the dispossessed. For lesbians of color, racism has certainly compromised the affirmation that they have expected from the lesbian and feminist communities, both of which have purported to speak on behalf of women as an oppressed class. For lesbians of color in battering relationships, that lack of support only further jeopardizes their ability to seek sanctuary from their violent relationships.

INTERNALIZED OPPRESSION IN COMMUNITIES OF COLOR AND ITS IMPACT ON LESBIANS OF COLOR

For many lesbians of color, the contradiction in feeling both inherently safe yet afraid as lesbians in their ethnic communities is evidence of the pervasive nature of both racism and sexism. There are a number of ways that both forms of oppression work independently and simultaneously to silence lesbians of color.

As stated in the previous section, there is such a critical tie between homophobia and sexism that perhaps it is unnecessary to make any distinction between the two concepts. Hatred of feminists is hatred of women who are not dependent on maintaining the patriarchy, i.e., women who do not *need* men for their daily survival, sense of self, or raison d'etre. By extension, lesbians are also perceived as living independent of the patriarchy, and therefore are also hated (whether or not they are "feminists"!).

In a complex combination of sexism and racism, many communities of color identify feminists, and therefore lesbians as a White phenomenon (Clarke, 1983; Giddings, 1984; Smith, 1983). While partially justified in their attribution of the mainstream, political-social feminist movement to White women, it is more likely that the powerful influence of sexism in communities of color results in many people of color "blaming" the existence of lesbians on White feminism. In addition, by relegating lesbians to "White-ness," people of color can protect themselves from further racist attack by dissociating themselves from "social deviants" that not even White people want to have in their midst.

At the opposite end of the same racist-sexist continuum, however, the adherence by communities of color to sexism as a means of controlling women actually becomes a point of commonality with the oppressor, i.e., White, male, heterosexual systems. The fact that sexism is an institution that both White and non-White communities support is one of the ways that men of color, in particular, can maintain a sense of equal status to White men. The existence of lesbians, however, is evidence that the patriarchy — whether in White or non-White communities — is fallible. That there would be a class of women who could exist and thrive independent of males implies that sexism as an institution has not been totally effective in controlling all women. When communities of color, i.e., men of color, acknowledge the existence of lesbians of color, it forces them to acknowledge not only that they have failed to control "their" women, but also that they are not as equal in status to White men as they believe. As a result, communities of color are reluctant to recognize, much less affirm, lesbians of color.

Another way that lesbians of color threaten their communities is the implication that they are obviously choosing same-sex bonding for reasons other than reproduction of the species. Especially for communities of color, this perception becomes interpreted as having serious ramifications for continuation of the race as many ethnic minority groups historically have been subject to mass genocide due to racism. Homophobic attitudes about lesbians of color become focused on the perceived betrayal that lesbians manifest by not adhering to heterosexism and therefore, to perpetuation of the race. It is clear, however, that the perpetuation of non-White races is not incumbent on heterosexual *or* lesbian women of color having babies. Rather, the fear of extinction which is deeply rooted in racism so threatens communities of color that sexism is used to scapegoat lesbians of color in order to defend against White, male, heterosexist institutions.

The dual effect of racism and sexism on lesbians of color is that they are silenced in the very communities which should be havens from the racist, sexist, classist institutions that comprise majority culture. If racism compromises the ability of lesbian communities to support lesbians of color, and heterosexism in combination with racism prevents feminists from acknowledging their lesbian of color sisters, there is always the expectation of a historically viable, ethnic culture that lesbians of color can "belong" to. Unfortunately, the rejection of lesbians within their ethnic communities is very common (Hidalgo & Hidalgo-Christensen, 1979). As Smith and Smith (1983) so painfully state about homophobia in the Black community, "There's nothing to compare with how you feel when you're cut cold by your own" (p. 124).

In summary, it is somewhat surprising that lesbians of color would ever feel safe in the world. The triple jeopardy they face as women living in a sexist society, as lesbians living in a homophobic society, and as people of color living in a racist society forms a complex web of silence and vulnerability with very little protection. In this oftentimes isolated existence, lesbians of color in violent relationships are further hidden due to the shame and fear associated with domestic abuse.

COMMUNITY RESPONSE
TO THE PROBLEM OF BATTERING
IN LESBIAN OF COLOR RELATIONSHIPS

For all of the reasons previously discussed, and perhaps others, lesbians of color take enormous risks to come out in lesbian, feminist, or ethnic communities, and of course, in society-at-large. For lesbians of color who are in violent relationships, "coming out" about being battered is further compromised due to the history that many of the communities mentioned above have had in dealing with the problem of domestic abuse in male-female relationships. For battered lesbians of color, their abusers, and all of us who are concerned about violence and its relationship to complex institutions of oppression, we are facing the uncovering of another class of people whose presence blatantly reminds us of the continuing impact of sex, race, class, and other forms of oppression in our society.

The acknowledgement of lesbians of color in battering relationships will threaten many of us in the communities that we have so carefully nurtured over the years to protect us from those painful effects of oppression. For feminists, the existence of violence in lesbian of color relationships will represent the failure of the mainstream women's movement to adequately address the interface of sexism, racism, violence, and homophobia. If the women's movement over the last 25 years has built a credible base against White, male patriarchy at least in part by minimizing non-White and lesbian perspectives in the early development of feminism, acknowledging lesbians of color in battering relationships will surely shatter some of that stability.

For the battered women's movement, the discussion of violence in lesbian of color relationships will raise the same questions and criticisms as did the acknowledgement of lesbian battering, about our heretofore well-founded analysis of sexism and male violence. In addition, the progressive sexual assault and battered women's movements will undoubtedly be forced to confront the role of lesbians of color — as clients, residents, participants, staff, and as leaders — in our local, state, and national programs.

For lesbian communities, the exclusion of lesbians of color in many of the lifestyle norms of lesbian culture will become more apparent when battering in lesbian of color relationships is recognized. While domestic abuse is now more widely viewed as a social problem, it still has implications of deviancy not only for the victim ("Why does she stay?") but also for the abuser ("batterers are sick"). With the stigma of pathology that is still attached to homosexuality, as well as the growing conservative backlash which has marked the U.S. social-political climate in the 1980s, the fear of increased homophobic retaliation towards the entire lesbian and gay community will surely be intensified by lesbians of color coming out about their abusive relationships.

Finally, for communities of color that have built strong ties based on ethnic pride and solidarity against racism, dealing more openly with lesbians of color in battering relationships will make those communities more vulnerable to racist attacks by attributing lesbian violence in non-White populations to "problems in the race." In addition, those communities will have to confront the sexism and homophobia in their own neighborhoods that continue to hurt lesbians of color who are their mothers, daughters, and sisters.

CLINICAL PERSPECTIVES ON BATTERING IN LESBIAN OF COLOR RELATIONSHIPS

There has not been adequate study or research on lesbian battering to make definitive comparisons between lesbians and heterosexuals who experience violence in their primary relationships. Many clinicians and battered women's advocates who have worked with both populations suggest that there are more similarities than differences (Hart, 1986; Kanuha, 1986; Klauda, 1984; Lobel, 1986). Violence in lesbian of color relationships, however, has not been examined in much depth due to the small number of lesbians of color that have sought assistance from domestic abuse and other service providers.

For many lesbians of color in violent relationships, the isolation connected with racism in both the lesbian and women's communities makes it exceedingly difficult to seek help. While many lesbian communities are holding educational-discussion sessions on lesbian battering, along with offering support groups for battered lesbians, outreach to lesbians of color has not been very effective (Knollenberg, Douville, & Hammond, 1986). Not only are many lesbian events targeted towards "the lesbian community" as one seemingly homogeneous group, but the small and connected nature of many predominantly White lesbian communities often results in lesbians of color feeling uncomfortable and out of place. For lesbians of color who are in battering relationships, seeking help within the lesbian community for a problem as serious as partner abuse is only another barrier to overcome.

While more therapists, battered women's programs, and gay/lesbian social service agencies are becoming sensitive to racism issues and working with people of color, very few have received training about lesbian battering. Even less have a solid base in both anti-racist and lesbian violence work. Besides The Gay and Lesbian Anti-Violence Project in New York, and individual therapists and support groups scattered in different cities around the country, there are few programs that are specifically focused on services for either lesbian abusers or survivors (Lobel, 1986; NiCarthy, Merriam, & Coffman, 1984; Porat, 1985). One severely battered lesbian of color stated firmly that she would never go to a battered women's shelter; however, she was unsure whether or not her reluctance was due to racism or homophobia in that particular shelter. Other lesbians of color have preferred to seek help from therapists — lesbian or straight, White or non-White — due to the relative privacy and confidentiality of the therapeutic context. In every case, however, the task for lesbians of color in battering relationships always involves a troubling balancing act in finding providers who are not only sensitive to the issues of lesbians, women of color, and domestic abuse, but who are also competent. Most women are not faced with that same complexity of barriers when seeking help in dealing with battering relationships.

In the United States, the violence against women movement was begun over 15 years ago largely through the efforts of White feminists. Recently, however, people of color have been challenged by feminist women of color to acknowledge the existence of domestic abuse in their communities (Burns, 1986; Richie, 1983). Due to institutionalized racism, most people of color are well-aware of the subtle and direct repercussions that will result from their admission to the dominant White society that their communities are experiencing a serious social problem such as domestic violence. History has proven that Whites need very little rational justification to label non-White people as pathologic, and thereby to maintain systematic oppression against them. Not only is there legitimate fear of punishment by White society for "just having a problem," but attempts to then seek help from the very systems that should be helping them (police, courts, hospitals) are often fraught with insensitivity, hostility, and incompetence (American Indian Women Against Domestic Violence, 1984; White, 1985; Zambrano, 1985).

If we consider the racist society in which we live, and place within it the heterosexist attitudes and practices of some communities of color, lesbians of color have good reason to believe that their ethnic communities will not provide them safety from the domestic violence they are experiencing. While escape from racism in society-at-large usually reinforces among people of color loyalty to one's ethnic community, the sense of belonging and protection for lesbians of color in battering relationships is usually compromised due to their sexual preference. In addition, many lesbians of color who are experiencing relationship violence express a need to protect both their communities and themselves from the retaliation of the dominant White and heterosexual society that would use lesbian battering to further stigmatize and oppress them.

In the final analysis, the conflicting loyalties to their community, to their relationships, and to themselves become so overwhelming that lesbians of color are oftentimes trapped into remaining in battering situations. Dealing with these conflicts by clearly delineating the multiple issues involved in "coming out" about being women of color, being lesbians, and experiencing violence, along with identifying appropriate responses to each of those situations would empower lesbians of color to alleviate the violence in their relationships.

A number of lesbians of color who have been in battering relationships with White women have suggested that the power issues inherent in biracial relationships had an effect on the violence with their partners. One battered lesbian of color stated that her partner, who was White, verbally abused her using racial epithets and negative racial stereotypes while also physically abusing her. Another woman of color described an S & M ritual based on a master-slave scenario with her White partner that eventually deteriorated into non-consensual sexual and physical abuse.

Since there are no studies of the effect of racism on the dynamics of relationship violence (in either heterosexual or lesbian couples), we can only speculate on its impact and/or meaning. For White lesbians who are in battering relationships, the power implied in White privilege may manifest itself either by rationalizing the use of violence to control their partners, or by justifying the battering by their partners who are women of color as an irrational attempt to "equalize" the relationship. For lesbians of color who are in battering relationships with White partners, one of the results of institutionalized racism could be a form of internalized oppression where violence is well understood as one of the behaviors that people of color are accustomed to experiencing. This is not to imply that lesbian relationships with/between women of color are more violence-prone, since there is absolutely no evidence to support such a conclusion. Rather, lesbians of color who are in biracial relationships have often reported that the use of violence to control others is part and parcel of racism, and therefore is sometimes used to explain why one could batter, or be battered. In our work with lesbians of color who are either abusers or survivors, clinicians need to be aware of the possible effects that racism has on the dynamics of violence and control in intimate relationships.

Many of the public agencies that deal with domestic abuse — police, courts, social services — have notoriously poor training or sensitivity not only about women, but certainly about women of color and lesbians. The rampant heterosexism and racism of these key service providers in domestic abuse intervention always jeopardize women, but even more so women of color and lesbians. For lesbians of color in battering relationships, their legitimate fear of these systems cannot be underestimated. Many lesbians of color will refuse to call the police, obtain orders for protection, or press charges against their abusers due to the retaliation that they will have to endure by those agencies. It is important to understand the critical role of systems advocacy, in addition to supportive counseling when working with lesbians of color who are attempting to access these services. Clinicians must be careful and thorough in assessing the inherent dangers to lesbians of color who utilize traditional institutions that work with heterosexual battered women, and should respect the choices that lesbians of color must make with regard to those systems.

Finally, the role of psychotherapy in the "treatment" of domestic abuse has received mixed reviews by many feminists due to the traditional tendency of the male-dominated mental health profession to blame women who are the victims of violence (Bograd, 1984; Schecter, 1982). Over the last five years, training and monitoring of therapists who work in the area of domestic abuse has given therapy more credence as an option for battered women and their families (Edelson, 1984; Walker, 1984). However, there is still an absence of training on issues related to women of color, lesbians of color, and lesbian battering throughout the various mental health disciplines. Therapy for lesbians of color in battering relationships requires that the therapist not only be competent in evaluating the appropriateness of psychotherapy (vs. support, advocacy, or self-help), but that she have an understanding of all areas that affect the lives of lesbians of color, i.e., racism, sexism, and domestic abuse.

CONCLUSION

The multiple issues that affect lesbians of color in violent relationships are complex, confusing, and always painful. Therapists working with lesbians of color must not only be able to acknowledge this myriad of issues, but more importantly to understand the interface between them. The isolation, silence, and fear that many lesbians of color must live with daily can only be broken through that acknowledgement and understanding. By continued research, analysis, and clinical observation, the feminist therapy profession can make significant contributions in ending violence in the lives of this vulnerable group of women.

REFERENCES

Allen, Paula Gunn (1981). Beloved women: Lesbians in American Indian cultures. *Conditions: Seven*, 67-87.
American Indian Women Against Domestic Violence (1984). *Position paper.* (Available from the Minnesota Coalition for Battered Women, 435 Aldine St., St. Paul, MN 55104).
Bograd, Michelle (1984). Family systems approaches to wife battering: A feminist critique. *Journal of Orthopsychiatry, 54,* 558-568.
Burns, Maryviolet C. (1986). *The speaking profits us: Violence in the lives of women of color.* Seattle: Center for Prevention of Sexual and Domestic Violence.
Chapman, Marilyn & Karcher, Kim (1983). *Draft-Support group summary.* Unpublished manuscript.
Clarke, Cheryl (1983). Lesbianism: An act of resistance. In Cherríe Moraga and Gloria Anzaldúa (Eds.), *The bridge called my back: Writings by radical women of color* (pp. 128-137). New York: Kitchen Table: Women of Color Press.

Edleson, Jeffrey L. (1984). Working with men who batter. *Social Work*, May-June, 237-242.

Giddings, Paula (1984). *Where and when I enter: The impact of Black women on race and class in America*. New York: William Morrow.

Hart, Barbara (1986). Lesbian battering: An examination. In Kerry Lobel (Ed.), *Naming the violence: Speaking out about lesbian battering* (pp. 173-189). Seattle: Seal Press.

Hidalgo, Hilda & Hidalgo-Christensen, Elia (1976). The Puerto Rican lesbian and the Puerto Rican community. *Journal of Homosexuality*, 2, 109-121.

Hull, Gloria, Scott, Patricia Bell, & Smith, Barbara (Eds.). (1982). *All of the women are White, all the men are Black, but some of us are brave: Black women's studies*. Old Westbury, NY: The Feminist Press.

Irvine, Janice (1984, January 14). Lesbian battering: The search for shelter. *Gay Community News*, pp. 13-17.

Kanuha, Valli (1986). *Violence in intimate lesbian relationships*. Unpublished manuscript.

Kaye, Janet (1984). Breaking the silence on lesbian battering. *Los Angeles Herald Examiner*, pp. A-1, A-13.

Klauda, Ann (1984, May 16). Violence in intimate lesbian relationships. *Equal Time*, pp. 1, 3.

Knollenberg, Sue, Douville, Brenda, & Hammond, Nancy (1986). Community organizing: One community's approach. In Kerry Lobel (Ed.), *Naming the violence: Speaking out about lesbian battering* (pp. 98-102). Seattle: Seal Press.

Livingstone, Betty (1982). *Domestic violence in the Madison lesbian community*. Unpublished manuscript.

Lobel, Kerry (Ed.). (1986). *Naming the violence: Speaking out about lesbian battering*. Seattle: Seal Press.

Lorde, Audre (1983). The master's tools will never dismantle the master's house. In Cherríe Moraga and Gloria Anzaldúa (Eds.), *This bridge called my back: Writings by radical women of color* (pp. 98-101). New York: Kitchen Table: Women of Color Press.

Meyer, Pat & Hunter, Phoebe (1983). *Iowa City survey and results*. Unpublished report. Iowa City, IA: Domestic Violence Project.

Moraga, Cherríe & Anzaldúa, Gloria (Eds.), (1983). *This bridge called my back: Writings by radical women of color*. New York: Kitchen Table: Women of Color Press.

NiCarthy, Ginny, Merriam, Karen, & Coffman, Sandra (1984). *Talking it out: A guide to groups for abused women*. Seattle: Seal Press.

Noda, Barbara, Tsui, Kitty, & Wong, Z. (Spring, 1979). Coming out: We are here in the Asian community: A dialogue with 3 Asian women. *Bridge: An Asian American Perspective*.

Paisley, Christine A. & Krulewitz, Judith E. (1983, March). *Same-Sex assault: Sexual and non-sexual violence within lesbian relationships*. Paper presented at the National Conference of the Association for Women in Psychology, Seattle, WA.

Pharr, Suzanne (1988). *Sexism and homophobia*. Manuscript submitted for publication.

Porat, N. (Ed.). (1985). Lesbian issue [Special issue]. *WCDV Review, 10*(2) (Available from Western Center on Domestic Violence, 870 Market Street, San Francisco, CA 94102).

Richie, Beth E. (1985). Battered black women: A challenge to the black community. *The Black Scholar, 16*(2), 40-44.

Roberts, J.R. (1981). *Black lesbians: An annotated bibliography*. Tallahassee: Naiad Press.

Schecter, Susan (1982). *Women and male violence: The visions and struggles of the battered women's movement*. Boston: South End Press.

Smith, Barbara (Ed.). (1983). *Home girls: A Black feminist anthology*. New York: Kitchen Table: Women of Color Press.

Smith, Barbara (1985). Home truths on the contemporary Black feminist movement. *The Black Scholar, 16*(2), 4-13.

Smith, Barbara & Smith, Beverly (1983). Across the kitchen table: A sister-to-sister dialogue. In Cherríe Moraga and Gloria Anzaldúa (Eds.), *This bridge called my back: Writings by radical women of color* (pp. 113-127). New York: Kitchen Table: Women of Color Press.

Steinem, Gloria (1978). The politics of supporting lesbianism. In Virginia Vida (Ed.). *Our right to love: A lesbian resource book* (pp. 267-269). Englewood Cliffs, NJ: Prentice Hall.

Vida, Virginia (Ed.). (1978). *Our right to love: A lesbian resource book*. Englewood Cliffs, NJ: Prentice Hall.

Yamada, Mitsuye (1983). Asian Pacific American women and feminism. In Cherríe Moraga and Gloria Anzaldúa (Eds.), *This bridge called my back: Writings by radical women of color*, (pp. 71-75). New York: Kitchen Table: Women of Color Press.

Walker, Alice (1982). *The color purple*. New York: Harcourt Brace.

Walker, Lenore E. (1979). *The battered woman*. New York: Harper and Row.

Walker, Lenore E. (Ed.). (1984). *Women and mental health policy*. Beverly Hills: Sage Publications.

Western Center on Domestic Violence (1984). *Lesbian battery: Selected articles*. (Available from Western Center on Domestic Violence, 870 Market Street, Suite 1058, San Francisco, CA 94102).

White, Evelyn C. (1985). *Chain, chain, change: For Black women dealing with physical and emotional abuse*. Seattle: Seal Press, New Leaf Series.

Zambrano, Myrna Z. (1985). *Mejor sola que mal accompanada: For the Latina in an abusive relationship*. Seattle: Seal Press, New Leaf Series.

Resolving "Other" Status: Identity Development of Biracial Individuals

Maria P. P. Root, PhD

SUMMARY. The current paper describes the phenomenological experience of marginal socio-ethnic status for biracial individuals. A metamodel for identity resolution for individuals who struggle with other status is proposed. Subsequently, multiple strategies in the resolution of ethnic identity development are proposed among which the individual may move and maintain a positive, stable self-image.

Half-breed, mulatto, mixed, eurasian, mestizo, amerasian. These are the *"others,"* biracial individuals, who do not have a clear racial reference group (Henriques, 1975; Moritsugu, Foerster, & Morishima, 1978) and have had little control over how they are viewed by society. Because of their ambiguous ethnic identity and society's refusal to view the races as equal, mixed race people begin life as *marginal people*. Freire (1970) observes that *marginality is not a matter of choice, but rather a result of oppression of dominant over subordinate groups*.

The challenge for a nonoppressive theory and therapy, as femi-

---

Maria P. P. Root is half Asian (Filipino) and half white, born in the Philippines and raised in California. This bicultural context has been the catalyst for many interests which appear diverse but are related through integration of the diversity represented in her cultural background, e.g., psychosomatic symptomatology, family therapy, identity development, and issues of underserved populations.

The author wishes to acknowledge feedback from Carla Bradshaw, PhD, Laura Brown, PhD, Christine C. Iijima Hall, PhD, and Christine Ho, PhD which helped shape revisions of this paper.
Correspondence may be addressed to the author at: 2457-26th Ave. E., Seattle, WA 98102.

nist perspectives attempt, is twofold. First, racism must be recognized and challenged within the therapist's and theorist's world. Without meeting this challenge, it is unlikely that nonpathological models of mental health for mixed race persons can be developed. Second, theoretical conceptualization and application to therapy must become multiracial and multicultural to accurately reflect the process of more than a single racial group. New templates and models for identity development are needed which reflect respect for difference. Necessarily, these theories will need to deviate from traditional linear or systemic models which both have singular endpoints to define mental health. These models are based upon male mental health or, more recently, alternative models define white women's mental health. Current models of mental health do not accommodate the process by which individuals who have "other" identities, such as biracial and or gay/lesbian, arrive at a positive sense of self-identity or maintain a positive identity in the face of oppressive attitudes.

In this paper, the phenomenological experience of "otherness" in a biracial context is described and its socio-political origins explored. The integration of biracial heritage into a positive self-concept is complicated and lengthy. An alternative model for resolution of ethnic identity is offered which takes into account the forces of socio-cultural, political, and familial influences on shaping the individual's experience of their biracial identity. The uniqueness of this paper's approach is that several strategies of biracial identity resolution are offered with no inherent judgment that one resolution is better than another. Instead, the problems and advantages inherent with each type of resolution are discussed. It is proposed that the individual may shift their resolution strategies throughout their lifetime in order to nurture a positive identity.

While early sociological theory might suggest that such a model as proposed here describes a "marginal personality" (Stonequist, 1937), or in DSM-III-R nosology (American Psychiatric Association, 1987) inadequate personality or borderline personality, recent research suggests that biracial young adults are generally well adjusted (Hall, 1980; Pouissant, 1987). Thus, the resolution of major conflicts inherent in the process of racial identity development may result in a flexibility to move between strategies which may reflect positive coping and adaptive abilities and be independent of the integrity of the individual's personality style.

ASSUMPTIONS ABOUT THE HIERARCHY OF COLOR IN THE UNITED STATES

Several general assumptions are made throughout this paper which are important for understanding the origins and dynamics of conflict surrounding the biracial individual. These dynamics further influence the developmental process of identity resolution.

First, in the United States, despite our polychromatic culture, we are divided into white and non-white. The positive imagery created by the "melting-pot" philosophy of the United States is relevant to white ethnic groups of immigrants such as the Irish, French, and Scandinavian people and not Africans, Asians, Hispanics, or even on home territory, American Indians. Cultural pluralism is neither appreciated nor encouraged by the larger culture.

Second, white is considered superior to non-white: the privileges and power assumed by whites are desired by non-whites. It is from this assumption attempts are made to prevent racial mixing because free interaction assumes equality. A corollary of this assumption is that mixed race persons who are part white and can pass as such will be very likely to strive for this racial identity in order to have maximum social power and to escape the oppression directed towards people of color.

The third assumption is that there is a hierarchy of racial/cultural groups based upon their similarity to middle-class white social structure and values. Thus, in general, Asian Americans have a higher social status than Black Americans in white America.

The hierarchical social status system based upon color has oppressed biracial people in two major ways. Both reasons stem from American society's fear of "racial pollution" (Henriques, 1975) (an attitude that was acutely reflected in Hitler's Germany). First, biracial persons have been given little choice in how they are identified. Any person with non-white ethnic features or traceable non-white blood is considered non-white (cf. Henriques, 1975). As a result, Poussaint (1984) notes than any individual with one black and one non-black parent is considered black. Because Asian ethnic groups can be equally oppressive in their fear of "racial pollution" (cf. Murphey-Shigematsu, 1986; Wagatsuma, 1973), a child that is half Asian and half anything else, particularly black, is identified by the blood of the non-Asian parent. Mixed race persons from two minority groups are likely to experience oppression from the racial group of heritage which has higher social status. This method of "irrational," incomplete racial classification has made identity resolution for the biracial individual very difficult and oppressive.

The second source of oppression stems from society's silence on biracialism as though if it is ignored, the issue will go away. It was only as recently as 1967 that the Supreme Court ruled in the *Lovings* case of Virginia that anti-miscegenation laws were unconstitutional, a ruling based on an interpretation of the 14th amendment (1868) to the Constitution that could have been made any time in the previous 100 years (Sickels, 1972). Subsequently, the last 12 states with anti-miscegenation laws were forced to overturn them. However, this ruling does not change attitudes. Society still prohibits interracial unions (Petroni, 1973).

The last assumption about the hierarchy of color is necessary for understanding the marginality of biracial persons who are part white. Because whites have been the oppressors in the United States, there is a mistrust by people of color of those accepted by or identified as white. Subsequently, those biracial individuals who are part white (and look white) will at times find it harder to gain acceptance by people of color by virtue of the attitudes and feelings that are projected onto them because of their white heritage and the oppression it symbolizes to people of color (Louise, 1988).

Being mixed race, like interracial marriages has meant different things at different times (e.g., whether it reflects sexual oppression of a minority group, or equity and similarity of racial groups). Nevertheless, mixed race persons have always had an ambiguous ethnic identity to resolve. *It is the marginal status imposed by society rather than the objective mixed race of biracial individuals which poses a severe stress to positive identity development.* There are few if any role models due to the lack of a clear racial reference group. Friends, parents, and other people of color usually do not comprehend the unique situation and intrapersonal conflict inherent in the resolution of an ambiguous ethnic identity for mixed race persons.

THE BEGINNINGS OF "OTHERNESS"

The themes described in the development of awareness of otherness in biracial persons have been highlighted in several recent research reports, e.g., Asian-White (Murphy-Shigematsu, 1986), Black-Asian (Hall, 1980), and Black-White mixes (Pouissant, 1984). The themes of the early years are around race, family, acceptance, difference, and isolation. It is suggested that the intrapersonal and interpersonal conflicts which emerge out of these themes are circular and transitory. They reemerge at different points in development with a chance for a greater depth of resolution and understanding with each cycle.

The awareness of "otherness," or ambiguous ethnicity begins early when a child starts to be aware of color around age three (Goodman, 1968) but before a sense of racial identity is formed. An ethnic name or non-ethnic name, which may not be congruent with how a child is perceived can intensify this awareness. Initially this awareness develops from being identified as different from within any ethnic community. Questions and comments such as, "Where are you from?" "Mixed children are so attractive," and "You are so interesting looking," heighten the feeling of otherness. This acknowledgment of a child's ethnic mix or differentness is natural and not in and of itself harmful or particularly stressful. In fact, the special attention initially may feel good. It is the combination of inquisitive looks, longer than passing glances to comprehend unfamiliar racial-ethnic features (an "unusual or exotic look"), and comments of surprise to find out that the child is one or the other parent's biological child *along with* disapproving comments and nonverbal communication that begin to convey to the child that this otherness is "undesirable or wrong." Suddenly, previously neutral acknowledgment or special attention is interpreted as negative attention. It is with these reactions that the child in her or his dichotomous way of knowing and sorting the world may label her or his otherness as bad. The child's egocentrism can result in assuming blame or responsibility for having done something wrong related to their color; subsequently, one may notice in young children peculiar behaviors to change racial characteristics such as attempts to wash off their dark color (Benson, 1981). Because the child is not equipped to resolve this conflict at such an early age, the conflict in its complexity is suppressed. It emerges only when negative experiences force the conflict to the surface.

During the early grade school years, children start comprehending racial differences consciously (Goodman, 1968). Self-concept is in part internalized by the reflection of self in others' reactions (Cooley, 1902). Subsequently, a significant part of identification of self in reference to either racial group is influenced by how siblings look, their racial identification, and people's reactions to them. Racial features can vary greatly among the children of the same parents; for example in a Black-White family, one child may look white, one may look black, and one may look mixed.

They are teased by their schoolmates, called names, and or isolated — all the result of the prejudice that is transmitted by relatives, the media, and jokes. For those children who are products of interracial unions during foreign wars (i.e., WW II, Korean War, Vietnam War), fear of the "enemy," translated into national hatred towards the "enemy," may be projected onto interracial families and their children.

Once the child comprehends that there is a concept of superiority by color, she or he may attempt to achieve acceptance by embracing membership in the "hierarchically superior" racial group of their heritage, and rejecting the other half of their heritage. For example, Black-White children may want their hair straightened if it is kinky; Asian-White children may want blue eyes.

A teacher's oppressive assumptions and projections can also contribute to the marginality of the biracial child. This child may be singled out in ways that set her or him apart from peers. Unrealistic expectations of the child may be assumed, and misperceptions of the child's environment perpetuated. For example, in assuming that the child identifies with a culture unfamiliar to the teacher, she or he may be asked to "teach" the class about their racial/cultural group (while other children are not asked to do the same). By her or his action, the teacher is likely to project stereotypes onto the child with which they may not identify.

During the process of ethnic identity development, the biracial child from mid-grade school through high school may be embarrassed to be seen with one or both parents. This embarrassment reflects internalized oppression of societal attitudes towards miscegenation, possible internalized family oppression, as well as more typical American adolescent needs to appear independently functioning of their parents.

The Role of Family

The family environment is critical in helping the child and teenager to understand their heritage and value both races. A positive self-concept and view of people is promoted in interracial partnerships and extended families in which a person's value is independent of race though race is not ignored. This environment, whether it be as a single or two parent household, gives the individual a security that will help them weather the stress of adolescence. It is this unusual objectivity about people which determines the options the biracial person has for resolving their identity.

Unfortunately, the stress that has been experienced by interracial families, particularly those that have developed during wartime (e.g., Vietnam and the Korean War), has often resulted in a lack of discussion of race, discrimination, and coping strategies for dealing with discriminatory treatment. This silence has perhaps reflected these families' needs for a sanctuary from the painful issue of racial differences. Similar to issues of sexuality, the silence may also reflect the difficulty most people appear to have in discussing race issues.

Being identified with a minority group that is oppressed can generate feelings of inferiority within the biracial person, particularly if this parent is treated as such in the extended family. If the extended family is primarily composed of the socially dominant racial group, overt or covert prejudicial remarks against the parent with less racial social status will increase the child's insecurity about their acceptance. He or she may subsequently also devalue cultural and racial features associated with this parent in an attempt to be accepted.

Outright rejection of the parent with less racial social status, in the aspiration of being conditionally accepted by the dominant cultural group, reflects internalization and projection of discriminatory, oppressive attitudes towards one's own racial heritage (Sue,

1981) and creates tremendous intrapersonal conflict in resolving racial identity. Rejection at this age stems from the awareness that one is judged by those with whom they affiliate; color is a social issue that regulates acceptance and power.

In general, the intensity of the child's reaction is mediated by the racial diversity present in the community, the amount of contact the individual has with other biracial individuals, and the presence of equity among racial groups in their community (Allport, 1958). A child is much less likely to be embarrassed or to reject that part of their heritage that is judged negatively by society if there are ethnic communities which live side by side, if the parent with less racial social status has pride in themselves, and if parents have equal social status within the family. (It is important to be aware that persons of different races in relationships are not exempt from acting prejudicially or in an oppressive manner towards each other.) Based upon the pervasiveness of racism and the widespread oppression of women in American culture, it hard to imagine equity in an interracial, heterosexual marriage.

Some families have a difficult start when an interracial relationship results in the severing of emotional and physical ties by the extended family such as in refusals to visit or accept a marriage or the children. It is a type of abandonment which contributes to mixed race children feeling more different and insecure from other children. Emotional cutoffs are more subtle than physical ones and can be equally damaging, e.g., biracial grandchildren are treated negatively compared to the rest of the grandchildren. This type of discrimination can be very subtle such as loving treatment of biracial child combined with a simultaneous refusal to acknowledge biracial features. Cutoffs can also occur by non-white families and communities. For example, more traditional Japanese grandparents may refuse to accept grandchildren who are any other race *and* ethnic background (e.g., Chinese). Rigid, impermeable physical, emotional, and psychological boundaries communicate hatred and judgment; they mirror to a greater or lesser extent community feelings.

The estrangement and isolation described above encourage denial and rejection of the part of self that has been unaccepted by the extended family; it is very difficult not to internalize this oppression and rejection. As in the case of people who are emotionally deprived of acceptance, some mixed race persons will subsequently try to obtain the approval or acceptance of those persons who are least willing to give it. In the case of biracial children, they may place extra importance on the opinions of persons whose race is the same as their grandparents who initiated the cutoff. Alternately, they may displace anger towards the extended family onto strangers of the same race.

Summary

The process of identity development so far mirrors what Atkinson, Morten, and Sue (1979) describe in their first two stages of minority identity development. In the first stage (Conformity Stage), there is a preference for the dominant culture's values (which in the case of the biracial person may be part of their heritage). In the second stage (Dissonance Stage), information and experiences are likely to create confusion and challenge the individual's idealization of the dominant culture. It is at this point that the individual is usually reaching the end of elementary school and entering junior high school.

Due both to the adolescent's motivation to belong to a community or group and to the adolescent's reaction to a sense of injustice, the biracial individual may seek refuge and acceptance with the group that represents the other half of their heritage. The Minority Identity Development Model predicts that in the third stage (Resistance and Immersion) there will be a simultaneous rejection of the other part of their racial heritage, e.g., being angry and distrustful towards whites (Atkinson et al., 1979) or the racial-social group with greater status. However, this is where models for identity development are not adequate for the biracial individual's unique situation.

For the biracial individual to reject either part of their racial heritage continues an internalized oppression. In reality, it appears that some biracial persons attempt to do this, but the attempts are likely to be very shortlived due to powerful reminders of both sides of their racial heritage. To reject the dominant culture is to reject one parent and subsequently, an integral part of themselves that is unchangeable, particularly if it is the same sex parent. And because racial groups other than white have their prejudices and fears, the biracial individual may feel neither fully accepted nor fully privileged by their other reference group. The individual is harshly reminded of their ambiguous ethnic/racial status; they are an *other*. They are *marginal* until they achieve a unique resolution for themselves that accepts both parts of their racial heritage. In order to move out of marginal status they need to place less importance on seeking social approval and even move beyond the dichotomy of thinking about the world and self as white versus non-white, good versus bad, and inferior versus superior. This strategy towards resolution requires the child to do something that in all likelihood they have few models to emulate.

FACING RACISM: THE END OF CHILDHOOD

In retrospective reports, biracial adults report differing degrees of awareness of the extent to which their biracial heritage increased the stress of adolescence (Hall, 1980; Murphy-Shigematsu, 1986; Seattle Times, April 1988). This awareness seems to be effected by the communities in which they have lived, parental support, acceptance by the extended family, racial features, and friends.

Junior high and high school are difficult developmental years as teenagers seek a balance between establishing a unique identity while pursuing conformity to peer values. For many biracial individuals, the teenage years appear to be encumbered by a more painful process than the monoracial person. Racial identity conflict is forced to the surface through increased peer dependence, cliques, dating, and movement away from the family.

Turmoil is generated when acceptance at home is not mirrored in the community. At an age that one depends on peers' reactions as the "truth," the teenager may be angry at their parents for failing to prepare them, or for leading them to believe that they are wonderful, lovable, and likable. This inconsistency results in confusion, grief, and anger. Subsequently, conflicts of vague origin increase between children and parents; the adolescent sentiment, "You don't understand; no one understands!" takes on added meaning. Teenagers feel increasingly isolated when they do not know who to trust and as a result may become vulnerable to interpreting environmental cues. For those biracial individuals who feel a tremendous amount of alienation, they may dismiss the positive feedback about self and become extra sensitive to negative feedback. They may overcompensate academically and or in social relationships in order to prove their worth.

A dual existence may be reported by the biracial person; they may appear to be accepted and even popular, but may simultaneously continue to feel different and isolated. Morishima (1980) suggests there may be more identity conflicts for Asian/White children because of their ambiguous appearance. Many White-Asians reflect feeling different regardless of growing up in predominantly white or Asian neighborhoods (Murphy-Shigematsu, 1986). In contrast, Black-White and Black-Asian persons' racial identities appear to be more influenced by their neighbors' color (Hall, 1980), though this difference may simply reflect the continuing, strong oppression of Blacks leading to less freedom of choice for persons who are part Black. However, the biracial adolescent may not relate their feelings of alienation to their biracial status, particularly in the case of those persons who have appeared to move well between and among racial groups. For therapists working with biracial persons, this source of alienation should always be kept in mind, especially with vague complaints of dissatisfaction, unhappiness, and feelings of isolation.

Dating brings many of the subtle forms of racism to the surface. For mixed race persons, all dating is interracial and can be fraught with all the tensions that have historically accompanied it (Petroni, 1973). For the teenager who has seemingly been accepted by different racial groups and has friends of different races they may be confronted with the old slur, "It's okay to have friends who are Black (Asian, White, etc.), but it's not okay to date one, and definitely not okay to marry one." A more subtle form of this racism occurs with parental encouragement of interracial friendships and even dating. However, more covert communication imparts the message, "you can date one, but don't marry one." For those biracial persons who can "pass" as white on the exterior, but do not identify as such, their attraction to non-whites may be met with statements such as, "You can do better than that." This statement is interpreted as a prejudicial comment towards their internal perception and identification of themselves. For some biracial persons this will be the first time that they experience barriers because of color or their socially perceived ambiguous race. For the child who has grown up in an extended white family and has been encouraged to act white and identify white, dating is painful. The teenager or young adult may avoid much dating and or continue in their activities in which these conflicts are absent.

A form of racism which surfaces during adolescence and may continue throughout life is "tokenism," which occurs both personally and vocationally. The biracial person's racial ambiguity and partial similarity by values or appearance may be used by a dominant group as a way of satisfying a quota for a person of color who is less threatening than a monoracial person of color (despite how the biracial person identifies). What makes this type of recruiting oppressive is that the group is using this person to avoid dealing with their racism; furthermore, they are assigning racial identity for the person and not informing her or him of their purpose. The group or organization subsequently uses their association with this person as evidence of their affirmative action or antiracist efforts. As a result, they have actually made this person marginal to the group.

Gender Issues

Like women, non-white persons have had to work harder to prove themselves equal by white, male standards. This observation is true for mixed race persons who may have to fight misperceptions that mixed race persons may be abnormal. The arenas in which biracial men and women have particular difficulties are different. Non-white men, because they have more social, economic, and political power than most women, are particularly threatening to White America. It is hypothesized that mixed race men will have a more difficult time overcoming social barriers than mixed race women; they will have to work harder to prove themselves and experience an oppression, which while shared by other minority group men, may exist also within their minority reference groups towards them.

On the other hand, because women in general are less threatening to the mainstream culture than men, mixed race women may not experience as much direct oppression as mixed race men. Biracial women may in fact be perceived as less threatening than monoracial women of color. They are likely to have difficulty comprehending, and then subsequently coping with pervasive myths that mixed race women are "exotic" and sexually freer than other women (Petroni, 1973; Wagatsuma, 1973). These myths appear to stem from myths that interracial relationships are based upon sex (cf. Petroni, 1973). Coupled with a lack of acceptance, some biracial women become sexually promiscuous in a search for acceptance (Gibbs, 1987). Mixed race women may also have more difficulty in relationships because of intersections of myths, lower status as women, and their search for an identity.

Summary

Racism challenges adolescent optimism. The young person's sensitivity to social approval and the human need for belonging make the resolution of biracial identity a long, uncharted journey. The path is determined by family, community, and peer values and environments. Racial features including skin color of self and family members also shape one's sense of racial identity.

To assume that the biracial person will racially identify with how they look is presumptive, but pervasive. Besides, the biracial person is perceived differently by different people. *Many persons make the mistake of thinking that the biracial person is fortunate to have a choice; however, the reality is that the biracial person has to fight very hard to exercise choices that are not congruent with how they may be visually and emotionally perceived.* She or he should have options to go beyond identifying with one or the other racial group of their heritage; the limitations of this dichotomy of options is oppressive and generates marginal status. To be able to have an expanded slate of options may shorten the journey and reduce the pain involved in resolution of biracial identity.

STRATEGIES FOR RESOLUTION OF "OTHER" STATUS

Several models for identity development exist both in the psychological and sociological bodies of literature. Minority models for identity development share in common the rejection of white values in order to appreciate minority values. However, as pointed out in the Atkinson et al.'s (1979) model, there is an inherent difficulty in rejecting "whiteness" if one is part white. In fact, the author proposes that for those individuals who are part white to manifest hatred towards whiteness probably reflects oppression within the nuclear and extended family system. For biracial persons who are a minority-minority racial mix, it is not clear how to apply this model.

A Beginning Schematic for Identity Development

I am proposing a schematic metamodel that might be used to understand the process of identity development for persons with different types of "other" status. This model is schematically a spiral where the linear force is internal conflict over a core sense of definition of self, the importance of which is largely determined by socialization (e.g., race, gender). Different sources of conflict may move the individual forward. It is proposed, however, that in each person's life there are at least one or two significant conflicts during critical developmental periods that move them forward. The circular or system forces encompass the political, social, and familial environments.

I suggest that in the identity development of the biracial person, the strongest recurring conflict at critical periods of development will be the tension between racial components within oneself. Social, familial, and political systems are the environments within which the biracial person appears to seek a sense of self in a circular process repeatedly throughout a lifetime. Themes of marginality, discrimination, and ambiguity are produced by these systems.

At all times, biracial persons contend with both parts of their racial heritage. Early in the process of identity development, after the child has become aware of race, she or he is likely to compartmentalize and separate the racial components of their heritage. The attention they give to aspects of their heritage may alternate (though not necessarily equally) over time. This alternating represents conflict and lack of experience and strategies for integrating components of self. Resolution reflects the lack of need for compartmentalizing the parts of their ethnic heritage.

The rest of this paper is dedicated to outlining four general resolutions of biracial identity. That there is more than one acceptable outcome confronts the limitations of traditional psychological theory which allow for only a single healthy endpoint. If there is another step in the contribution that feminist theory can make to personality development, it might be to provide flexibility and tolerance for more than a single definition of mental health.

The factors and criteria that determine each resolution are outlined. All resolutions are driven by the assumption that an individual recognizes both sides of their heritage. The resolutions that are proposed are an articulation of what appears on the surface: acceptance of the identity society assigns; identification with a single racial group; identification with both racial groups; and identification as a new racial group.

Acceptance of the Identity Society Assigns

Biracial people growing up in more racially oppressive parts of the country are less likely to have freedom to choose their racial identity. They are likely to be identified and identify as a person of color which will be equated with subordinate status. This strategy reflects the case of a passive resolution that is positive but may stem from an oppressive process. However, it is possible for it to be a positive resolution if the individual feels they belong to the racial group to which they are assigned. Affiliation, support, and acceptance by the extended family is important to this resolution being positive.

Individuals who have largely been socialized within an extended family, depending on them for friendship as well as nurturance are likely to racially identify with this group regardless of their visual similarity or dissimilarity to the extended family. One will tend to identify with the ethnic identity with which society views the family. The advantage of this identification is that the extended (well-functioning) family is a stable, secure reference group whose bonds go beyond visual, racial similarity.

This resolution is the most tenuous of the strategies outlined in that the individual may be perceived differently and assigned a different racial identity in a different part of the country. Because one's self-image in the mind's eye is stable across significant changes, the conflict and subsequent accumulated life experience would need to be tremendous to compel the individual to change their internally perceived racial identity. In the event of this challenge, the biracial person may work towards a more active resolution process. However, it is likely that she or he will still racially identify the same way but based on a different process such as identification with the extended family. Evidence of a positive resolution is that the individual would educate those persons with whom they interact of their chosen identity.

Identification with Both Racial Groups

Some biracial persons identify with both racial groups they have inherited. When asked about their ethnic background, they may respond, "I'm part Black and part Japanese," or "I'm mixed." This resolution is positive if the individual's personality remains similar across groups and they feel privileged in both groups. They may simultaneously be aware that they are both similar and different compared to those persons around them. However, they view their otherness as a unique characteristic of self that contributes to a sense of individuality.

This may be the most idealistic resolution of biracial status, and available in only certain parts of the country where biracial children exist in larger numbers and mixed marriages are accepted with greater tolerance by the community such as on the West coast. This strategy does not change other people's behavior; thus, the biracial person must have constructive strategies for coping with social resistance to their comfort with both groups of their heritage and their claim to privileges of both group.

Identification with a Single Racial Group

The result of this strategy sometimes looks identical to the strategy of assuming the racial identity that society assigns. It is different, however, by the process being active rather than passive and not the result of oppression. In this strategy, the individual *chooses* to identify with a particular racial/ethnic group regardless if this is the identity assumed by siblings, assigned by society, or matching their racial features. This is a positive strategy if the individual does not feel marginal to their proclaimed racial reference group and does not deny the other part of their racial heritage. This is a more difficult resolution to achieve in parts of the country which have the strongest prohibitions against crossing color lines (e.g., the South).

A major difficulty may be faced with this strategy when there is an incongruous match between how an individual is perceived by others and how they perceive themselves. With this strategy, the biracial person needs to be aware and accept the incongruity and have coping strategies for dealing with questions and suspicion by the reference group. Some individuals will need to make a geographic move to be able to live this resolution more peacefully.

Identification as a New Racial Group

This person most likely feels a strong kinship to other biracial persons in a way that they may not feel to any racial group because of the struggle with marginal status. Identification as a new race is a positive resolution if the person is not trying to hide or reject any aspect of their racial heritage. This individual may move fluidly between racial groups but view themselves apart from these reference groups without feeling marginal because they have generated a new reference group. There are few examples of biracial groups being recognized in a positive way. Hawaii perhaps sets one of the best examples with the Hapa Haole (White-Asian) (Yamamoto, 1973).

A clear problem with this resolution is that society's classification system does not recognize persons of mixed race. Thus, this individual would continually experience being assigned to a racial identity and would need to inform people of the inaccuracy when it felt important to them.

Summary

I suggest that these strategies are not mutually exclusive and may coexist simultaneously, or an individual may move among them. Such movement is consistent with a stable, positive sense of identity if the individual does not engage in denial of any part of their heritage (internalized oppression). Two themes are common to the resolutions listed above. First, it is important that the biracial person accept both sides of her or his racial heritage. Second, the biracial person has the right to declare how they wish to identify themselves racially—even if this identity is discrepant with how they look or how society tends to perceive them. Third, the biracial person develops strategies for coping with social resistance or questions about their racial identity so that they no longer internalize questions as inferring that there is something wrong with them. Rather, they attribute questions and insensitivities to ignorance and racism.

Resolution of biracial identity is often propelled forward by the internal conflict generated by exposure to new people, new ideas, and new environments. Subsequently, it is not uncommon that many individuals emerge out of college years with a different resolution to their racial identity than when they graduated high school. Furthermore, geography plays a large part in the options the individual has. Living in more liberal parts of the country may be necessary to exercise a wider range of options with less social resistance.

CONCLUSION

The multiple strategies for resolution of other status in this paper constitutes a proposal, challenge, and appeal to theorists of human personality development to be more flexible in considering the range of positive psychological functioning. Psychological theories have been oppressive by their narrow range of tolerance and allowance for positive mental health. As a result, many different types of people can relate to the search for a resolution of other status, though not necessarily based on racial/ethnic ambiguity. If theories of identity development allowed for a slate of equally valid resolutions of conflict around basic components of identity, fewer people may struggle with "identity crises." Because of the role that feminist theory has played in attempting to validate the experience of persons with "other" status by sexual orientation, religious/ethnic identity, etc., *it seems that feminist theorists and therapists may be the persons most able to develop flexible models of mental health that truly allow for diversity.* But first, more feminist theorists and therapists will have to reach out beyond their boundaries of cultural safety to understand issues of race.

Although it appears that the biracial person may have the best of both worlds, this is a naive assumption which presumes that she or he has unopposed freedom to choose how she or he wishes to be perceived. In reality all racial groups have their prejudices which when projected onto the biracial person are the creators of marginal status. The biracial person does not have a guaranteed ethnic reference group if they leave it to the group to determine if they can belong.

The key to resolving other status derived from ethnic ambiguity requires an individual to move beyond the dichotomous, irrational categorization of race by white versus non-white, which in turn has been equated with degrees of worth and privilege in our culture. Towards this goal, three significant assumptions can be made about the experience of the biracial person which subsequently affects their process of identity resolution.

First, the biracial person does not necessarily racially identify with the way she or he looks (Hall, 1980). Because self-image is an emotionally mediated picture of the self, one's perception of self is governed by more than racial features. One's image of self is shaped by the presence or absence of other people similar to them, the racial features of siblings, exposure to people of both races which they inherit, identification with one parent over another, peer reactions, and how the extended family has perceived them as children.

Second, unlike monoracial people of color, the biracial person does not have guaranteed acceptance by any racial reference group. Thus, minority models of identity development do not reflect the resolution of this situation which is the crux of the biracial person's marginal status. *Looking for acceptance from others keeps the biracial person trying to live by the "irrational" racial classification rules which may keep her or him marginal to any group.*

The third assumption is that there is more than one possible, positive resolution of racial identity for biracial persons. This assumption reflects a departure from traditional European, male originated identity models which have a single, static, positive outcome. Furthermore, the *resolution strategies for biracial identity can change during a lifetime.* It is this ability to be flexible that may indeed determine both self-acceptance and constructive, flexible coping strategies.

Marginality is a state created by society and not inherent in one's racial heritage. *As long as the biracial person bases self-acceptance on complete social acceptance by any racial reference group, they will be marginal.* Freire (1970) clearly articulates the origin and subsequently difficult resolution of marginality,

> . . . marginality is not by choice, (the) marginal (person) has been expelled from and kept outside of the social system . . . *Therefore, the solution to their problem is not to become "beings inside of," but . . . (people) . . . freeing themselves; for, in reality, they are not marginal to the structure, but oppressed . . . (persons) . . . within it* (author's emphasis). (pp. 10-11)

REFERENCES

Allport, Gordon W. (1958). *The nature of prejudice.* Reading, MA: Addison-Wesley.

Atkinson, D., Morten, G., & Sue, Derald W. (1979). *Counseling American minorities: A cross cultural perspective.* Dubuque, IA: Brown Company.

Dien, D. S., & Vinacke, W. E. (1964). Self-concept and parental identification of young adults with mixed Caucasian-Japanese parentage. *Journal of Abnormal Psychology, 69*(4), 463-466.

Freire, Paolo (1970). *Cultural action for freedom.* Cambridge: Harvard Educational Review Press.

Gibbs, Jewelle Taylor (1987). Identity and marginality: Issues in the treatment of biracial adolescents. *American Journal of Orthopsychiatry, 57*(2), 265-278.

Goodman, M. E. (1968). *Race awareness in young children.* New York: Collier Press.

Hall, Christine C. Iijima (1980). *The ethnic identity of racially mixed people: A study of Black-Japanese.* Doctoral Dissertation, University of California, Los Angeles.

Henriques, Fernando (1975). *Children of conflict: A study of interracial sex and marriage.* New York: E. P. Dutton & Co., Inc.

Louise, Vivienne (1988). Of Color: What's In a Name? *Bay Area Women's News, 1*(6), 5,7.

Morishima, James K. (1980). *Asian American Racial Mixes: Attitudes, Self-Concept, and Academic Performance.* Paper presented at the Western Psychological Association convention, Honolulu.

Moritsugu, John, Foerster, Lynn, & Morishima, James K. (1978). *Eurasians: A Pilot Study.* Paper presented at the Western Psychological Association convention, San Francisco, 1978.

Murphy-Shigematsu, Stephen (1986). *The voices of amerasians: Ethnicity, identity, and empowerment in interracial Japanese Americans*. Doctoral Dissertation, Harvard University.

Petroni, Frank A. (1983). Interracial Dating—The Price is High. In I. R. Stuart and L. Edwin (Eds.). *Interracial marriage: Expectations and Realities*. New York: Grossman Publishers.

Poussaint, Alvin F. (1984). Benefits of Being Interracial. In the Council on Interracial Books for Children, *Children of interracial families*, *15*(6).

Sickels, Robert J. (1972). *Race, marriage, and the law*. Albuquerque, NM: University of New Mexico Press.

Stonequist, Everett (1935). The problem of the marginal man. *The American Journal of Sociology*, *41*, 1-12.

Sue, Derald W. (1981). *Counseling the culturally different: Theory and practice*. New York: John Wiley & Sons.

Wagatsuma, Hiroshi (1973). Some Problems of Interracial Marriage for the Japanese. In I. R. Stuart and L. Edwin (Eds.), *Interracial Marriage: Expectations and Realities*. New York: Grossman Publishers.

Yamamoto, George (1973). Interracial Marriage in Hawaii. In I. R. Stuart and L. Edwin (Eds.), *Interracial Marriage: Expectations and Realities*. New York: Grossman Publishers.

What Has Gone Before:
The Legacy of Racism and Sexism in the Lives of Black Mothers and Daughters

Beverly A. Greene, PhD

SUMMARY. The role of mother is an important one for many Black women, and it is accompanied by tasks not shared by their white counterparts, specifically, racial socialization of Black children. It is important therefore that psychotherapists understand the additional stressors brought to bear on Black women as mothers as well as the effect of those stressors on their parenting skills. This paper focuses on the legacy of adaptive strengths Black women have exercised in coping with an antagonistic environment; potential complications in the task of racial socialization; traditional resources found in Black families, as well as psychotherapeutic interventions which may enhance this process when problems occur.

> The grace with which we embrace
> Life in spite of pain, the
> Sorrow
>
> Is always a measure of what has
> Gone before
>
> — Alice Walker
> "Fundamental Difference" (1970)

Beverly A. Greene is Director of the Inpatient Child and Adolescent Psychology Service at Kings County Hospital in Brooklyn, NY, and Clinical Assistant Professor in the Department of Psychiatry, Downstate Medical Center. She also has a private clinical and consulting practice in Brooklyn. She is a Black American whose grandmother's grandfather was a Cherokee Indian who remained in Tennessee when the Cherokee nation was exiled to Oklahoma.

Correspondence may be addressed to the author at: 26 St. Johns Place, Brooklyn, NY 11217.

207

In the continuing conspiracy of silence and distortion about the history and culture of Black persons, little attention has been given to the question of what has gone before. The legacy of racism and sexism in the lives of Black women may be seen as quite relevant to what occurs now in their children's lives and what may occur in their children's futures. How this legacy is communicated to Black females by their mothers and what kinds of outcomes are associated with various communications is often misunderstood and warrants further inquiry.

A commitment to feminist principles includes an understanding and interest in the effects of discrimination on the lives of all women, not simply the lives of women from the culture's dominant groups. Feminist psychotherapy, in any attempt to understand Black women and their development must understand the role of racism in their past as well as in their present. For most women their relationships with their own mothers influence how they come to see themselves, and can be a salient factor in the way they socialize their own daughters. It follows that feminist psychotherapy should extend its concern and understanding of the effects of racism and sexism in Black women's lives to its effect on their parenting interactions, skills, and subsequent messages to their children, then integrate this understanding into the current theoretical understanding of feminist psychotherapy and into the treatment process itself.

The role of mother itself is an important one for many Black women and is accompanied by tasks not required of their white counterparts. Psychotherapists must understand the additional stressors that impinge on Black mothers as well as the effects of various mechanisms of mastery against racism and sexism that Black mothers either consciously or unconsciously teach young Black females. It may be helpful to determine which strategies or mechanisms are adaptive versus maladaptive, how well the adaptive strategies function, and under what conditions they function optimally.

The dominant culture's disparaging view of Black persons is pervasive and institutionalized. Much of the deficit oriented literature generated about Black persons appears to have been designed to simply reaffirm and perpetuate popularly held beliefs and stereotypes about Black persons, rather than yielding pertinent information about their adaptive skills and resilience. These views and the both subtle and overt ways that they are communicated have been reviewed in detail elsewhere (Giddings, 1984; Greene, 1985, 1986; Guthrie, 1976; Karier, 1986; Mays, 1985; Noble, 1978; Powell, 1983; Thomas & Sillen, 1972; Williams, 1987; Willie, Kramer & Brown, 1973).

Much has been written about the debilitating effects of racism on Black persons. Less is known, however, about what may be called "racial socialization" among Black folk. Specifically, this refers to what Black parents communicate to Black children about what it means to be a Black American, what they may expect from Black and white persons, how to cope with it, and whether or not the disparaging messages of the broader culture are true. What has gone before in the life of the Black mother and her subsequent adjustment may greatly influence the extent to which she reinforces or mitigates the dominant culture's contempt for Black persons to her children.

The phenomenon of racial socialization between Black mothers and their daughters in the context of a hostile environment, problems which may occur during its course, and psychotherapeutic interventions which may facilitate passing on a legacy of pride and coping skills rather than a legacy of shame and self-denigration will be explored below.

DISTINCTIVE CHARACTERISTICS OF BLACK CULTURE

Boykin (1985) suggests that the essence of Black culture may be defined as that which emphasizes the spirit of the matter rather than the letter of things. He delineates more specific and salient cultural characteristics as the following: an emphasis on style, or the notion that it is not what you do but how you do it that is valued; admiration for personal attributes rather than status or office; a heightened sensitivity to nonverbal modes of communication; a person rather than object oriented focus; a response to wholes or gestalts rather than discrete parts; a particular value of personal distinctiveness and spontaneity reflected in the improvisational styles of Black music; an emphasis on emotional sensibilities, emotional expressiveness, and interdependence among individuated group members; and a preference for oral and auditory modes of communication. Here, the spoken word is used to convey deep textural meanings which may be lost in the grammatical structure required of the written word. The use of Black English or specific language styles has been explained by Levine (1977) as a means of promoting and maintaining a sense of group unity and cohesion among Black persons who live in the midst of a hostile society.

Young (1970) cautions observers of Black parents and their children that Black parents tend to socialize modes or styles of behavior rather than emphasizing rules that govern behavior. An emphasis on style may be more difficult to observe and quantify than rule-governed behavior and may as a result go unnoticed.

Akbar (1985) notes that derivatives of African thinking may still be observed in Black Americans of African origin in the essence of the concept "I am because We are," rather than the Cartesian notion that has influenced European American thought of "I think therefore I am." Dixon and Foster (1971) suggest that an African philosophical orientation would be captured in the notion, "I feel, therefore I think, therefore I am." Here, it is the experience that counts rather than words, thoughts, or what is said. The concept "I am because We are" underscores the value of placing the needs of the group or tribe over the needs of the individual as well as an emphasis on interdependence and collective responsibility.

Measures of intelligence based on Cartesian thought emphasize the ability to manipulate material objects of the external world rather than the African value system which emphasizes adequacy in negotiating cooperative, amiable human relationships. It should be noted that technology and the development of technological skills, associated with the former, are not to be eschewed. However, their pursuit and idealization to the exclusion of other skills, values, and modes of thinking can lead to what Haskins and Butts (1973) refer to as an "incomplete knowledge of the world." Further, the use of the Cartesian as the standard, normative, or corrective mode against which other modes are seen as inferior, rather than as a preferred or valued mode for a numerical majority of persons, has served to arbitrarily devalue and stigmatize persons whose values or modalities are simply different.

THE BLACK FAMILY AND RACIAL SOCIALIZATION

The Black mother-daughter dyad and racial-sexual socialization will constitute the focus of this inquiry. This does not imply that father-daughter, mother-son, extended family or peer group relationships and interactions are of minimal importance. It is fair to say, however, that mothers, in this case Black females, are usually charged with the task of socializing Black children. In 1982, 81.9% of Black children who did not live with both parents lived with their mothers, 14.5% lived with neither parent, and only 3.6% lived with their fathers (Edelman, 1985). Further, 55.3% of all Black children are born to a single mother (National Center for Health Statistics, 1982).

Black women parent Black daughters in the context of a society which devalues all women to some extent when their status is compared to that of men. Among women, however, the dominant culture idealizes white women while devaluing and assigning a subordinate status to Black women. Ladner (1971) notes that race can operate as a more powerful social variable than others and can transcend the effects of class, education, occupation, and religion. As a result, race may transcend the effect of gender for Black women, who do not share similar status, roles, values, or sets of expectations as white women. Black females are not simply seen as women, but rather as Black women. Parameters of their roles are influenced by race and the existence of racism. It therefore becomes difficult if not impossible to completely disentangle the effects of sex and race in the lives of Black women. Traditionally, Black women have not received the customary courtesies for femininity. They have been required to work as hard and as frequently as Black men while being held accountable to standards of femininity based on the white female ideal (Cade, 1970; Epstein, 1973; Freudiger & Almquist, 1980; Harley, Terborg & Penn, 1978; Lerner, 1972; Myers, 1980; Robinson, 1983). While all women were regarded as the biblical originators of sexual sin, white women were elevated to a pedestal of sexual purity and virtue. Black women were characterized as the embodiment of sexual evil and lust (Greene, 1986).

Bell (1971) writes that motherhood has been an historically important role for Black women. A close bond with her children may be seen as the derivative of an important role for Black women in pre-colonial Africa where children were highly prized and the roles of childbearer and childrearer were taken seriously and valued.

Ladner (1971) notes that African women were often considered the founders or mothers of tribes and the primary carriers of culture. Nobles (1974a) points out that a special bond observed in the relationships between Black women and their children cannot be simply attributed to the fact that in slavery, a Black family was legally defined to include only a mother and her children. Rather, it reflects deep roots in an African heritage and a philosophical orientation which places a special value on children because they represent the continuity of life.

It must be clear that Black females served important functions in cultural transmission, economic and parenting roles. It would seem logical that a young Black woman's understanding of what it means to be a Black woman may most certainly be heavily influenced by her mother's phenomenological understanding of racism and sexism and their respective roles in shaping her mother's own life.

Traditionally, Black women have been blamed for the family ills and stresses which are in fact caused by institutional racism. A disparaging social science literature then measures Black persons and their family structures against an idealized white mythology with the view that, owing to the Black female's alleged domineering and matriarchal nature, the Black family represents a tangled web of pathology. Paradoxically, Hill (1972) reminds us that Black women have always represented strong and competent mother figures, as even slaveholders entrusted their white children to her care. This need to pathologize Black persons, in this case Black women, has resulted in a line of distorted research inquiry which focuses on deficits. In so doing, it overlooks strengths and resources which could be utilized when problems occur. Further, this serves the purpose of reaffirming and legitimizing the original racist stereotypes, and provides the appearance of a justification for the very racist and sexist practices which blatantly contradict the American ideal of equality and fair play.

Hill (1972) identifies what he considers to be five major characteristics of Black families which reflect both the derivatives of their

African culture roots as well as their need to adapt to a racist and sexist society. Strong kinship bonds exist between family members, often including people who are not biologically related but who are clearly experienced as family members. Hence a young Black child's family may include her family of origin as well as aunts, uncles, cousins, grandparents, close family friends and neighbors, all of whom may be directly involved in childrearing in some capacity. Black females in this system play important roles in childrearing regardless of their biological relationship to those children.

What Hill (1972) describes as a strong achievement motivation among Black families is reflected in the emphasis Black mothers have always placed on the importance of an education for their children. This is frequently communicated overtly to a child with the clear admonition that they will have to outperform their white counterparts to have any chance of success. Adaptability and flexibility of family roles is a characteristic reflecting the African principles of cooperative work and collective responsibility. As Black women were always a part of the labor force, America's structure of sex roles was never particularly suited to the needs of Black families whose economic and social realities differed from the dominant cultural norm.

A strong religious and spiritual orientation has long been an important aspect of Black life. What is important to note here is the opportunity for Black children to see their mothers as role models, exercising leadership and utilizing talents in ways they were not permitted to do in the dominant culture but were encouraged to do within Black churches.

Finally, Hill (1972) cites a strong work orientation or ethic as a Black family trait. This is reflected in the conspicuous presence of working Black women throughout history. In most Black middle class households, male and female wage earners are a common necessity for maintaining middle class status. Young Black females are socialized to expect that they will have to work to support themselves as well as their families, to think about the kind of work they will do, and to educate themselves to obtain appropriate skills. They generally do not expect that marriage will relieve them of being a part of the labor force (Jones, 1985; Rollins, 1985).

The family may be seen as the traditional buffer between a child and the outside world, and the major source of communicating cultural values and practices. Parents are usually, but not exclusively, the persons responsible for the nurturance and guidance of a child through its developmental periods into adulthood (Franklin & Boyd-Franklin, 1985). It must be noted that biological parents may not necessarily perform this function, or perform it exclusively, particularly in Black families where extended kinship patterns are prevalent and of cultural significance. A major task of the parenting persons is that of interpreting the outside world's messages to a child about who she or he is with respect to Black and white persons, and what her or his respective place in the world is or can be. This must be done in addition to teaching the child the skills required to survive and negotiate the cognitive, social, and, for Black children, racial tasks of the world.

This is a complex task for any parent. However, it is further complicated for Black parents, as they must perform in what may be described as the ubiquitous environment of real and/or potential racial discrimination and prejudice.

Nobles (1975) writes that the task of the Black family is to prepare its children to live among white people without becoming white people, and to mediate between two often contradictory cultures. This process may require an ability to be different people at different times, a duality of socialization. Black families are required to teach Black children to be aware of, and able to imitate, the majority culture whether they accept its values or not. The need to be bicultural in an antagonistic environment may produce competing and conflicting developmental tasks and tensions. An understanding of what those conflicts are for Black children, how they may be manifested, and how they are or may be successfully negotiated has never been adequately explored.

A special task and added stressor confronting Black parents involves finding ways of warning Black children about racial dangers and disappointments without overwhelming them or being overly protective. Either extreme will leave a child inadequately prepared to negotiate the world. This process in its essence may be seen as racial socialization.

Ferguson-Peters (1985) writes that the supportive child-rearing strategies of Black families buffer some of the cruel and demeaning messages received by Black children from the dominant culture. Spencer (1987) adds that race consciousness provides a necessary foundation for the coping strategies needed by Black children.

The pressure of racism and the varied effects and methods used by Black parents to minimize its damaging effects on their children can be accurately perceived as a major source of stress not shared by their white counterparts. It is reflected in the amount of energy consumed in, and the distractions presented by, the ongoing requirements of coping with the dominant culture's prejudices and barriers.

Peters (1985) interviewed Black parents in an attempt to discern factors relevant to the socioemotional development of young Black children, and the childrearing behaviors, attitudes, and goals of their parents. A majority of parents interviewed reported that being Black made a difference in the way they raised their children. They reported that special things were required to prepare Black children for being Black in this society, and that this placed additional stress on their lives, as well as their children's lives.

Many of the parents in this study reported that they did not feel they had been adequately prepared by their own parents to cope with the prejudice and discrimination they faced. While it is questionable if any amount of preparation can sufficiently dull the pain of racism, the failure to recognize the existence of racism and its sequelae and to understand how it proceeds has implications. An inability to identify factors which facilitate an awareness of racism and which lead to adaptive coping skills, as well as to identify factors which may undermine this awareness may lead to problematic outcomes.

THE BLACK CHILD

Black children, like other Black persons, have historically been the targets of a deficit-oriented research model which measures them and their performance against an idealized standard of the behavior of those white children living in adequate economic and educational environments. It is against this background that Black children have been judged dysfunctional, inadequate, and low in self-esteem, despite the fact that little empirical evidence supports this rampant assumption. Black children have been found to have similar distributions of self-esteem scores as found in other populations (McAdoo & McAdoo, 1985). It is suggested that the socioemotional environment of Black children represents a major factor contributing to their adaptive development.

The image of childhood as a protected developmental period during which children mature and explore the world unencumbered by many of life's stark and dangerous realities does not hold true for a majority of Black children, particularly those who are economically impoverished. The vulnerability of Black parents to the whims of an institutionally racist society, and particularly the vulnerability of Black mothers who tend to occupy the ranks of the least well paid, are shared by their children, and in ways that the parents cannot protect them from. This is not so universally the case for white parents and their children. This is reflected by the fact that 50% of Black children live in poverty, as compared to 20% of all American children (Edelman, 1985).

Garbarino (1982) defines risk as the impoverishing of a child's world of the basic social and psychological necessities of life, leaving them at risk for impaired development. As the context of racism and sexism is antithetical to the optimal development of individual endowments, Black female children may be seen as being at risk for impaired development (Powell, 1983; Wyatt, 1985).

Black children may grow up under conditions which clearly contradict those of white children and the formally espoused values of the dominant culture. This is manifested in the limits placed on their opportunity for optimal development (Spencer, 1987). They enter a world which views them with fear, suspicion and as the antithesis of all that society defines as beautiful. The conspicuous omission of their images in children's books and the media's derogatory portrayal of Black persons represent examples of the sources of this message. While large numbers of black children live in neighborhoods where violence, drugs, traffic and filth are the day to day reality, those who do not still remain Black in a culture which treats them with contempt regardless of their social class. They are bombarded from different directions with the clear message that society places a low premium on their existence.

The ''at risk'' status of Black children is reflected concretely in significant differences between Black and white children on a number of dimensions. Black children are six times as likely to show excess exposure to lead; six times as likely to contract tuberculosis; ten times as likely to die before the age of one year from nutritional deficiencies; and four times as likely to suffer from gastritis and gastrointestinal infections and disorders as their white counterparts (Edelman, 1985). Black children are found in correctional facilities at 400 times the rate of their white counterparts and are placed in psychiatric, foster care, and health care facilities at a rate 75% higher than that of their white peers (Edelman, 1985).

Daily survival becomes an ongoing struggle for most Black mothers and their children. A major task confronting Black children rests in the challenge to survive in a society where they must incorporate the dominant values of the society, which include an insidious devaluation of non-white persons, while simultaneously incorporating the values of a Black community. Another task involves developing one's natural abilities and endowments when a large portion of one's creative energy must be used simply to survive.

Operating in a context where they are frequently double-bound, where different standards apply to the same phenomena, Black children, especially females, face an inability to predict whether certain behaviors on their parts will be regarded positively and rewarded, or negatively and punished (Holiday, 1985). In this atmosphere, the opportunity to succeed against the odds may represent an underpinning of exceptional performance. It may also lead to frustration, indifference, hostility (Holiday, 1985) and behaviors that appear self-defeating. It is puzzling why theoreticians and behavioral scientists do not frame their research and observations around the questions of why more Black children are not more dysfunctional or deficit-ridden, and what it is that occurs among Black folk which has historically mitigated or worked successfully against that negative outcome.

Spencer (1987) writes that a Black child's preparation by parents and other socializing agents to understand and take pride in her own culture can be a major source of resilience and coping; and that its absence leaves a Black child at additional risk for impaired development.

POTENTIAL COMPLICATIONS IN BLACK MOTHERS' ROLES IN RACIAL SOCIALIZATION

Black persons are often understood as if they passively react to racism and oppression, and as if they unthinkingly accept the dominant culture's values and views of them. Such assertions occur despite the evidence of the use of various creative and resourceful methods of adaptation. These resources and coping mechanisms have historically and continue to be manifested in the use of different strategies, tailored to different periods of time, geographical regions, and racial environments in the United States, as well as to different points of developmental racial awareness of an individual.

Richardson (1981) suggests that sociocultural and racial environments and experiences of mothers can greatly influence their perception of social reality, and that these perceptions will effect childrearing values and behavioral strategies. He writes that Black mothers are required to mediate the hostile external society for their children.

It should be clear that a delicate balance is required of Black mothers in the process, particularly when it is complicated by the pernicious effect of sexism and, for Black Lesbian mothers or daughters, homophobia (Lorde, 1987; Parker, 1987). These and other factors influence the way a Black mother views herself. In what ways might it influence her socialization of her daughter?

Black mothers must prepare their daughters to become Black women. They must communicate the racial and sexual dangers and realities of the world that confront Black women, how to make sense of them, when and how to respond to racial dangers if at all. It may be incumbent on Black mothers to provide more positive messages and alternatives (to the white middle class ideal) to their daughters to offset the negative reflections they see of themselves in the eye of the dominant culture. Clearly, if a natural mother is unable to do this, extended or other family members, peers, educational and mental health environments may do so. It should be noted, however, that these extended family influences may be less intense and powerful than that of a natural mother, particularly in the early rather than later stages of childhood. A mother's failure, however, to mitigate the dominant culture's devaluing message, and rather to reinforce it, can be associated with maladaptive adjustments in her daughter.

Black mothers perform this task in many different contexts. However, it may be most problematic for the child in the context of rejection or maternal failure. Franklin and Boyd-Franklin (1985) write that racial socialization is enhanced in the context of love and support for the child; however, it is negatively affected when it occurs in the context of parental contempt, rejection, or failure. Mother-daughter dyads in isolated environments, in the presence of overwhelming or severe maternal stressors, or maternal psychopathology may be at risk for maternal failure. The existence and degree of poverty, marital difficulty, illness and other stressors may also jeopardize the success of this process. Good coping skills have been observed in children whose parents were models of resilience and who were available to their children with encouragement, comfort, and reassurance (Anthony & Cohler, 1987).

Racial socialization may be further complicated by great differences between the mother's racial experiences and those of her daughter. This may be particularly difficult in contemporary environments where the signposts of racism are less visible and more subtle than in previous generations.

Over and covert racism may require grossly different response strategies. The parent whose experiences were limited to overt forms of discrimination may feel less able to assist a child who confronts its more subtle forms. It has been noted that those confronted early in life with direct and open racial discrimination may be better prepared to manage it later in life than those persons who were either protected from it, or confronted only its more subtle forms (S. Greene, personal communication, 1988). I would suggest that the expectation of discriminatory treatment may be a salient factor in the development of skills and strategies required to recognize and manage this phenomenon when it occurs. This may be particularly relevant when discrimination occurs in its less visible manifestations. Generally there may be a higher level of preparedness for such events among skilled copers.

The function and effect of the presence or absence of a "living racial memory" (L. Polite-Henderson, personal communication, 1988), defined as a repertoire of direct confrontations and conscious responses to episodes of both overt and subtle racism in the life of a Black mother may also represent a salient variable in racial socialization. Inquiry by therapists into this phenomenon might be framed as a series of questions which ask if the client has conscious access to personal memories of episodes of racism; if such memories are absent or denied; the frequency and intensity of these events; how they were responded to, and how the client feels about the adequacy of her solutions. Answers may provide insight into the kinds of skills and level of preparedness passed along to the child. At one end of the spectrum, maternal denial of racial differences and their meanings may be observed. On the other end, a Black daughter may be unconsciously given license to act out racial anger that her mother was or is unable or unwilling to express. There are a variety of other scenarios which may be elicited via such inquiry, and which may result in the creation of maladaptive solutions for the child.

Just as the signs of racism may be overt or covert, the Black mother's communications to her daughter may be overt or covert. Harrison-Ross (1973) stresses the need for Black parents to directly and openly discuss race with Black children. Its omission, like that admonition that "everyone is the same" can be a destructive communication when a child knows and sees otherwise. It can also communicate shame in the mother about herself, racial difference, and those same issues in the child. Internalized racism in a parent may be observed and warrants inquiry by a clinician. Harrison-Ross (1973) notes here that attention to a child's name may reveal a parent's discomfort with Blackness. Names such as Crystal, Lily, Diana, etc. can in the presence of other factors suggest wishes for lightness, paleness, or whiteness. Further, if the mother is employed, are her employers Black or white? Is the relationship with them perceived as exploitative, benevolent, paternalistic, or benign, and how is that communicated to her children?

Within the mother-daughter dyad, physical appearance is a salient variable. As physical attractiveness for women was and continues to serve a functional role analogous to social power among men, the things a Black mother communicates to her Black daughter about the relative attractiveness of her physical characteristics and what, if any, extremes must be taken to alter them is important to understand. This is particularly true in the context of a culture where Black facial features are considered unattractive, and where women are clearly rewarded for approaching the white beauty standard. If a Black mother has accepted the dominant culture's standard of beauty, that standard and whatever conflicts or internal tension that accompany it may be passed on to her daughter (Lightfoot, 1988).

In slavery, lighter-skinned Black persons, usually the progeny of white slave masters, were sometimes given the illusion of better treatment. This often meant simply less abusive treatment; nevertheless, jealousies and resentments between darker and lighter skinned slaves were fueled by it. As a result, many Black and white persons developed skin color preferences and resentments that persist to this day. The most salient aspects of this notion are that lighter skinned Black persons, particularly women, are seen as more attractive and acceptable, and hence better treated by the dominant group (Greene, 1986). It is no surprise the skin color variations within Black families can be a source of difficulty between family members.

A Black mother's messages regarding skin color preferences may also transmit her conflicts about skin color to her daughter. As the child's skin color can affect the quality of parenting, the level of parental aspirations for her daughter, and the child's position in the family, this represents an important area of scrutiny for therapists (Harrison-Ross & Wyden, 1973). The importance of bleaching creams, hair straighteners, and attention to facial features in the mother's life may suggest what she is predisposed to communicate to her daughter about the suitability of the latter's appearance. It may be helpful to make inquiries about hair styles, texture, and length, and feelings about the above, as well as to ask who in the family was or is considered beautiful, and why. In addition, how does or did the mother in question respond to comments and questions from others about her child's skin color, particularly if the mother's and child's colorings are distinctly different?

Examples of ways in which skin color conflicts in the Black mother may have relevance to her daughter's development may be observed and explored with little direct inquiry. If a dark or light skinned mother idealizes her lighter skinned child, what might the dynamic implications be? Would that child feel devalued for being rewarded for an attribute that she has nothing to do with? Is her mother predisposed to expect more of this child, perhaps as a result of the assumption that life's obstacles are more easily negotiated if one has light skin? Would that mother, if dark skinned, feel envious and induce guilt feelings in her lighter skinned child? Would that mother be more predisposed to attribute her daughter's success to her skin color rather than to her abilities? In that same context, would this mother be predisposed to suggest to her daughter that she need not put forth much effort to succeed, leaving the daughter with unrealistic notions about how difficult life should or should not be?

Another relevant line of inquiry is related to the question of whether or not a Black mother is predisposed to be more protective of her darker skinned children, either as a result of her own conflicts about skin color or perhaps the realistic notion that the dominant culture will be even less hospitable to these children. What effect might this have on the child's development and how that child might perceive her level of competence? It is important to raise the question of whether or not the darker skinned child would experience her mother's heightened sense of protectiveness as her mother's lack of faith in her abilities rather than her mother's understanding of the dominant culture's obstacles. It may be difficult to clearly distinguish maternal racial conflicts from a Black mother's honest attempts to protect or prepare in some special way the child she perceives to be more vulnerable or at risk from a rejecting environment. It should be noted that special skill and sensitivity are required of the Black mother who faces this challenge so that her child is not left feeling doubly rejected.

There are many different scenarios and outcomes along this line of inquiry. These questions are raised here to suggest a way for the therapist to organize and think about them, and to suggest some of the subtle ways in which parental racial conflicts may be passed along to the next generation.

As the existence and effects of racism have been historically denied, so have the racial pain, hurt and rage which may often result. How a Black mother responds to her own racial pain will influence how she teaches her daughter to respond to it. One may need to determine if open acknowledgement of such feelings is acceptable or unacceptable, to whom, and why.

All women are discouraged to some extent from overtly expressing anger, particularly when it is in response to their discrimination or exploitation. However, prevailing, stigmatizing, and dichotomous views of Black females as either angry, volatile, castrating bitches; nurturing, universally accepting and caring mammy figures; or as morally loose and sexually promiscuous may predispose some Black females to feel a need to act out or assiduously avoid acting out any behavior which might be associated with any of these aforementioned stereotypes. In addition to the stress created out of the perceived need to maintain a constant state of vigilance around expressing certain feelings, there is a concomitant loss of spontaneity required for authenticity in interpersonal relationships.

This dilemma may leave some Black women feeling reluctant to overtly express their anger lest they be viewed as the stereotypic character, the hostile Sapphire. Sapphire was the Black, nagging wife of a simpering, scheming Black male character, Kingfish, in the 1950s radio (and later television) show Amos and Andy (Hooks, 1981). The character of Sapphire was the antithesis of the traditional and safe Black character of Mammy, as Sapphire openly and forcefully expressed her anger or rage, no matter who the target might be. Thus, Sapphire became the embodiment of the quintessential evil, bitchy, angry Black woman who was treacherous and contemptuous of Black men.

The implicit message to Black women was and is that they have a narrow choice of roles acceptable to and often created by the dominant culture. They may either be the Mammy, who knows her place and happily remains there, stalwart, denying her own needs and pain, thus appearing ever cheerful and content to take care of others, particularly her own master and mistress, requiring nothing in return. Or she may be the shrewish Sapphire, a hostile angry person who is never satisfied with anyone and consequently does not warrant the slightest deference to her feelings. The alternative to these roles is to attempt to approximate the dominant culture's idealized image of femininity which was to be passive and white and in so doing, obliterate as much of one's Black physical and cultural identity as possible. As this was always impossible to do, and the rewards elusive, many Black women found themselves back in the no-win situation.

Once overt expressions of anger or rage become synonymous with being labeled an evil, domineering bitch, it is no surprise that many Black women would consciously or unconsciously repress, deny, or displace that anger, often directing it at themselves and others like them, hence often at their own daughters. It is my belief that the above constellation of racist images was created to prevent or limit the expression of Black women's anger, and that Black mothers who have been taught to do this will teach their daughters to do the same. It is essential to assist a client in understanding this as internalized racism, the difficulty of resolving this dilemma, and how she arrived at her particular solution.

Teaching Black children to suppress or repress racial anger or to deny racial pain has in some situations and may continue to be of lifesaving importance. However, it always carries a price. This is particularly true if such repression is used to address a chronic continuous stressor. It is not advisable to teach any child to simply act on angry feelings. Milner (1983) suggests that it is important to help children understand and accept their angry feelings; in this case, their racial anger. This will leave them with a greater ability to accept negative feelings without being threatened by them and therefore have less of a need to project them onto others.

It may also be helpful to assist a Black mother in planning a discussion with her child about angry feelings in response to racial rejection or hostility. Such a discussion might include: setting priorities about what kinds of situations call for a direct or indirect response and why; in what situations a direct response might be dangerous to the child; and explore alternate ways of expressing or managing angry feelings.

Rich (1976) writes, "We are none of us either mothers or daughters. To our amazement and confusion and greater complexity, we are both." As Black females are often given responsibility for the care of siblings as well as household tasks at an early age, many Black women may have an early motherhood identification (Hale-Benson, 1986). This may be reinforced by extended kinship patterns, and the role of interdependence and connectedness specific to Black families; it may also be supported by the less protected status of Black children by the dominant culture and the subsequent assumption of higher levels of responsibility for themselves at an earlier age than their white counterparts. A broader question in this area is that of the relationship between these factors and the development of autonomy and competence.

Black children develop autonomy primarily as a result of being given external tasks to do directly, rather than being told about them. Problems may occur in this area for children prepared for autonomy in nonautonomous contexts, particularly in an atmosphere where interdependence is stressed. An example is of children who are given overly protective verbal messages (i.e., that the world is hostile and dangerous to them, that no one is to be trusted) simultaneous with being given separating or autonomous tasks to perform (R. Eversley, personal communication, 1988).

Minuchin and Fishman (1981) use the term "parental child" to describe the role of a child to whom a parent delegates a certain level of responsibility in the care of herself or her siblings. Advantages of this role exist for both the parent and the child. It can be problematic, however, for a child who is given autonomous tasks to do or parentified prematurely. That is, when the responsibilities delegated to the child interfere with her age-appropriate developmental tasks, this may lead to the development of a precocious or pseudo-autonomy (D. Gartner, personal communication, 1988; Greene & Pilowsky, 1986).

THERAPEUTIC STRATEGIES

It is important to help a client to identify and understand the racial tradition in her family and to speculate about how she carries or does not carry on that tradition. It may help the client to understand this as a generational issue. The therapist should raise the client's curiosity about what her mother instructed her to do when confronting racism, how to determine if racism was present, and what she can recall about how her mother actually behaved in similar situations. It is important to note discrepancies between the mother's actual behavior and what she instructed her daughter to do. This can represent a source of confusion for a child. A client's mother's relationship with her own siblings and parents (the client's aunts, uncles, and grandparents) may provide clues as to the nature of the racial tradition in the family. Who in her mother's (or father's) family was "favored" and who was not; was there a pattern of skin color or physical features correlated with favor or disfavor; all of these may be relevant questions to raise.

Different geographical regions and rural versus urban origins of Black mothers may also be a factor in their sense of the conspicuous presence or absence of racism in their lives, the importance of skin color variations, and adaptive strategies. It is important that clients who are mothers be encouraged to talk directly to their children about how they view the world and their rationale for using certain strategies when dealing with racism.

When maladaptive patterns are present, it can be of therapeutic importance to assist a client in understanding that she is a witting or unwitting partner in a generational pattern. This can be communicated with the notion that she had no choice about the way her mother regarded herself or her children, but that the client can break this generational cycle by reflecting consciously on what she does and how or from whom she learned to do so. A Black mother can benefit from this perspective in understanding more fully what she communicates to her own daughter.

It is of additional importance to assist a client in appreciating that, as a Black mother, she has added parenting tasks that require particular skill and sensitivity and represent an additional source of stress for her. When extended family or community supports are available, their utilization should be encouraged.

Black mothers should be encouraged to address racial issues directly with their children while exploring symbols of Black culture with them. This may be accomplished by reading stories to or with their daughters about historical achievements of Black women and men, as well as sharing other facts pertinent to the strengths and uniqueness of Black culture and Black persons. It may also be helpful for Black mothers to talk to their daughters about what it was like to grow up as a Black person and a woman in her time, and particularly about the conditions and barriers that have changed, and what efforts were needed to bring those changes about. Finally, Black mothers must be aware of their potency as role models for daughters who will imitate what they see their mothers do before they can understand much of what she says.

CONCLUSION

This paper has attempted to raise the current level of inquiry about how Black mothers, under the most difficult of circumstances, have successfully negotiated the task of teaching adaptive racial socialization skills to their daughters. The impact of living in an antagonistic environment upon the Black mother-daughter dyad has been explored. Strategies for therapists working with Black women who are encountering difficulty with or are unaware of their roles in this process have been presented, with a particular emphasis on working with Black women who have children, especially daughters.

There are developmental difficulties in the dynamics and mechanisms of the mother-daughter relationship which are common to all women. However, the full impact of racism superimposed upon sexism and, for Black Lesbians, homophobia, and the special tasks of racial socialization which must be performed by Black mothers, remains an important area for further exploration by theoreticians and therapists.

REFERENCES

Akbar, N. (1975, October). *Address* before the Black Child Development Institute Annual Meeting, San Francisco CA.

Akbar, N. (1985). Our destiny, authors of a scientific revolution. In Harriet McAdoo & John McAdoo (Eds.), *Black children.* (pp. 17-31). Beverly Hills: Sage Publications.

Anthony, E.J. & Cohler, B.J. (Eds.) (1987). *The invulnerable child.* New York: Guilford Publications.

Bell, R. (1971). The relative importance of mother and wife roles among Negro lower class women. In Robert Staples (Ed.), *The Black family: Essays and Studies,* Belmont CA: Wadsworth.

Boykin, A.W. (1983). The academic performance of Afro-American children. In Janet Spence (Ed.), *Achievement and achievement motives.* San Francisco: Freeman.

Boykin, A.W. & Toms, F.S. (1985). Black child socialization: A conceptual framework. In Harriet McAdoo & John McAdoo (Eds.), *Black children*. (pp. 33-51). Beverly Hills: Sage.

Cade, Toni (1970). *The Black woman: An anthology.* New York: New American Library.

Dixon, V. & Foster, B. (1971). *Beyond Black & white.* Boston: Little, Brown and Co.

Edelman, Marian Wright (1985). The sea is so wide and my boat is so small: Problems facing Black children today. In Harriet McAdoo & John McAdoo (Eds.), *Black Children.* (pp. 79-82). Beverly Hills: Sage.

Epstein, Cynthia F. (1973). Positive effects of the multiple negative: Explaining the success of Black professional women. *American Journal of Sociology, 78,* 912-935.

Ferguson-Peters, Marie. (1985). Racial socialization of young Black children. In Harriet McAdoo & John McAdoo (Eds.), *Black children.* Beverly Hills: Sage.

Franklin, A.J. & Boyd-Franklin, Nancy (1985) A psychoeducational perspective on Black parenting. In Harriet McAdoo & John McAdoo, (Eds.) *Black children* Beverly Hills: Sage.

Freudiger, Patricia & Almquist, Elizabeth M. (1980). Sources life satisfaction: The different worlds of Black and white women. In *Black working women debunking the myths: A multidisciplinary approach* Proceedings of a conference, Berkeley: Center for the Study, Education, and Advancement of Women.

Garbarino, J. (1982). *Children and families in the social environment.* New York: Aldine.

Giddings, Paula (1984). *When and where I enter: The impact of Black women on race and sex in America.* New York: William Morrow and Co.

Greene, Beverly (1985). Considerations in the treatment of Black parents by white therapists. *Psychotherapy: Theory, Research, Practice, Training, 22,* 398-393.

Greene, Beverly (1986). When the therapist is white and the patient is Black: Considerations for psychotherapy in the feminist heterosexual and lesbian communities. *Women & Therapy, 5,* 41-66.

Greene, Beverly & Pilowsky, Daniel (1986). Absent parents revisiting: Its contribution to intrapsychic conflict in emotionally vulnerable foster children. Manuscript submitted for publication.

Guthrie, R.V. (1976). *Even the rat was white: A historical view of psychology.* New York: Harper and Row.

Hale, Janice (1980). The Black woman and child rearing. In LaFrances Rodgers-Rose (Ed.), *The Black woman.* (pp. 79-87). Beverly Hills, Sage.

Hale-Benson, Janice (1986). *Black children: Their roots, culture, and learning styles (Revised Edition).* Baltimore: Johns Hopkins University Press.

Harley, S. & Terborg-Penn, R. (Eds.) (1978). *The Afro American woman: Struggles and images.* Port Washington, NY: Kennikat Press.

Harrison-Ross, Phillis & Wyden, Barbara (1973). *The Black child: A parents' guide.* New York: Wyden Publishing.

Haskins, J & Butts, H.F. (1973). *The psychology of Black language*. New York: Barnes and Noble.

Hill, R. (1972). *The strengths of Black families*. New York: National Urban League.

Hooks, Belle (1981). *Ain't I a woman? Black women and feminism*. Boston: South End Press.

Holiday, Bertha G. (1985). Developmental imperatives of social ecologies: Lessons learned from Black children today. In Harriet McAdoo & John McAdoo (Eds.), *Black children*. Beverly Hills: Sage.

Jones, Jacqueline (1985). *Labor of love, labor of sorrow: Black women, work and family from slavery to the present*. New York: Basic Books.

Karier, C. (1986). *Scientists of the mind: Intellectual founders of modern psychology*. Champaign, IL: University of Illinois Press.

Ladner, Joyce (1971). *Tomorrow's tomorrow: The Black woman*. Garden City, NY: Doubleday.

Lerner, Gerda (1972). *Black women in white America: A documentary history*. New York: Vintage Books.

Levine, L. (1977). *Black culture and Black consciousness*. New York: Oxford University Press.

Lightfoot, Sarah Lawrence (1988). *Balm in Gilead*. Reading, MA: Addison Wesley.

Lorde, Audre (1987). Turning the beat around: Lesbian parenting 1986. In Sandra Pollack & Jeanne Vaughn (Eds.), *Politics of the heart: A lesbian parenting anthology*. (310-315). Ithaca, NY: Firebrand Books.

Mays, Vickie M. (1985). The Black American and psychotherapy: The dilemma. *Psychotherapy: Theory, Research, Practice, Training, 22,* 379-388.

McAdoo, Harriet & McAdoo, John (Eds.) (1985). *Black children: Social, educational, and parental environments*. Beverly Hills: Sage.

Myers, Lena (1980). *Black women: Do they cope better?* Englewood Cliffs, NJ: Prentice Hall.

Milner, D. (1983). *Children and race*. Beverly Hills: Sage.

Minuchin, Salvador & Fishman, H.C. (1981). *Family therapy techniques*. Cambridge, MA: Harvard University Press.

National Center for Health Statistics (1982). Advance report of final natality statistics, 1978. *Monthly Vital Statistics Report, 31.*

Noble, Jean (1978). *Beautiful also are the souls of my Black sisters*. Englewood Cliffs, NJ: Prentice Hall.

Nobles, W. (1974a). African root and American fruit: The Black family. *Journal of Social and Behavioral Sciences.*

Nobles, W. (1974b). Africanity in Black families. *Black Scholar Magazine, 5,* 10-17.

Nobles, W. (1975). The Black family and its children: The survival of humaneness. Unpublished manuscript.

Parker, Pat (1988). Gay parenting, or, Look out Anita. In Sandra Pollack &

Jeanne Vaughn (Eds.) *Politics of the heart: A lesbian parenting anthology* (94-99). Ithaca, NY: Firebrand Books.

Powell, Gloria (Ed.) (1983). *The psychosocial development of minority group children*. New York: Brunner/Mazel.

Rich, Adrienne (1976). *Of woman born: Motherhood as experience and institution*. New York: W.W. Norton.

Richardson, B.B. (1981). Racism and child rearing: A study of Black mothers. *Dissertation Abstracts, 42*, 125-A.

Robinson, Christine (1983). Black women: A tradition of self reliant strength. *Women & Therapy, 2*, 135-144.

Rollins, Judith (1985). *Between women: Domestics and their employers*. Philadelphia: Temple University Press.

Spencer, Margaret Beale (1985). Racial variations in achievement prediction: The school as a conduit for macrostructural cultural tension. In Harriet McAdoo & John McAdoo (Eds.), *Black children*. (pp. 85-111). Beverly Hills: Sage.

Spencer, Margaret Beale (1987). Black children's ethnic identity formation: Risk and resilience of castelike minorities. In Mary Jane Rotheram & Jean S. Phinney (Eds.), *Children's ethnic socialization*. (pp. 103-116). Beverly Hills: Sage.

Thomas, Alexander & Sillen, Samuel (1972). *Racism and psychiatry*. New York: Brunner/Mazel.

Walker, Alice (1970). These dissenting times (originally Fundamental Difference) In *Revolutionary petunias and other poems*. New York: Harcourt, Brace.

Williams, Juan (1987). *Eyes on the prize: America's civil rights years*. New York: Viking Press.

Willie, C., Kramer, B. & Brown, B. (Eds.) (1973). *Racism and mental health*. Pittsburgh: University of Pittsburgh Press.

Wyatt, Gail (1985). The sexual abuse of Afro-American and white women in childhood. *Child Abuse and Neglect, 9*, 507-519.

Young, V.A. (1970). Family and childhood in a Southern Georgia community. *American Anthropologist, 72*.

Perceptions of the Sexual Self: Their Impact on Relationships Between Lesbian and Heterosexual Women

Diane Palladino, PhD
Yanela Stephenson, MSW

SUMMARY. This paper explores the role of women's sexual self in the formation of friendships between lesbian and heterosexual women. The Stone Center (Wellesley College) developmental theory is used as a framework through which to identify and examine the gaps in current thinking about the definition of women's sexual self and the impact of the erotic on "women bonding." Recent literature exploring women's friendships is used to illuminate the ambiguous, and sometimes distorted, definition of women's sexual self. A multi-ethnic, multi-racial approach is applied to reflect the diverse experience of American women.

The purpose of this article is to explore the question: what is the role of the sexual self in the development of friendships between lesbians and straight women?

There are four major sources of material which provide descriptions of women's sexuality: (1) modern sexology, both medical and

---

Diane Palladino is a feminist activist and a psychotherapist focusing on women's issues, with an emphasis on lesbian issues. *Author note*: "I self-identify as a second generation Italian-American woman, of working class background." Correspondence may be addressed to: P.O. Box 232, Northampton, MA 01060.

Yanela Stephenson is a social worker and a psychotherapist in New Jersey interested in exploring the dynamics within relationships between women. *Author note*: "I am a Black Cuban who has lived in the United States since 1987." Correspondence may be addressed to: 14 Renaissance Lane, New Brunswick, NJ 08901.

231

non-medical; (2) social construction theory; (3) the writings of sex radicals; and (4) writings on women's friendships. The work of Kinsey (1953) and Masters and Johnson (1960) has documented the physiological response of women to sexual and erotic stimuli and has brought to light the multi-faceted nature of the erotic. Along with the earlier feminist analyses of women's sexual response (Lydon, 1970; Sherfey, 1966) research from both these areas has resulted in reassessing the requirement of vaginal orgasm to prove sexual maturity and the act of penile penetration as the premier event in sexual activity; each has been relegated to a lesser and more appropriate place in the repertoire of sexual enjoyment.

Feminist analyses of the condition of women have relied heavily on social construction theory. By re-examining women's experience, feminism was able to illuminate what lay below the surface of patriarchal reality and to name the unspoken; these analyses exposed the extent of the oppression against women and made connections between and among a variety of threads which make up women's experience.

While feminist analysis has made possible the re-visioning of women's lives, one area that has been neglected is that of women's sexuality. Carol Vance (1984) discusses the gap in the analysis:

> What directions might a feminist politics on sex take in the future? . . . feminism must be a movement that speaks to sexuality, that does not forfeit the field to reactionary groups who are more than willing to speak. We cannot be cowardly, pretending that feminism is not sexually radical. Being a sex radical . . . is *less a matter of what you do, and more a matter of what you are willing to think, entertain, and question* . . . feminism must speak to sexuality as a site of oppression, not only the oppression of male violence, brutality and coercion . . . but also *the repression of female desire* that comes from ignorance, invisibility, and fear. Feminism must put forth a politics that resists deprivation and supports pleasure. (p.23, author's emphasis added)

At this time, the writings of sex radicals have provided a perspective which raises new questions about the relationship between gender and sexuality, the interstices of oppression and agency, and the right of women to reclaim their sexuality.

It is through the writings on women's friendship that the meanings, processes, effort, the uniqueness of women coming together, and the implications that arise from the process of this union can be found. We have chosen female friendship as the background against which to examine women's perceptions of the sexual self because women bonding is an intricate part of women's acculturation and development. Although the characteristics of bonding and alliances are the same for most women, the implication of their manifestations differ when it comes to two heterosexual women, between two lesbians and between a heterosexual woman and a lesbian woman. It is the dynamic of bonding that takes place between a lesbian and a heterosexual woman which, we feel, provides a unique vantage point from which to examine women's sexual self and the process of being in relation to another. Women talk about friendship, gyn/affection, eroticism and merging, all of which describe the intensity and intertwined dynamic that occurs in the process of the coming together of women. The process of strong bond between women is the core of any friendship. It is this process which we have called bonding and alliance.

We conceive of the sexual self as one component under the umbrella term "women's sexuality." The sexual self, as we define it, contains the physical responses which exist perhaps *despite* socialization attempts. For the purposes of our examination, the sexual self is defined as: (1) passion for a physical encounter; (2) letting go of the "self" (intellectual/ego) to merge with another in order to attain self expression; (3) fantasizing of a sexual nature; (4) allowing for physical exploration and for new encounters without monitoring or judgement; (5) expanding the boundaries around the self while knowing that one can regain them after the encounter; and (6) allowing the body to act and react without the judgements, expectations and rules of gendered role.

In order to explore the relationship of the concept of the sexual self to the development of friendships between lesbians and straight women, we examine the developmental theory of Jean Baker Miller (1986) and the clinicians at the Stone Center (Jordan, 1987; Kaplan, 1984; Stiver, 1986; Surrey, 1985) for its usefulness as a tool in illuminating women's sexual development. We also analyze the literature on the formation of women's bonding and alliances in an attempt to raise new questions concerning the dynamics which occur between lesbians and straight women.

We have established the following three working hypotheses which inform the direction of this exploration. First, women grow and develop in *relationship to* rather than through *separation from* one another. Second, bonding and friendships among and between women have been and continue to be a critical context in which women grow and develop. Lastly, the development of women's sexuality is distorted through patriarchally constructed definitions of female sexuality and the social presumption of heterosexuality. We postulate that the distortion of women's sexual self has negatively influenced the potential for bonding and alliances among lesbian and straight women, and that it is only when women come to define and accept their sexual self that relationships between these two groups can proceed in a clear and unencumbered manner.

THE STONE CENTER DEVELOPMENTAL THEORY

Feminist clinicians at the Stone Center, Wellesley College, have been in the process of creating a developmental model which reflects women's experience. The basis for this model was outlined by Dr. Jean Baker Miller (1976) in her book *Towards a New Psychology of Women*. The theory continues to be expanded primarily through the working papers produced by Stone Center associates. The various aspects of the current theory are reflected in the second edition (1986) of Miller's book and the working papers.

Overview of the Self-In-Relation

The central concept of the theory is the "self-in-relation." Simply stated, this means that "for women, the primary experience of self is relational . . . the self is organized and developed in the context of important relationships" (Surrey, 1985, p.2). The model postulates that women's self development occurs within constructing, building, and maintaining relationships where mutuality and reciprocity form the foundation of the relationship. The individual is both giver and receiver within the relationship, while obtaining validation for herself and giving validation to others. The self-in-relationship model contains the following premises (Surrey, 1985):

> 1) relationship is seen as the basic goal of development; 2) other aspects of the self develop within the primary context of relationships; 3) there is no inherent need to disconnect or to sacrifice relationships for self-development.

There are a number of factors which are involved in the concept of a mutually constructed relationship. For the purposes of this paper, relationship can be summarized as:

> a two-way interaction which . . . at its best (is) a mutual process . . . (where each party) participates in the development of (the) other . . . (through) attaining a capacity to be attuned to the affect of (the) other, (thereby being) understanding (of) and being understood by the other; (this mutual interaction results in) . . . both parties feel(ing) enhanced and empowered . . . through their empathic connection with the other; . . . connection, then, is a key component of action and growth. (Kaplan, 1984, p.3)

This focus shifts the emphasis from male centered assumptions of progressive developmental separation to the female experience of relationship as the basis for self-experience and development. Forces which enable growth are considered in terms of a relational model with mutual empathy and mutual dependence playing central roles (Stiver, 1986).

Women's experience of connection is formulated early in the female's development, through the mother-daughter bond, and leads to an expectation of continued self-development-in-relation. As Surrey (1985) observes:

> the child's increasing ability for mutual empathy (is) developed in a matrix of emotional connectedness . . . this sense of connection forms the framework . . . for the process of differentiation and clarification which will follow . . . key is the mutual sharing process (which) fosters a sense of mutual un-

derstanding and connection . . . Girls, then, develop the expectation that they can facilitate *the growth of a sense of self*
through psychological connection and expect that the mutual
sharing of experience will lead to psychological growth. (p.5,
author's emphasis added)

This expectation is frequently not met in the female's later experience with male relationships. The female continues to value relationships with the result that the maintenance of the relational
connection often requires that she subordinate other parts of herself
in order to keep the connection. Miller (1986a) points out that,
"Eventually, for many women the threat of disruption of connections is perceived not as just a loss of a relationship but as something closer to a total loss of self" (p.83).

Overview of Sexual Development in the Theory

For the purposes of this article, female sexual development has
been divided into three areas: the sexual "self-in-relation," the experience of adolescence, and the effect of imbalance in relational
mutuality. Each of these are considered separately.

The description of the development of women's sexual self is
embedded in the core concept of self-in-relation. That is, women
experience and grow in the discovery and the application of their
sexual selves in relation to others as they experience mutuality in
sexual relationships. Surrey (1983), in discussing women's capacity for pleasure in relatedness, writes that different relational connections involve the ability to identify with the other in the sense of
connectedness through feeling states and empowerment based on
the complex awareness of the needs and realities of another person
(Jordan, Surrey & Kaplan, 1983). Thus, the young female expects
that her sexual development will proceed through mutually enhancing sexual relatedness, just as she expects that her whole being will
be so developed. This expectation is not met, however, and the
theory suggests that the splitting off of the sexual self begins in
adolescence.

Three major changes occur in adolescence which impact on the
female's sexual development: she becomes aware of physical sexual impulses, she learns that her sexual feelings are not given vali-

dation by males, and she begins to question her right to sexual desires and her need to fulfill those desires. This process may be foreshadowed in latency when girls are very intensely involved in all of their relationships; it is in this stage when girls may learn to hide the sexual responses that they are beginning to discover make up a "new" side of themselves (Miller, 1984, p.7). This "hiding" process continues into adolescence when, according to Miller (1984),

> most girls . . . learn that their own sexual perceptions, sensations, and impulses are not supposed to arise from themselves, but are to be brought forth by and for men . . . this is in contrast to what has been going on in the girl's earlier representations of herself . . . She still seeks to act on these desires within relationships with others . . . But she meets opposition . . . (p.8)

It is during adolescence when the girl learns that assumptions she had made about how she could act included some problematic areas. One of these areas is that of bodily and sexual experience. The girl's attempt to act on the basis of her own sexuality leads to conflict with potential male partners and sexuality is thus made an unacceptable aspect of her internal sense of self; she is prevented from bringing a large part of herself into the relationship (Miller, 1984). She is given "the message that her own perceptions about her bodily and sexual feelings are not acceptable and she will . . . tend to experience her physical desires and stirrings as wrong, bad, evil, dirty and the like" (Miller, 1984, p.8). She begins to reject her own sexuality and disallow herself sexual pleasure. "This situation can lead to an attempt to deal with this experience by turning to passivity and submission" (Miller, 1984, p.8). Thus, adolescence is a time when girls not only begin the experience of sexual maturation, but it is also a time when they begin to confront the barriers placed around their sexual selves by patriarchal culture. Girls begin to understand that their autonomous sexual feelings are not to be discussed and certainly not to be acted upon. The hiding process that was begun in latency has now proven to be a useful coping mechanism in dealing with her newly found sexual responsiveness; unfortunately, it may also become a permanent part of the female's perception of her sexual self.

When mutuality is absent in relationships with men, women take on the role of primary giver and nurturer *to others* in the area of sex as well as in other areas. Many women still cannot engage in sexual relations without the feeling that they are "primarily" giving to the other person (Miller, 1986a). The denigration of the expectation of relational reciprocity by both society in general and the specific men with whom they are involved has made women's sexual needs and desires invisible; women begin to question the justification and validity of these needs and desires and to doubt them. In "sexual learning," women do not have their own experiences validated; they become ashamed of their "deficiency" and deny their own experience and adopt male norms and withdraw interest in sexuality and desire (Jordan, 1987).

This submersion of the sexual self forces fragmentation of the self which may result in a one sided sexual involvement that can mean the loss of the complete sense of self. Miller (1986a) elaborates that, "If a woman . . . thinks of sex as bad, then it is sometimes easier to engage in it (to even enjoy it) if she can maintain the concept that it is the man's doing" (p.107). When this occurs, one ceases to be an agent and has to rely on another person to act for her; she ceases to be an agent for herself; she becomes an object.

The Role of Racism and Homophobia

While this process of sexual objectification is part of all women's experience under patriarchy, racism and homophobia are two other dimensions of women's experience which are relevant to women of color and to lesbians. For example, historically, in the United States, Southern white men had legal license freely to abuse Black women and then labeled them immoral, loose and sexually degraded. These myths about Black women's sexuality, which serve to attack Black women's morals and character, have continued into the present. Black women's perceptions of themselves as sexual beings and agents may become distorted (Turner, 1984).

The ingrained assumption, even among feminist theorists that relational maturity is possible only through heterosexual union supports the institution of compulsory heterosexuality (Gartrell, 1984). Thus, most women are encouraged to seek sexual complementarity from men. The lack of examination of this homophobic assumption, according to Gartrell (1984), has impacted lesbians in two ways. First, they are seen as a direct threat to the institution of compulsory heterosexuality, and second, lesbianism has come to be defined only as a sexual behavior. In these ways, racism and homophobia have served to caricature both heterosexual women of color and lesbians and to further alienate them from their sexual selves.

Self-in-relation theoreticians are calling for sexual frankness and a redefinition of female sexuality in women's terms rather than as it is perceived by men. This requires an elimination of the role of sexual object and an understanding that women's self awareness grows from attunement to *our* bodies, responses, and feelings which include the validation of our responses by others to help form and crystallize this self knowledge (Jordan, 1987). The Stone Center theory provides a useful critique of the social construction of female sexuality from a psychological perspective. It describes, from a constructionist point of view, the impact that patriarchal theories and definitions of female sexuality have had on the sexual development of women.

Evaluation of the Stone Center Theory

The concept of the "self-in-relation" appears to provide an important perspective in the further investigation of women's sexual self. First, it defines sexual connection as a mutual interplay between people and an essential part of the integrated self. A sexual relationship with another can be a viable mutually empathic experience without having to be "in love." Second, it emphasizes the importance of the self as an "agent" capable of bringing forth its own sexual reality and sexual self. That is, it emphasizes the critical stance of being for the self as well as being for the other. Third, it places relationships between women in their proper perspective. If women find connection an essential way to develop, it explains why many women often feel emotionally closer to women friends than to male lovers/partners.

It seems inevitable, given the connectedness of many female-female relationships, that the sexual self would emerge as an issue in the relationship. The denial of this aspect of the self may force women to fragment themselves and feel dishonest in the relationship. Especially when there is difference in sexual preference, this cannot continue to be seen as a divisive difference, but rather as an area that warrants recognition, definition, and honest and open discussion.

The self-in-relation theory has several gaps which need to be addressed in order to account for sexual, racial, ethnic, and class differences. There is no explanation for the female adolescent's shift to men as love objects. We would suggest that the presumption of heterosexual development within the theory has obscured the need for more investigation and thought in this area. The omission of an explanation is especially glaring because while the model underscores the female's loss of agency upon learning that she is not allowed to act *for herself* sexually, it fails to explain her response to this loss or other perceived options. There is a tendency in this model to equate sexual activity with an emotionally bonded relationship and make the latter the primary or even preferred context in which sexual behavior occurs. Only Jordan (1986) appears to suggest an alternative perspective when she says, " . . . in sexual engagement there is such a rich potential for expression of exquisite attunement and the possibility to give one's attention in equibalance to self and other . . . a mutual surrender to shared reality" (p.8), but there remains only the suggestion of how the self can be in relation to another in a physical, and passionate coming together. The authors suggest that to ignore the purely physical sexual self is to support the destructive injunction to women that mandates "being in love" in order to express oneself sexually; this has resulted in the creation of what we term "pseudo-relationships" to justify acting on female sexual passion.

There has been very little attempt to apply the theory to the experiences of women from differing racial and ethnic backgrounds. The only application done in this area was by Clevonne Turner (1984) who found the theory relevant to the Afro-American women's experience:

This theory represents a significant part of the Black women's developmental experience as she adds on other relationships which start with the mother/daughter bond and tend to heighten rather than diminish her sense of self . . . daughters are usually taught very early in life *to rely on themselves* as well as to *learn how to care for others*. (pp.3-4)

In addition to broadening the application of the theory to include sexual, racial, ethnic and class differences, an attempt to link the meaning of women's emotional bondings to each other with women's sexual responses needs to be constructed. As it now stands, the theory addresses emotional bonding in male/female relationships, female/female relationships and the stages of female sexual development as separate facets of a woman's life. We feel that is necessary to consider the dynamic and perhaps dialectical relationships formulated as a result of the coming together of all of these aspects of women's experience with relationship.

While the Stone Center Theory represents a beginning in the exploration of women's sexual development and of the social barriers which constrain this development, further examination is needed in order to assess its relevance to all women's experience in the United States.

THE INTERPLAY BETWEEN WOMEN'S SEXUAL EXPERIENCES, WOMEN'S FRIENDSHIPS AND BONDING

Ehrenreich, Hess, and Jacobs (1986) assessed the meaning of the sexual revolution of the last 20 years for women. They pointed to the re-definition of sex, during this period, from a phallocentric act to be experienced in the missionary position to one where either partner can be the giver or receiver of interchangeable sexual pleasures. For middle and upper class women, sex became recreational and something to enjoy rather than one's "duty." Their perception and experience of sex underwent a drastic change as they were freed from the oppression of the "madonna/whore" syndrome and they put off love, children, and marriage for career and independence.

This analysis, while attempting to define the results of the sexual revolution in terms of women's experience, does not integrate the effects of the interaction of additional variables such as race, class, and sexual preference into the discussion, nor does it consider the significance of women's friendships in relationship to women's sexuality. To provide an inclusive examination of the meaning of this period for all women, the examination must be broadened to take these factors into account. Further exploration of the meaning of female sexual desire as experienced, but perhaps not discussed, by women is needed to describe and fully understand the nature of the sexual self. As Carole Vance has stated (1985), "The subtle connection between how patriarchy interferes with female desire and how women experience their own passion . . . is emerging as a critical issue to be explored" (p.4).

Bonding and Alliance

Bonding and alliance are inherent in the experience and history of women; this is evidenced by group participation in quilting bees, coffee clatches, consciousness raising groups, and women's church groups, as well as the individual experiences of the marriage resisters, the spinsters, women in convents, and also within the Latina and Black women's cultures. The bonding and alliance which occurs between women has been described in many different ways and by many different authors. We have selected to review the literature on friendship because it makes up a significant part of women's experience; the experience of friendship includes erotic and romantic connections, as well as emotionally non-sexual bonding.

Since we are using the word erotic frequently, it is important to clarify its meaning; in Webster's Dictionary (1983), the word erotic is defined as "arousing sexual feelings or desires amatory." Audre Lourde (1984) expands the definition of the erotic to include not only the sexual, but also to the spiritual depth filled with passion and exploration of the self, presenting a wholistic representation of a woman. She states:

> The erotic is a resource within each of us that lies in a deeply female and spiritual plane, . . . rooted in the power of our unexpressed or unrecognized feelings! The erotic has often been misnamed by men and used against women . . . made

into the confused, the trivial, the psychotic, the plasticized sensation. The erotic is measured between the beginnings of our sense of self and the chaos of our strongest feelings. It is an internal sense of satisfaction to which, once we have experienced it, we know we can aspire. For having experienced the fullness of this depth of feeling and recognizing its power, in honor and self-respect we can require no less of ourselves. (p.54)

Louise Eichenbaum and Susie Orbach (1988) talk about the development of women's sense of self in relation to feminine gender and how gender influences the personality construct; this influence can extend to the prescribing of women's actions and re-actions. They trace this phenomenon to the mother-daughter relationship, which is both an enabling and a disabling one. This phenomenon is referred to as "the grammar of women's emotional experiences" (Eichenbaum & Orbach, 1988), where behaviors are prescribed as being grammatically correct or incorrect. A woman is grammatically correct when she is "all giving," dependent, and connects to anyone around her; conversely, if a woman wants to be her own person, seeking and exploring new ways of independence, and exhibiting assertive and challenging behaviors, she would be considered grammatically incorrect. This male construction has been internalized by women. The authors view this situation as problematic because the duality represses women's need to self actualize.

Miller (1986) and Eichenbaum and Orbach (1988) view women's developmental process as relational and molded by the construct of the feminine gender. In the process of relating to others, women expect to become stronger, yet generally lose their sense of self which they then attempt to regain in the joining in an intimate relationship—be that a friendship or an amorous/sexual relationship. Eichenbaum and Orbach (1988) have defined this process as a "phenomenon of merged attachment which is the fabric out of which adult female friendships are fashioned" (p.63). This process is perceived as detrimental to women because it promotes a sense of selflessness, creating a being who cannot make decisions for herself and who exists in relation to others in order to validate herself. They note the implications of the "merging attachment" of women and between women as the experiencing of unexpressed or expressed anger, pain, betrayal, abandonment, competition, jealousy, disagreements, and/or threat. This type of acculturation is oppressive and it infiltrates all aspects of women's lives, jobs, sexual relationships and, of course, friendships.

Eichenbaum and Orbach (1988) advocate for a "separate attachment/connected autonomy" where women can express themselves by connecting, agreeing, disagreeing, supporting each other, soothing one another, and through feelings of love and support and the powerful use of intuitive judgment. These experiences can exist while maintaining a different and/or separate reality—where they no longer have to feel that they must be in total agreement with someone else in order to be validated.

While Eichenbaum and Orbach (1988) acknowledge lesbian relationships and the intensity that two women bring to a relationship based on their developmental and cultural makeup, they did not explore existing implications of sexual preferences for the development of friendship. They also failed to recognize or point out the eroticism and intensity that can evolve between friends, regardless of sexual preference, as happened in their experience with each other and described as follows:

> We remember the first times we saw each other. Susie was in a colloquium. A young woman . . . read a paragraph she had prepared . . . for an upcoming event . . . It was a powerful and passionate statement. Susie turned to her friend Carol Bloom . . . "Who is she?" "Oh, that's Luise Eichenbaum" . . . in a class on women and film, a young woman with a long suede skirt, tall purple boots, a trendy London shag haircut, an English accent, confidently commented on the film . . . "Who is she?" Luise asked Carol. "That's Susie Orbach," . . . Luise was interested. (p.2)

In this example we can hear the intensity which took place between the two women. If the names of one of these two women were changed to that of a male, it could be assumed that this would be the beginning of a love affair. The importance of this passage is that these two women are heterosexuals—but if they would have been lesbians, it would again be interpreted as having a sexually erotic overtone. Since they are heterosexual women, the erotic element is left unexplored.

In *A Passion for Friends*, Janice Raymond (1986) talks about and reclaims the uniqueness and essence of friendships. Raymond uses the term gyn/affection as a new term for female friendship. She adds, "the basic meaning of gyn/affection is that women affect, move, stir and arouse each other to full power" (p.7). The author defies the premise that women exist in relation to men (hetero-relationally), and, in so doing, underscores the significance of woman's relation to herself and to other women. Raymond, as well as Eichenbaum and Orbach, makes a point of not romanticizing women's experiences. Raymond highlights this by enumerating the obstacles that exist between women: women hating women, women internalizing the statement that "women are their own worst enemies," the disassociation of women to their culture, and the male-identification of women. In spite of the unfortunate experience of some women when they reject their unique gender characteristics, Raymond (1986) expands on her definition of gyn/affection:

> women who affect other women stimulate response and action; bring about change in the living; stir and arouse emotions, ideas, and activities that defy dichotomies between the personal and political aspects of affection. Thus, gyn/affection means personal and political movement of women toward each other. As personal is political, so too, the political is personal. (p.8)

In reviewing Black feminist literature, it was difficult locating literature that used the word "friendship." Initially, this seemed strange and incomprehensible since there is always a "woman" in the Black experience. It was not until we read Raymond's definition of gyn/affection (cited above) that it brought to light the strength that is generated when women come together. This was instrumental in allowing us to make a direct connection with our own experiences and also make connections with the term "sister" which is used in literature written by Black women.

During the 19th century, in the United States, Black women's clubs were of great importance because they promoted a space where Black women could meet, talk, and write about their interests. In *1894, Women's Era*, a 19th century Black women's publication, it is stated that the "Clubs will make girls think seriously of their future lives, and not make women think their only alternative is to marry" (1986, p.36). However, the presumption of the norm of heterosexuality, as well as the exclusion of the erotic, as they apply to Black women's lives, remains omnipresent.

This is evidenced in the experience of Gloria T. Hull who researched and wrote about the life of Alice Dunbar-Nelson, the wife of Paul Laurence Dunbar, one of America's first Black Nationalist poets. Alice Dunbar-Nelson was a Clubwoman known for her political activism, writing, and speaking. In her research, Hull was shown a diary which Dunbar's niece had in her possession. In it, Dunbar talks of at least two women friends with whom she had sexual and romantic ties. The question of how the romantic issue was going to be managed led to the attempt, by the niece, to erase or exclude Dunbar-Nelson's "gyn/affection" in the publication of the diaries. This move was successfully opposed by Hull, as she viewed this aspect of Dunbar-Nelson's life as essential to who she was as a woman. Hull writes:

> Only the power emanating from within herself and strengthened by certain external networks of support enabled Dunbar-Nelson to transcend these destructive political and socio-economic forces. Her mother, sister, and nieces in their inseparable, female centered household constituted a first line of resistance. (Ascher, DeSalvo, & Ruddick, 1984, p.109)

Bonding and alliance has always existed in the history of Black women. This is evident in friendships, the female centered family, the clubs of the 19th century, the use of the word "sister," lesbian relationships, and through the unique and special connection between "mother-daughter-auntie" relationships. "Auntie" is included in this triad because of the important role that an aunt plays in the Black experience. Her role is similar to that of a mother; an aunt is always able to pick up where the mother leaves off and, at times, be as active as the natural mother in providing nurturing and connection. Similar connections are captured by Myrtha Chabran in her essay "Exiles," found in *Between Women* (Ascher, DeSalvo, & Ruddick, 1984). Chabran writes to her mother, reminiscing about her childhood and also discloses her new definition of herself — as an exile from Puerto Rico. In doing so, Chabran draws existing similarities between her mother and Julia De Burgos (a Puerto Rican poet) and herself. Chabran uses this process of connecting to others (including to Doris Lessing and Jean Rhys) in seeking to clarify who she is in relation to significant people in her life. Chabran writes:

> I came into contact with the English very early in life, because as it turns out, my father was an Englishman . . . it was not until I had been in England for some time that I understood my father; Doris (Lessing) wrote about her father's *genio*, his character. It was you, *nani*, I did not understand until I came to terms with my being a woman. (Ascher, DeSalvo, & Ruddick, 1984, p.167)

The concept of women "in relationship to" others is crystallized, as we see the connections that Chabran makes. It is also clear that it had been easier for her to understand her father (men) better than her mother (women), due to the fact that developmentally the differences of roles and gender are not meshed with her own roles and gender proscription; it is not until she becomes a *self* that Chabran understands her similarities to her mother.

In this literature, there is a consensus that women grow in relation to other women. This phenomenon occurs through nurturing, support, love, and validation, to the extent that there seems to exist an "original primary attraction of women for women" (Raymond, 1986, p.5). It seems that in the bonding between friends, there is an innate connection that exists beyond friendship — the sensual, sexual, and erotic which evolves in the union between women.

In heterosexual friendship, if this erotic component is recognized, "it" can be scary; if it is not handled properly, it will be ignored as if the intensity of the feelings did not exist. On the other hand, when connections of great intensity are felt between lesbians, the *possibility* of sexual interaction or the expression of the attraction is more readily accepted because the women are in touch with their sexual—emotional attractions to women. In the case of the sexual and emotional joining of two lesbians, the beginning of the relationship is more likely characterized by the tensions brought on by "lust" rather than the anxiety generated by the fear of losing the sense of self. The lesbian is more likely to experience the merging as gaining power through the union with another woman. In essence, "lesbianism has pushed friendship beyond the intimacy of a personal relationship to a political affective state of being" (Raymond, 1986, p.15).

In an unpublished paper, a student interviewed a heterosexual woman on the topic of friendships and attractions between women. In response to the question, an interviewee stated:

> Women are very sensual and sexual; it is easy to become confused with feelings of friendship you have for a woman. In our society, the feelings you have for a friend, of friendship and love, are often supposed to be the kind of feelings reserved for members of the opposite sex, even though these feelings are part of friendship too. We are very physical with each other. We walk arm and arm . . . She knows my life story and I know hers. When we first became friends it was a strong feeling we had for one another; we did not know if it was right. I'm heterosexual and so is she. We didn't want to be sexually involved but there was a sexual undertone. It wasn't sexual though; there needs to be another word for it. We talked about it, if it wasn't such a cultural thing to be heterosexual, would we be more physical with each other, just because we love each other. Culture has a lot to do with it. (Barone, 1987)

Here both women appeared to have been eroticized by each other, yet they chose to discuss and examine their attraction within the framework of social norms and constraints. In addition, these two women have a connection as friends, and as such, were able to openly discuss their sexual and erotic attraction to each other without losing their sense of self or their sexual identity.

Clearly, women can build alliances with other women and they do not have to translate into sexual behavior. However, the conflict that arises as a result of experiencing the erotic cannot be ignored. For the most part, the definition and expectations that men have imposed on women have weakened women's relationships, stifling the potential toward self actualization both sexually and, at times, emotionally.

Other reasons for the lack of actualization can be attributed to the fear of being judged by society for being different, fear of the assumed loss of self, and fear of one's own passion — one's emotional and sexual desires. In applying the Stone Center's developmental theory to this phenomenon, it becomes clear that many women, when confronting the *potential* of an intense friendship or union, will experience conflict and fear because of the underlying unarticulated eroticism inherent in the relationship. Much of this anxiety results from the need to redefine who they are and to confront the erotic facet of themselves which has usually been denied.

CASE ILLUSTRATIONS

What then happens between friends who are "one of each"? We have suggested the hypothesis that the avoidance of the definition and confrontation of women's sexual self, along with the erotic element which is contained within, effects the formulation of friendships and potential friendships between lesbian and heterosexual women. We will present examples from our clinical work with women to illustrate the variety of ways in which women's sexual self is circumvented and/or distorted in the development of lesbian-heterosexual relationships.

In the first case, *the denial of commonality between two people is used to justify the impossibility of lesbian-heterosexual bonding.* A white lesbian reports that she finds it difficult to relate to straight women because "they don't have anything in common" with her. Her assumption of lack of commonality allows her to justify avoiding contact with heterosexual women; the result for her is a paucity of intimate contact which results in isolation because she cannot develop intimate friendships with women who do not share her sexual preference. While this example is from a lesbian's experience, we have received corroborating evidence from other therapists who have seen the same response in heterosexual women. The denial of commonality can be seen particularly when a lesbian in a long term friendship (from childhood, perhaps) comes out to the heterosexual woman and the relationship "cools off" and eventually disintegrates.

In the second case, *the woman recognizes a sexual attraction and feels she "has to" act on it.* A black heterosexual woman feels conflicted about her erotic attraction towards a self-identified lesbian. She does not know how to deal with these feelings. The lesbian acknowledges that she shares the sexual attraction. The result is physical contact in the form of kissing, but no discussion about either the feelings or what has happened. The conflict for each of these women, and the difficulty they experienced in verbally acknowledging erotic feelings for each other, resulted in the inability to clarify the choices present for each one.

For many women, the emergence of sexual feelings results in the polarization of their perceived choices; they act on the feelings because the feelings have surfaced. Frequently, this response is accompanied by emotional turmoil and crisis. The acknowledging of same sex attraction, and perhaps a bi-sexual component, is too threatening a possibility to accept. Equally, for straight women, the attraction to a lesbian does not necessarily evidence her latent lesbianism. If the existence of a multi-faceted sexual self is acknowledged, the possibility that this physical attraction may represent another aspect of emotional intimacy can be entertained; the attraction can be acknowledged verbally and not necessarily acted upon. The choice of "no action" needs to be recognized but cannot be if the sexual self is not explored.

In the third case, there is *acknowledgement of emotional intimacy and bonding but a denial of the erotic element.* A white heterosexual woman admits that she has her emotional needs filled by women, including lesbians, but she relates sexually only to men. She does not identify as a lesbian. She accepts her emotional connection to women, but is fiercely protective of her heterosexual life style. This response is commonly found with heterosexual women who self-identify as feminists.

Part of the struggle which plagued the women's movement of the early 1970s was the definition of a "women identified woman" (Rich, 1980; Ferguson, Zita, & Addelson, 1980). The debate was framed in political terms. We would suggest that the essence of the issue is women's lack of clarity in defining the sexual self, and the lack of acknowledgement of the erotic for women and their lives. In case #2, the women acknowledged their sexual attraction through "compulsory" action and denied it through lack of verbal discussion, while in this case, the sexual self is taken out of the realm of the erotic and denied by using a strictly political definition of it.

In the last case, *an oversensitivity to the potential sexual definition of relationship results in one person assuming inappropriate responsibility for the relationship.* A Latina lesbian reports that she protects her heterosexual friends by making certain that their interactions are not sexualized. On one occasion, there was an accidental brushing against the friend's breast with her elbow as the lesbian was reaching for something. Her immediate reaction was a fear of what the friend would think of the accidental touching since she is a lesbian and her friend a heterosexual. She did not want the friend to be uncomfortable as a result of the contact. In this case, a commonplace contact became magnified out of proportion because of the distortion in the definition of the sexual self and the nature of the erotic in this woman's life.

These examples are culled from the consulting room because women have identified these concerns as representing "problems" for them. It is assumed that the response to the sexual self, as to all other ways of being, is mediated by women's religious, cultural and ethnic background. Although there were different races and cultures represented in the cases presented, the effect of this diversity requires more specific explorations than this paper has provided.

CONCLUSION

It has been our intent to illustrate the difficulty experienced by women in the process of connecting to the sexual self and, that one of the many layers of complexity contained in friendships between women involves the experiencing of the erotic which can be elicited by another female. Once the layer of the erotic is recognized, the process of connection automatically demands another level of participation — a profound and purposeful verbal communication which will shape the direction of the relationship and which will enable each woman to become empowered within the relationship. We hope that we have opened up the issue of women's sexual self to exploration by others. We would suggest that if a healthy model of women's sexual self was developed, open discussion of this issue would yield a greater understanding and re-definition of women's sexual response so that inclusiveness rather than exclusiveness will be the result.

REFERENCES

Ascher, Carol, DeSalvo, Louise, & Ruddick, Sara (1984). *Between women*. Boston: Beacon Press.

Barone, Jodi (1987). *Women's friendships*. Unpublished manuscript, West Chester University, West Chester, Pennsylvania.

Ehrenreich, Barbara, Hess, Elizabeth, & Jacobs, Gloria (1986). *Remaking love, the feminization of sex*. Garden City, New York: Anchor Press.

Eichenbaum, Luise, & Orbach, Susie (1988). *Between women*. New York: Viking Penguin Inc.

Ferguson, Ann, Zita, Jacquelyn N., & Addelson, Kathryn Pyne (1981). On compulsory heterosexuality and lesbian existence: Defining the issues. In Nannerl O. Keohane, Michelle Z. Rosaldo & Barbara C. Gelphi (Eds.), *Feminist theory: A critique of ideology* (pp.147-188). Chicago: University of Chicago Press.

Gartrell, Nanette (1984). *Issues in psychotherapy with lesbian women*. (Working paper No.83-04). Wellesley, Massachusetts: Wellesley College. The Stone Center.

Jordan, Judith V. (1987). *Clarity in connection: Empathic knowing, desire and sexuality*. (Working paper No.29). Wellesley, Massachusetts: Wellesley College. The Stone Center.

Jordan, Judith V. (1986). *The meaning of mutuality*. (Working paper No.23). Wellesley, Massachusetts: Wellesley College. The Stone Center.

Jordan, Judith V. (1984). *Empathy and self boundaries*. (Working paper No.16). Wellesley, Massachusetts: Wellesley College. The Stone Center.

Jordan, Judith V., Surrey, Janet L., & Kaplan, Alexandra G. (1983). *Women and empathy—implications for psychological development and psychotherapy*. (Working paper No.82-02). Wellesley, Massachusetts: Wellesley College. The Stone Center.

Kaplan, Alexandra G. (1984). *The "self-in-relation": Implications for depression in women*. (Working paper No.14). Wellesley, Massachusetts: Wellesley College. The Stone Center.

Kinsey, Alfred (1953). *Sexual behavior in the human female*. Philadelphia: Saunders.

Lorde, Audre (1984). *Sister outsider*. Trumansburg, New York: The Crossing Press.

Lydon, Susan (1970). The politics of orgasm. In Robin Morgan (Ed.), *Sisterhood is powerful: An anthology of writings from the women's liberation movement* (pp.219-228). New York; Vintage Books.

Masters, William H. & Johnson, Virginia E. (1960). *Human sexual response*. Boston: Little Brown.

Miller, Jean Baker (1986a). *Toward a new psychology of women*. Boston: Beacon Press. Second edition.

Miller, Jean Baker (1986b). *What do we mean by relationships?*, (Working paper No.22). Wellesley, Massachusetts: Wellesley College. The Stone Center.

Miller, Jean Baker (1984). *The development of women's sense of self*. (Working paper No.12). Wellesley, Massachusetts: Wellesley College. The Stone Center.

Miller, Jean Baker (1982). *Women and power*. (Working paper No.82-01). Wellesley, Massachusetts: Wellesley College. The Stone Center.

Raymond, Janice (1986). *A passion for friends: Toward a philosophy of female affection*. Boston: Beacon Press.

Rich, Adrienne (1980). *Compulsory heterosexuality and lesbian existence*. Denver, Colorado: Antelope Publications.

Sherfey, Mary Jane (1966). A theory of female sexuality. In Robin Morgan (Ed.), *Sisterhood is powerful: An anthology of writings from the women's liberation movement* (pp.245-256). New York: Vintage Books.

Stiver, Irene P. (1986). *Beyond the oedipus complex: Mothers and daughters*. (Working paper No.26). Wellesley, Massachusetts: Wellesley College. The Stone Center.

Surrey, Janet L. (1985). *Self-in-relation: A theory of women's development*. (Working paper No.13). Wellesley, Massachusetts: Wellesley College. The Stone Center.

Turner, Clevonne (1984). *Psychosocial barriers to black women's career development*. (Working paper No.84:08). Wellesley, Massachusetts: Wellesley College. The Stone Center.

Vance, Carole S. (Ed.). (1984). *Pleasure and danger: Exploring female sexuality*. London: Routledge & Kegan Paul.

Webster's New World Dictionary. (1983). (Second College Edition). New York: Warner Books, Inc.

Developing a Feminist Model
for Clinical Consultation:
Combining Diversity and Commonality

Sandra J. Coffman, PhD

SUMMARY. Feminist therapists have often felt outside the mainstream of clinical practice. The on-going process of developing our theoretical base has both strengthened our effectiveness and decreased our sense of professional isolation. Few mentors, colleagues or supervisors share this feminist philosophical base. One response to this dilemma has been the development of feminist organizations, such as the Feminist Therapy Institute and the Association for Women in Psychology. A complementary response is the creation of local feminist consultation groups for ongoing clinical consultation and for personal support.

This paper discusses the process of developing one such group and the role that the interaction that commonality and diversity has played in its creation and evolution. The dialectical relationship between commonality and diversity is also explored in a broader sense. Finally, the beginning of a developmental view of this group's evolution is offered, emphasizing the links for women between connectedness and learning.

Author note: "My ethnic background is Caucasian and Western European on both sides of my family. My mother's father was a second generation immigrant from Bavaria in Germany; her mother's ancestors came from England many generations ago. My father's family were farmers who left England and Scotland because of their Mennonite religion."

The author acknowledges with warmth and respect the help and support for writing this paper given by her colleagues Dorsey Green, PhD, Carol Henry, PhD, and Susan Shaul, PhD. She also thanks Ginny NiCarthy, MSW, for her astute editorial comments.

Correspondence may be addressed to the author at: Market Place One, 2001 Western Ave., Ste. 340, Seattle, WA 98121.

255

INTRODUCTION

In the 1960s and 1970s feminist scholarship emphasized the similarities between women and men (Bem, 1975, 1976; Maccoby & Jacklin, 1974). This attempt to describe the immense similarities in human capabilities and desires provided necessary groundwork for a feminist analysis of society and psychology. This early analysis exposed the false ideology of differences that supported the economic inequalities that still discriminate against women in our culture.

More recently, attention has also been paid to the psychological differences between women and men, as feminist theorists strive to better explain and validate women's experience. Chodorow (1978), Miller (1976), Gilligan (1982), Eichenbaum and Orbach (1988), and Clunis and Green (1988) have all delineated positive ways in which women's experience differs from men's. An example of this can be seen in the importance of connection in women's lives. Belenky, Clinchy, Goldberger and Tarule (1987) elaborate the importance of connection in the ways women learn and know the world.

Berlin (1987) and Hare-Mustin and Marecek (1988) have subsequently reviewed the strengths and weaknesses of these two theoretical positions regarding gender difference. Both articles point out the danger that recent feminist psychodynamic theories, which emphasize women's positive qualities, might ignore or underestimate the influence of economic conditions and social conditioning. Hare-Mustin and Marecek also remind us that exaggerating differences between groups (such as between women and men) may also minimize within group variability, especially for subordinate groups:

> Thus, men are viewed as individuals, but women are viewed as women. As a result, most psychological theories of gender have not concerned themselves with differences among women that are due to race, class, age, marital status, and social circumstances. (1988, p. 459)

This analysis of the similarities and commonalities between the members of a small consultation group will focus on the issues raised by Hare-Mustin and Marecek.

The focus on differences between women and men has also had

positive results, such as allowing feminist theorists to "assert the worth of certain 'feminine' qualities. This has the positive effect of countering the cultural devaluation of women and fostering a valued sense of identity in them" (Hare-Mustin & Marecek, 1988, p. 459). The sense of connectedness and of interpersonal commitment fostered within our group will be discussed as examples of positive experiences more common to women than to men in American culture.

Fine (1985) reviewed feminist psychology and described feminist scholarship as that which: (1) exposes gender inequities; (2) aims for contextual validity; and (3) describes the dialectical nature of inquiry by focusing on conflicts and contradictions (rather than on consistencies and harmonies). She also criticized the lack of feminist description of group process. This description of our consultation group process draws both on previous feminist scholarship and on personal experience to illustrate the interplay between diversity and commonality.

COMMONALITY AND DIVERSITY
IN ONE CONSULTATION GROUP

This consultation group began as a dissertation support group for three of our members (Susan, Carol and Dorsey) as they were finishing graduate school in counseling in educational psychology. They invited me and two others to join them when they reconvened to study for the licensing exam in psychology.

Studying together definitely proved to be the most enjoyable and lasting benefit (apart from the licenses we earned) of the licensure procedure. In a situation which could easily have been keenly competitive, we were able to help and challenge ourselves in a completely supportive way. This foundation must have come somewhat from the trust built during the dissertation process, as well as from our feminist ideas of sisterhood and supporting others to do their best. Within the consultation group the common goal of becoming licensed, and helping each other to do so, provided a shared immediate external focus.

When this immediate goal was accomplished, the four of us met again as a consultation group several months later. Meeting every three weeks for several hours, we evolved a process of discussing personal and professional issues at first, then dividing the bulk of our time together based on each person's need for consultation that evening. As we have learned more about each other's personal and professional histories, we are better able to reinforce our strengths and be alert for areas of weakness or unawareness.

Our group has now been in existence for over five years with the same four therapists. We have developed a tremendous sense of commitment to the group itself, as well as to each other. We very seldom miss meetings except for illness, both because we realize the gap this leaves in the group and because we each gain tremendously from our sessions together. We have learned to challenge each other in a supportive way. Our shared sense of commitment and caring is unique in my experience and has greatly strengthened my clinical work.

The continuity of this group may reflect a successful balance for us between commonality and diversity. Commonalities between us include the following: a commitment to feminist therapy; humanistic psychology training; race (Caucasian); motherhood; middle class background; and age (late 30s to mid-40s). Areas of diversity include: sexual orientation; theoretical emphasis (including cognitive-behavioral, systems, and developmental); religious/spiritual background and current choices; and degrees and focus of political, community and professional activity.

Beyond the context of our group, all of us have sought diversity in other aspects of our lives. We have friendships and collegial relationships with women and men of other cultures and races, ages, sexual orientation and different kinds of physical abilities. Our political work has different foci including peace and justice work, the battered women's movement, the movement for equal rights for lesbians and gays, and working to influence professional organizations to be more sensitive to the needs of women and people of different cultures. All of us have chosen to live in areas of Seattle that are ethnically and economically mixed. The composition of our group and of our client population reflects the white dominant (75%) population base of Seattle.

Despite these differences, the homogeneity of this group could predispose us to a smug or limited perspective, particularly because of our membership in the dominant culture in terms of race and economics. We have attempted to be aware of this danger and to compensate for it in various ways. Because we are all Caucasian, we have tried to keep an eye out for racism, subtle or blatant, by reading and talking about these issues in our consultation group and by consulting with women of color. Our middle class backgrounds have also meant that we need to check for erroneous assumptions or anti-working class bias, especially when working with working class clients.

Although we are all able-bodied and hearing, two members of the group are familiar with sign language and have experience working with clients with various kinds of abilities. Our collective experience with this issue was also enlarged as the other members supported me during the three years my older child was temporarily disabled.

Our similarity in age is probably most limiting when working with clients over 45, who are walking roads none of us has yet travelled. Consequently, several of us routinely consult with women significantly older than ourselves who are knowledgeable about aging and the special dilemmas and challenges it presents older women in this culture.

Having only one lesbian member is another limitation even though we are sensitive to issues of homophobia and the special concerns of lesbian clients. We all enjoy working with lesbian clients and couples. However, Dorsey did feel isolated and like an outsider as the only lesbian member. She became aware of this during our second year together and explored the issue initially outside of the group with a close lesbian friend and colleague. With her friend's support, she challenged us about her sense of isolation and expressed her desire to have her lesbianism always acknowledged as a difference, while feeling also an integral part of the group. She said that the shocked look on our faces as she asked whether we could appreciate her as a member of the group with some special issues and difficulties was even more reassuring than our words.

We realize that the group provides an ongoing opportunity for us all to be aware of our homophobia. The heterosexual members also appreciate the opportunity to check with Dorsey about certain aspects of our clinical work with lesbian clients. Recently we were all delighted when we suggested to Dorsey that some of a client's problems might be the result of workplace homophobia; she and her client had not yet explored this possibility together. This demonstrates both the need for all of us in this culture to be on guard against homophobia and the positive power of the collective process in this area of vigilance.

We did try to enlarge our group and perspective at one time in our second year together. We invited a Black feminist psychologist we all knew, liked and respected to join the group, but she declined since she was leaving clinical work for an administrative position. She may also have been understandably reluctant to become the only woman of color in a white group. At this same time, we added another lesbian member, but she did not attend long and eventually dropped out of the group.

We are not clear about the failure of this process and it did make us reluctant to add other members. Obviously our previous history would make it difficult for anyone not to feel excluded in subtle ways, although we did do our best to include the new member. Our covert reactions may have contradicted our overt attempts to expand and welcome new members. The fifth member identified the problems as over-commitment and time constraints on her part, and also her own personal ambivalence about working to become an integral part of an existing group. As a result, we may have closed our ranks more tightly.

We were asked subsequently to add two additional members, both of whom were white and heterosexual. Although we all liked and respected both "candidates," both times we decided not to expand at that point in time. We talked both times about the feeling of safety that we have with each other and about our reluctance to risk that security. We also expressed our desire to gain in breadth and diversity if we do expand, by adding more lesbian members or women of color. However, since time constraints limit the size of the group, we could never become large enough to be truly multicultural, or we would have sufficient time for case consultation. This may mean that, even if we wish to expand in the future, lesbian and women of color might not wish to join us and replicate their experience of being in the minority yet one more time.

Despite their previously discussed limitations, the many commonalities in this group may have also allowed us to develop both a sense of connectedness and of safety from which we can better go out into a world that is challenging in so many areas. Our work with diverse clients is within a society and a professional community that are both still dominated by white middle class men. The prevailing white, heterosexual upper class bias and standards continually undermine women's sense of competency and safety. The ideas of feminists are particularly devalued and discounted. Everyone on our planet must now cope with an era of continual change in which our very survival as a species is daily threatened. Consequently, there often seems to be little that is certain or stable. Within this context of stress and struggle, we want some areas of our lives to feel safe and predictable, while so much else in the world is in flux.

COMMONALITY AND DIVERSITY: SHIFTING DEVELOPMENTAL NEEDS

Theories of group process have emphasized the importance of safety and commonality in the early stage in the group's development (Garland, Jones, & Kolodny, 1973; Yalom, 1975). Feminist theory suggests that women may have additional needs for bonding and creating a sense of alliance and friendship within a group setting (Eichenbaum & Orbach, 1988; Gilligan, 1982).

It is possible that human beings need a certain base, or critical mass, of security, to allow us to deal openly with diversity and change. If diversity is presented too soon or in overwhelming amounts, we may be more likely to be reactive or scared, possibly resulting in retrenchment or a conservative choice of homogeneity. As infants, we are better able to deal with separateness if we have previously experienced dependency and acceptance (Bowlby, 1965, 1985; Maccoby, 1980). Often the environment that provides that base is genetically and culturally our own, so that we can retreat from the discovery of diversity and conflict back to our home base of commonality. There our view of ourselves, of the world, and our role in the world is substantiated by common experiences, roles, myths, songs, and rituals.

Feminists have clearly documented the many ways in which our family structure can be oppressive to women and children (Barnard,

1982; Hare-Mustin, 1978; NiCarthy, 1984; NiCarthy, Merriam, & Coffman, 1984; Root, Fallon, & Friedrich, 1986). However, families can also provide strength and solace, especially to minority groups otherwise reminded of their otherness by the dominant culture. (Unfortunately gay men and lesbian women may not feel that sense of sameness until some of them later enter their own communities as adolescents or adults and recreate a new sense of family and reference group.)

Adolescence often presents a second critical period when security is needed, this time from a peer group so that separation can occur from the family of origin. The teen-age years are often characterized, therefore, by an avoidance of some kinds of differentness; at the same time other ways of expressing individual and generational uniqueness are cultivated. If these developmental needs for security are met, adolescents may be more likely to evolve into healthy adults who are capable of accepting and enjoying diversity. This developmental process and its critical periods needs to be further explored and better understood and appreciated in our shrinking world.

In the infancy of our consult group, all its members were themselves in the early stage of developing their professional identity as feminist psychologists. We had all had previous careers related to education and counseling. As returning students who had chosen counseling psychology inside a department of education, we felt like older step-sisters compared to the young clinical psychologists who so often come through graduate school directly after their undergraduate degrees. As women, we felt/feel in less powerful positions than men, both inside our profession and within the dominant male white culture. So, particularly in its early stages, our group provided a home base as we developed our individual and collective sense of our professional identity and competence.

We created a safe place to discuss our fears about our own competence, to brag about our clinical success and to ask for feedback, knowing it would come within a supportive framework. And, unlike other consult groups which have not endured as long, we have often discussed our personal lives in the group and have shared personal milestones and experiences. For instance, we discuss our various struggles with body image and weight and how this effects us individually, as well as how it relates to our work with clients with these issues. As two of our group members have taken on the primary financial responsibility for their families, we have more often discussed issues of money and power. Our seemingly "annual discussions" about the difficulties of setting fees are becoming more frequent and somewhat more heated. (For an interesting discussion of this dilemma from a feminist standpoint see Lasky, 1985.)

As trust grew, we were better able to deal openly with conflict. (This period of exploring conflict within the group may parallel the stage of adolescence in individual development.) For instance, we struggled more openly and directly with Dorsey's special needs as the only lesbian member. We also felt bold and secure enough to consider adding new members at this stage, although that did not materialize, perhaps because our covert process differed from our overt one of welcoming new members. As three members all had first and then second children, a new issue of diversity then was acknowledged as the fourth member, who was struggling with issues of infertility, felt increasingly isolated.

In an unpublished examination of types of conflict among feminists engaged in various kinds of collaboration, Clunis (1985) found that the most difficult conflict erupted when one member had a child. Luise Eichenbaum and Susie Orbach also comment on this in *Between Women* (1988). Noting that since childbearing now frequently extends into the late thirties and early forties, "women are continually confronted by friends, colleagues, and relatives who are pregnant and having children. An epidemic of powerful and deeply distressing feelings today surrounds pregnancy and childbearing in women's relationships" (p. 26).

When our group was first meeting as a study group for the licensing exam two of us already had children; Carol was pregnant and surrounded by beatific calmness. Her calmness was a boon to us all, and we all shared in the joy of the birth of her daughter, who emerged — to our relief and thanks no doubt to Carol's calmness — unscathed by all the collective anxiety with which the rest of us hopeful licensees had surrounded her. Dorsey and Sandra were already parenting sons and subsequently each gave birth to a second son. As this was Dorsey's first birth child (she previously was co-parenting her life partner's child) we listened and marvelled at her decision to get pregnant and at all the technology and choice involved. This process was particularly difficult for Susan, who was struggling with the legacy of infertility from a previous marriage and the question mark about whether any future partnerships would enable her to have a biologic child. Although the three of us attempted to be supportive, she had to remind us at different times about her feeling left out. After a second round of births, Susan asked us not to talk further about our children in our consultation sessions due to the personal pain and feeling of isolation that she experienced.

When Susan later became pregnant, only to be hospitalized for several months during an extremely difficult pregnancy, we all met in her hospital room for consultation, telephoned each other constantly with news and encouragement and visualized a healthy baby, doing anything we could imagine to support Susan and to strengthen the chances for a healthy child. Our joy was immense when her daughter Melanie was born perfectly healthy at full term. This was a particularly intense time for Carol who was pregnant with her second child. Since her pregnancy went well, it was important for us also to remember to inquire about her experience.

Thus, one difference between us, that of motherhood, has become a commonality as we all now share the experience of mothering young children. Yet, the process of mothering has been different for each of us. At this point, however, our shared experience overrides the differences, providing a commonality and source of mutual support. Although the struggle to accommodate difference strengthened us, Susan doubts that she could have remained in the group had she not had a child, since this difference represented such a painful personal issue for her.

Within this framework of building trust, both commonalities and differences were emerging and changing. Struggling with change was necessary and allowed us to build trust, but was also painful and raised the very real possibility that we might lose our group if we were unable to work through and respect our differences and diversity. Therefore, we also looked for ways to develop additional resources outside the group for help that we feared might not be available, or which might overtax the group process. For example, three of us are in separate additional consultation groups. We have all gone to other individual therapists for supervision with cases that seemed particularly difficult or which touched on our own personal issues; as group members we have sometimes advised each other to seek this kind of additional consultation. For a three-year period, I participated in a research project in order to strengthen my cognitive behavioral skills and to develop collegial relationships with clinicians working primarily from that theoretical framework.

In the most recent stage of our development as a group, the differences in our interpretations of feminist therapy and in other theories and skills are continually emerging. This willingness to acknowledge and explore differentness is only possible due to the common history and supportive environment that we have created during these five years.

THE DIALECTICAL RELATIONSHIP BETWEEN COMMONALITY AND DIVERSITY

Feminist therapists will be able to tell our daughters and sons that we were part of an important social movement that drastically changed the ways in which women and men, and women and women, relate to each other and to their society. As the feminist movement gathered strength, we can tell them, it began to appreciate the contributions of the first wave of American and English feminism in the late 1800s and early 1900s (Flexner, 1959; O'Neill, 1979; Spender, 1983) and of the many minority cultures that comprise the dominant American culture. Our movement, like many others, also made mistakes, particularly when it was under attack, by disregarding the multiplicity of needs that women of different economic classes and races bring to feminism (Brown, 1988).

In these somewhat later years of the second wave of feminism, we can no longer afford to disregard our diversity of needs. Therefore, a dialectical approach to understanding can enrich our examination of the interaction between commonality and diversity and help us avoid oversimplistic ideas. A dialectical approach is compatible with feminist analysis both in its emphasis on studying contradiction and in its insistence on understanding issues in their social context (Fine, 1985).

Using this approach, commonality and diversity can be viewed as opposites of each other, and therefore in dialectical contradiction to each other. Paradoxically, they are even partially defined by their opposition to each other. A creative tension exists between them, and they are always effecting and changing each other. Both contain negative and positive aspects. They are thesis and antithesis to each other and at times form a new synthesis. Then they may separate again into opposites but are both changed by the moment of synthesis and also by their ongoing interaction.

In the early years of our consult group a contradiction existed between the needs and experiences of the three members who were both therapists and mothers and the one who did not have children. There are certainly negative and positive aspects of both sets of experiences and needs. Sometimes the mothers needed or wanted to talk about the impact of mothering on their personal or professional lives; sometimes they even wanted to bring young babies to meetings so that they could nurse their infants. Each of these desires created tension and sadness for the childless member who, in this case, also wanted very much to have a child. Although this contradiction represented an extremely sensitive and difficult conflict in needs, we muddled through due to our caring for and commitment to each other.

We were all affected by sharing our different experiences in the group. This struggle affected all of us differently at different times, but we have all been strengthened and changed by this challenge — both individually and as a group. Now that we all have children, the contradiction regarding mothering revolves around the number and ages of our children, our different arrangements for co-parenting these children, and the different histories of our parenting experience. The form of these new contradictions is just beginning to unravel.

As defined by Klaus Riegel in *Foundations of Dialectical Psychology* (1979) dialectical psychology studies actions and changes, as opposed to most modern theories of development which emphasize stability. Instead, dialectical psychology,

> is primarily concerned with how individuals and groups succeed in overcoming their tranquility and balance. Conse-

quently, a dialectical psychology reinterprets crises and contradictions in positive terms . . . the long-term conception of dialectics is concerned with developmental changes in the individual and historical changes in society. (p. 15)

In this second era of feminism, we tend to speak of diversity as if it is completely good, and it would be easy to then assume that commonality is therefore all bad. Both a dialectical perspective and the history of our consult group provide examples that contradict this totally negative view. For example, diversity creates both richness and tension, which can be positive, negative, or both in different situations. People can speak in different dialects or even different languages, either impeding communication or enriching it. Certain steps can be taken to facilitate exchange, such as providing translators or learning each other's language or dialect. At times, however, communication will be slowed, and may even be distorted.

Another example of the positive and negative elements of diversity is found in building coalitions. Many of us have probably been involved in coalitions that attempted to define their principles of unity or to define their common goal as a means of respecting the diversity of groups or individuals brought together around a common issue. Sometimes this has worked well but at other times the issue got lost or was poorly attended to because of the amount of energy that was spent defining terms and on looking unsuccessfully for the thread of commonality that would allow united action or problem solving.

Likewise, commonality includes both positive and negative aspects which are at play in different ways depending on the societal and interpersonal context. The negative effects of commonality include the potential for narrow-mindedness, short-sightedness, and smugness. Racism, homophobia and other bigoted ways of viewing the world can flourish in homogeneous groups in this racist and homophobic society. By contrast, commonality of experience or world view can also have positive results, such as facilitating action. Common assumptions and language make it easier to plan and proceed. For example, our shared sex-role training as women may account for the generally polite and respectful behavior of our group members towards each other. (While this facilitates our group functioning, it may also contribute to our avoidance of conflict.) The middle and upper middle class upbringing of our group members results in some common behaviors and assumptions which make it easier for us to communicate and understand each other. For example, we are generally hopeful about the future, and we expect that our children will outlive us. We often feel optimistic about being able to act upon our environment and to know some professional success. Of course, the experience of sexism tempers this optimism somewhat. These expectations can help us empower our clients and help us persist in the difficult business of doing therapy.

The negative aspects of our common class background, however, are especially dangerous when we work with working class clients. We need to appreciate the ways in which working class women and men and their families may have absorbed society's view that they are of less value than middle and upper class people and that they should not expect to change their limited destiny (Rubin, 1969).

We also need to be aware of the ways in which people of color may view family responsibilities and role divisions differently than do white folks. Our common class background and our white skin privilege may keep us from really hearing and empowering some of our clients. The ease of our common language may keep us from noticing our biases and mistaken assumptions when we consult together about clinical cases and issues. This common language may have also sent a covert message of exclusiveness when we attempted to expand our group and diversify.

FRIENDSHIP AND LEARNING STYLES AMONG WOMEN

Belenky, Clinchy, Goldberger, and Tarule (1987) document the importance women place on connected learning and knowing. They document the frequency with which women are treated as if they are stupid and in which our concerns are discounted or denigrated in this misogynist society. They propose and describe five positions or modes of learning, the highest of which they call constructed knowledge, which will be subsequently described in more detail.

Having been labelled as the department feminist, I often felt extremely isolated in graduate school. I was lucky to be associated with feminist social workers and wished aloud that I had chosen social work as my field, with its strong history of social concern and its feminist organizations. It was only later, in the context of my association with this consultation group that I began to develop my identity as a feminist psychologist. This emerging professional identity was made possible by my sense of connection to other women with similar professional goals and feminist politics.

The theme of connectedness has also played an important role in the development of our consultation group. It continues to surface in our relationships with clients, and especially with female clients. The importance of connection to women, both as a vehicle for learning about ourselves and for our relationships, has both positive and negative aspects. In consultation, group members often help each other keep an eye on boundaries with clients. Maintaining distance and separateness is generally more difficult for us than is feeling connected to our clients. Therefore, we often have to spend a disproportionate amount of consult time dealing with borderline clients, partially due to their difficulty with boundaries. As therapists we also need to work hard to maintain appropriate therapeutic boundaries with survivors of various kinds of abuse. Clients who have been abused may not have learned how, or have not been allowed, to set appropriate limits and interpersonal boundaries, particularly if the abuse occurred when they were young. Issues of transference and countertransference are also more likely to emerge in these difficult cases, therefore requiring additional consult time and vigilance.

These particular issues are being raised much more often in the last two years of our group. This may be partially due to the fact that we are each more likely to accept more difficult cases now, since our sense of individual capabilities has strengthened with time. (We have also become better at limiting the kinds of cases we accept, as we become more insightful — with each other's help — of our personal and clinical weaknesses, limitations and areas of unawareness.) But we also suspect that we are challenging each other more frequently now, since we have built a sense of trust and caring from which to argue and question without risking our bonds of connection.

Viewed in the stages of relationship developed by Susan Campbell (1980), we have moved from the first stage of romance, emphasizing our similarities, through the second, third, and fourth stages (of battling differences and developing stability and then commitment), into the fifth stage of generativity, which Campbell labels co-creation. As individual feminist therapists, we have moved out into the world from the safe haven of our consult group. Examples of our increased activity in the wider world include the publication of two books and several articles, increased responsibility in professional organizations, presentations at conferences, community involvement and other political work. We have supported each other as we step out into more visible positions in the world, and have also cautioned each other when evidence of stress or overwork negatively impacts our work with clients or our relationships with each other.

As a group, we have also moved more into the world. This paper and another workshop given by another member on supportive consultation represent that expansion. As a group we also sponsored an in-service presentation by another professional for a small number of feminist therapists. We have also invited other therapists to speak to us about areas of their specific expertise for part of our consultation time.

Because of our fears of losing the group should conflict not be resolved, I suspect we move too quickly through the second stage of relationship, that of struggling with conflict and difference. Differences between us are currently being articulated more often and more intensely than in the past, so we seem to be repeating this stage of conflict resolution at the same time that we move from our base of relationship out into the wider world.

In closing, I would like to return to the fifth position of knowing described by Belenky et al. (1986), constructed knowledge, which reflects an integration of internal and external knowledge and voices. Although the authors apply this standard only to individuals and not to groups, it appears to me to describe many of the positive aspects of ourselves as we relate within the framework of our consultation group: "These women were articulate and reflective people . . . concerned with issues of inclusion and exclusion, separation and connection; each struggled to find a balance of extremes in her life. . . . Each wanted her voice . . . to make a difference in the world'' (p. 133). I feel extremely moved by this quotation, since it evokes the pride and warmth I feel for the members of my consultation group, each of whom fits this description. I have attempted to sketch our group history and to provide theoretical models to explain the process of developing our group so that our history, and possibly our format, might be of use to other feminist therapists. In particular, I have emphasized the ongoing dialectical relationship between commonality and diversity as it has evolved and changed within our group. But I cannot end without paying direct tribute to the individuals who comprise this group and to the many other feminist therapists who struggle with similar challenges. A final quote from Belenky et al. (1986) sums up my feelings of admiration and tribute:

> These women want to embrace all the pieces of the self in some ultimate sense of the whole — daughter, friend, mother, lover, nurturer, thinker, artist, advocate. They want to avoid what they perceive to be a shortcoming in many men — the tendency to compartmentalize thought and feeling, home and work, self and other. In women, there is an impetus to try to deal with life, internal and external, in all its complexity. And they want to develop a voice of their own to communicate to others their understanding of life's complexity. (p. 137)

REFERENCES

Barnard, Jessie (1982). *The future of marriage* (2nd ed.). New Haven: Yale University Press.

Bem, Sandra (1975). Sex-role adaptability: One consequence of psychological androgyny. *Journal of Personality and Social Psychology, 31*, 634-643.

Bem, Sandra (1976). Probing the promise of androgyny. In Alexandra G. Kaplan & Joan P. Bean (Eds.), *Beyond sex-role stereotypes: Readings toward a psychology of androgyny* (pp. 48-62). Boston: Little, Brown.

Belenky, Mary Field, Clinchy, Blythe McVicker, Goldberger, Nancy Rule, Tarule, Jill Mattuck (1986). *Women's ways of knowing.* New York: Basic Books, Inc.

Berlin, Sharon (1987). Women and mental health: anger, anxiety, dependency, and control. In Diane S. Burden & Naomi Gottlieb (Eds.), *The woman client: providing human services in a changing world* (pp. 146-161). New York: Tavistock Publications.

Bowlby, John (1965). Separation anxiety. In Paul H. Mussen, John J. Conger, & Jerome Kagan (Eds.), *Readings in Child Development & Personality* (pp. 140-151). New York: Harper & Row.

Bowlby, John (1985). The role of childhood experience in cognitive disturbance. In Michael J. Mahoney & Arthur Freeman (Eds.), *Cognition and Psychotherapy* (pp. 181-201). New York: Plenum Press.

Brown, Laura S. (1990). The meaning of a multicultural perspective for theory-building in feminist therapy. In Laura Brown & Maria P. P. Root (Eds.), *Diversity and Complexity in Feminist Therapy*. New York: Haworth Press.

Campbell, Susan (1980). *The couples journey.* San Luis Obispo: Impact Publishers.

Chodorow, Nancy (1978). *The reproduction of mothering.* Berkeley: University of California Press.

Clunis, Merilee. *Toward a feminist model of collaboration.* Presentation at the National Women's Studies Association National Conference in Seattle, WA, June 1985.

Clunis, Merilee & Green, Dorsey (1988). *Lesbian couples.* Seattle, WA: Seal Press.

Eichenbaum, Luise & Orbach, Susie (1988). *Between women.* New York: Viking Press.

Fine, Michelle (1985). Reflections on a feminist psychology of women: paradoxes and prospects. *Psychology of Women Quarterly, 9,* 167-183.

Flexner, Eleanor (1959). *Century of struggle.* Cambridge, MA: Harvard University Press.

Garland, James A., Jones, Hubert E., & Kolodny, Ralph L. (1973). A model for stages of development in social work groups. In Saul Bernstein (Ed.), *Explorations in Group Work*. Boston: Charles River Books.

Gilligan, Carol (1982). *In a different voice: psychological theory and women's development.* Cambridge, MA: Harvard University Press.

Green, Dorsey (1990). "Is separation really so great?" In Laura Brown & Maria P. P. Root (Eds.), *Diversity and complexity in feminist therapy.* New York: The Haworth Press.

Hare-Mustin, Rachel (1978). A feminist approach to family therapy. *Family Process, 17,* 181-194.

Hare-Mustin, Rachel T. & Marecek, Jeanne (1988). The meaning of difference: gender theory, postmodernism, and psychology. *American Psychologist, 43,* 455-464.

Kravetz, Diane (1980). Consciousness-raising and self-help. In Annette M. Brodsky & Rachel Hare-Mustin (Eds.), *Women and Psychotherapy* (pp. 268-281). New York: Guilford Press.

Lasky, Ella (1985). Psychotherapists' ambivalence about fees. In Lynne Bravo Rosewater and Lenore Walker (Eds.), *Handbook of feminist therapy.* New York: Springer Publishing Co.

Maccoby, Eleanor E. & Jacklin Carol N. (1974). *The psychology of sex differences.* Stanford, CA: Stanford University Press.

Maccoby, Eleanor E. (1980). *Social development, psychological growth and the parent-child relationship*. New York: Harcourt Brace Jovanovich.

Miller, Jean Baker (1976). *Towards a new psychology of women*. Boston: Beacon Press.

O'Neill, William L. (1979). *Everyone was brave*. Chicago: Quadrangle Books.

NiCarthy, Ginny (1986). *Getting free: a handbook for women in abusive relationships*. Seattle, WA: Seal Press.

NiCarthy, Ginny, Merriam, Karen, & Coffman, Sandra (1984). *Talking it out: a guide to groups for abused women*. Seattle, WA: Seal Press.

Riegel, K. F. (1979). *Foundations of dialectical psychology*. New York: Academic Press.

Root, Maria P. P., Fallon, Patricia, & Friedrich, William N. (1986). *Bulimia: A systems approach to treatment*. New York: W.W. Norton.

Rubin, Lillian Breslow (1969). *Worlds of pain: Life in the working-class family*. New York: Basic Books.

Spender, Dale (1983). *There's always been a women's movement this century*. London: Pandora Press.

Stiver, Irene P. (1984). *The meanings of "dependency" in female-male relationships*. Work in Press. No. 83-07. Wellesley, MA: Wellesley College.

Yalom, I. P. (1975). *The theory and practice of group psychotherapy* (2nd ed.). New York: Basic Books.

Feminist Psychotherapy and Diversity: Treatment Considerations from a Self Psychology Perspective

Joan F. Hertzberg, PhD

SUMMARY. This paper examines how one's ethnic, racial, and class identity is internalized and shaped by social relations and the external conditions of oppression and privilege. Psychotherapy issues are discussed from a Self Psychology perspective which emphasizes the role of the therapist's empathetic responsiveness in facilitating trust and disclosure and promoting psychological development through the vehicle of the transference relationship. Countertransference dynamics are explored with regard to social differences and distance between client and clinician. Issues of interpersonal trust and the effects of social conditioning toward prejudice are examined with respect to the therapeutic relationship. Finally,

---

Joan F. Hertzberg is a licensed clinical psychologist with a multi-cultural private practice in San Francisco. She is on the clinical faculty in the doctoral program at the California Institute for Integral Studies. Her background is middle class with a cultural heritage that is Jewish and of Rumanian and Latvian descent. She was in the first graduating class at Williams College which accepted women and graduated valedictorian. She received her doctorate in 1981 from University of California, Santa Cruz. She is also the recipient of a Clark Fellowship. Other publications include a chapter which she co-authored with Dr. Deborah Lee in *Women and Sex Roles: A Social Psychological Perspective* [Irene Frieze et al. (Eds.), W. W. Norton, 1978].

The author wishes to express special thanks to Dr. Karen Peoples for her valuable contribution to this paper. She would like to thank Dr. Deborah Lee, Dr. Maria P. P. Root, Dr. Laura Brown, Roger Lake, MFCC, and M. J. Lallo, MA, for their editorial help and encouragement.

Correspondence may be addressed to the author at: 1704 Church Street, San Francisco, CA 94131.

areas of compatibility between Feminist Therapy and Self Psychology are elucidated.

INTRODUCTION: CULTURAL ASPECTS OF THE SELF

The essence of this paper addresses the dynamics of the psychotherapeutic process with clients whose lives differ significantly from the health care provider from whom they seek treatment. In elucidating the dynamics of this relationship, social, interpersonal, intersubjective and intrapsychic levels of experience need to be addressed. Elements of the therapeutic relationship as experienced by each of the participants will be explored.

How do we as clinicians attend to the notion of internal representation of culture and its profound impact on the organization of self experience? Moffie (1983) recognizes the multi-level aspects of working with clients from divergent socio-cultural backgrounds. He conceptualizes the role of culture in psychological development as an additional aspect of consciousness known as the "transconscious" which is

> derived from the interaction of all aspects of the personality with the surrounding social groups. Regulation of drives, emphasis on particular perceptual modes, superego values, and the internal representation of the culture in the self would all be included. Similar patterns of responding to these developmental potentialities will then produce different group cultures and subcultures. (p. 48)

These internal representations for the minority individual include both the experience of the self within a particular subculture, as well as the experience of the self as an outsider of a larger, dominant culture. These affect-laden internal images of self and other are created through the interplay of developmental and social strivings within relational experiences. These relationships are further shaped and determined by the historical, economic, familial, and spiritual contexts in which they are embedded.

SOCIAL-PSYCHOLOGICAL CONSEQUENCES
OF EXTERNAL FACTORS:
INTERNALIZED OPPRESSION AND DOMINATION

The dominant culture's beliefs, stereotypes, prejudices and valuation of a group will often impact these internal representations of the self. Oftentimes, a person who is a member of a minority group may find herself or himself interacting with a larger culture which devalues, denigrates, and targets her/him as being different. S/he may find that s/he is unwittingly feared or despised based on other's responses to her/his culture, race, religion, appearance, or sexual preference. These beliefs and messages from the larger culture, in addition to direct experiences of discrimination and abuse, often affect one's sense of self. When these external beliefs and messages are introjected and become part of an autonomous internal dialogue and set of emotional responses, this is known as internalized oppression (Lipsky, 1977). These previously external messages now become part of how we see and feel about ourselves and how we function in relation to others. Children from less privileged backgrounds are often socialized to anticipate and be responsive to the needs and wants of members of the dominant culture. Feelings of worthiness, which affect one's sense of deserving, are transmitted consciously and unconsciously from generation to generation. Reich (1966) observed that psychically, "Character structure provides the necessary psychological support within the oppressed for those very external practices and institutions . . . which daily oppress them" (p. 18). Our psychic structures, according to Reich, are shaped, in part, by the external social conditions which correspond to different strata of society. These internal structures may, at times, serve to support the social status quo, rather than the individual's own best interests.

The effects of internalized oppression can lead to self-deprecation (Phillips, 1969; Lipsky, 1977), denial of one's affects and experiences, minimizing social differences and cultural identification, and invalidating one's perceptions of reality (Hertzberg & Eschbach, 1982). Another aspect of this self-devaluation is adapting to other's expectations in the establishment of a false self. This adaptation can take a variety of forms. One of the most insidious forms is the tendency to "pass" or conform to the dominant cultural expectancies. To "pass" as a member of the dominant culture by denying one's experiences, not acknowledging or bringing up differences, or minimizing their importance, all extract a high personal cost. These may be a loss of a positive sense of self, confusion as to one's true identity, a loss of familial and cultural connection, a devaluation of one's experience, and a sacrifice of self-respect. In more severe instances, this can lead to impairments in one's experience of self continuity as key elements of one's identity are repressed and denied.

These experiences of self-alienation and deprecation from within and without can contribute to a deep reservoir of rage which may be directed internally or externally. Due to women's conditioning cross-culturally, this rage is often directed inward in the forms of depression, psychosomatic illness, self-abuse, chemical dependency, and other self-destructive behaviors (Phillips, 1968; Chesler, 1977). Additionally, experiences of violence, abuse, and intense dehumanization constitute traumatic stress. The long-lasting effects of these experiences can manifest in Post-Traumatic Stress Disorders (American Psychiatric Association, 1987). Beyond the internalization of negative self-concept, such severe abuse can gravely impair one's sense of self-agency and self-expressiveness, leading to pervasive feelings of powerlessness, helplessness, and paralysis (Peoples, 1988).

There are many factors which mitigate against the devastating effects of dehumanization, some of which include family support and cultural identification, the availability of positive role models, a nurturing caretaking environment, a sense of community. Ethnicity and ethnic identification can provide connectedness to a larger group as well as a sense of historical continuity (Giordano, 1973). Group cohesiveness, familial support (Suchman, 1964), and positive role models all serve to combat the insidious forms of oppression. Strong bonding between parents and children (Joseph, 1981), the support of a larger extended family or community (Glazer & Moynihan, 1963), and pride and identification with one's ethnicity all serve as buffers against institutionalized and personal forms of oppression.

To the extent that these ameliorative experiences are lacking or entirely absent, the effects of discrimination, stress, and/or poverty can take a devastating toll on families and their members. When family members respond to one another in dysfunctional and unhealthy ways, the likelihood of experiences which bolster the positive elements of self in the developing child are limited. More often, the effects of oppression take their toll on the entire family. Parents may, in fact, turn to their children to provide caregiving. While this is often beyond their capacity to provide, children will attempt to respond in order to avoid emotional abandonment and in hopes of ultimately being cared for by their parents (Miller, 1981). It is important to note that these patterns emerge in dysfunctional family systems regardless of social, cultural, or economic factors.

As experiences of oppression are internalized, so are experiences of privilege and entitlement. When members of a privileged group introject feelings of superiority, elitism, self-aggrandizement, self-righteousness, "normalcy," and the acceptance of prejudice toward others, this constitutes internalized domination (Pheterson, 1986). This dynamic not only rationalizes and perpetuates the oppression of others, but has adverse consequences for the holder of these beliefs. In order to accept prejudices, one has to deny aspects of one's own humanity. Additionally, this can lead to alienation from one's own body and nature, as well as, restricting one's capacities for love, trust, empathy, and openness. This can gravely impair one's capacity for equal, intimate relationships. Instead, relationships are often characterized by distance, competition, one-upmanship, and an inability to be vulnerable. Members of privileged groups are often socialized to expect respect, to be taken seriously, and to be attended to by others. These expectations, however, may vary as experiences of privilege combine with those of emotional deprivation or family dysfunction. In many cases, this leads to dynamics in which both internalized oppression and domination appear intrapsychically within the same person and are manifested interpersonally. The two augment one another in what Pheterson refers to as "a mutually reinforcing web of insecurities and rigidities" (p. 159). While the social and political consequences of each are quite different, she notes that the psychological consequences are not dissimilar.

The fear of violence one feels as a victim of oppression reinforces the fear of revenge she feels as an agent of oppression. The isolation resulting from feelings of inferiority reinforces isolation resulting from feelings of superiority. The guilt felt for dominating others likewise reinforces the guilt felt for one's own victimization. (p. 159)

The complexity and interrelatedness of these interpersonal dynamics hold special consequences for the psychotherapy relationship. This is particularly true when the client is from a minority group seeking help from a professional or health care provider who is a member of the dominant, white, middle class, Anglo-Saxon, heterosexual background.

POWER DIFFERENTIALS
IN THE PSYCHOTHERAPEUTIC RELATIONSHIP

Feminist therapy looks at the power dynamics of society at large, as well as within the microcosm of the therapeutic dyad. While this relationship is inherently unequal due to its structure, the monetary exchange, and focus of treatment, these power differences may be exaggerated and highlighted due to social, cultural, and economic differences between client and therapist. Further, therapy can lead to reenactment of experiences of oppression and abuse in a context which is ostensibly to provide help. To minimize the potential of this occurring, it is essential that the therapist understand the dynamics of oppression. The types of oppression that need to be acknowledged are manifold and, at times, multiple. These include racism, sexism, classism, anti-Semitism, homophobia, ageism, and discrimination against disabilities and cultural background. The interactions of multiple forms of oppression can often be complex and confusing. For example, the experience of an upper class, educated Latina from Argentina who is married to an Anglo American male will be very different from a lesbian, migrant worker from Mexico who does not have legal residence or work status. The interface of class with race and culture can, at times, combine experiences of privilege with those of discrimination. These will also be reflected in attitudes of internalized oppression intermixed with those of internalized domination. Aside from these various affiliations and categories, each client needs to be seen and treated as a unique individual within the context of a particular familial, developmental, and socio-cultural background. This contextual approach is an essential aspect of a feminist perspective.

The extent to which we remain unaware of the cultural conditioning toward prejudice, our fear of differences, the use of vulnerable people and children as scapegoats (Miller, 1983), and the dynamics of entitlement and disenfranchisement, we are likely to act and react in ways that perpetuate various forms of invalidation in our personal and professional lives. This has particular consequences in the therapy context which "presumably helps patients overcome stereotypic views of themselves and to understand their own individuality, worth, and ability to utilize inner strengths in the service of growth and coping" (Greene, 1985, p. 389). For this process to occur, there are certain requirements of sensitivity and awareness that can promote a positive therapeutic outcome and relational experience. These will be addressed in the context of a Self Psychology perspective.

SELF PSYCHOLOGY:
A FEMINIST APPROACH TO DIVERSITY

According to Self Psychology, the psychotherapy context is an inherently intersubjective experience. This situation is one in which each participant attempts to organize and give meaning to the current relationship based on their own resources, past relational and emotional bonds, affective responsiveness, and ways of perceiving and processing interpersonal information. Stolorow, Brandchaft, and Atwood (1987) maintain that this "subjective reality becomes articulated through a process of empathetic resonance" (p. 7-8). This attitude of sustained empathetic inquiry is one in which the therapist "consistently seeks to comprehend the meaning of the patient's expressions from a perspective within, rather than outside, the patient's own subjective frame of reference" (Kohut, 1959, p. 10).

The centrality of this notion in Self Psychology provides a basis for a culturally-sensitive approach to working with individuals from diverse backgrounds. Within this therapeutic model, empathy is seen both as a primary analytic tool, as well as a major goal of psychological maturity (Gardiner, 1987, p. 231). Mahler, Pine, and Bergman (1975), in the tradition of an Object Relations perspective, tend to emphasize separation and individuation as primary developmental goals. In contrast, Self Psychology acknowledges the ongoing need throughout life to be embedded in a network of interrelationships which provide certain psychological and emotional functions. In this regard, the goal of development is one of self-differentiation and interdependence, or mature dependency, as the sine qua non of maturity. This emphasis on empathy, both as a central value and clinical methodology, is compatible with both feminist values and approaches to relatedness (Gilligan, 1982; Miller, 1976; Surrey, 1985).

Self Psychology views people's strengths and deficits within the constructs of a developmental model. Therapy is seen as a potential for reinstituting a stalled developmental process. It is through the transference relationship that internal patterns of relatedness emerge. Within this relationship, the client may learn to integrate affects, acknowledge emotional needs, develop self-regulatory capacities, and proceed in the process of self-differentiation. This theory recognizes the primary role of early caregivers in shaping the child's sense of self. Through the caregivers' responses of attunement and empathy, the child's emerging self begins to evolve. Parents serve the selfobject needs of the child by providing an external resource or relational vehicle through which psychological functions are performed. Stolorow et al. (1987) remind us that selfobjects are not persons, but rather, "a class of psychological functions pertaining to the maintenance, restoration and transformation of self-experience" (p. 16-17). The notion of selfobject provides a conceptual framework within which historical and social forces enter into the socialization process with significant others throughout life (Gardiner, 1987, p. 239). From a feminist perspective, this notion provides a psychological vehicle for the transmission of social forces and relations.

Parents or caregivers provide a variety of emotional and psychological functions which may become internalized in the service of the child's development. One key function that caregivers provide is attunement to and accurate reflection of the child's affects and needs. Developmentally appropriate mirroring responses to the child's grandiose and exhibitionist strivings are essential for the "consolidation of self-cohesion, self-esteem, and self-confident ambition" (Stolorow et al., 1987, p. 93). These strivings refer to the child's expansive self-expression and delight in her/his own vitality, mastery, and sense of greatness. When there is a consistent absence of attuned responsiveness in the caregivers, there will often be an impairment in affect integration. In this case, feelings and needs become disavowed or dissociated. When this unresponsiveness is consistent and the child feels ignored and disregarded, s/he becomes increasingly vulnerable to self-fragmentation (Stolorow et al., 1987, p. 67). Under less damaging circumstances, the developing child will become increasingly out of touch with her/himself and will often feel shameful about these unmet and unacknowledged needs and affects. There is a strong cultural component as to how grandiosity is responded to and what needs and affects will be recognized and reflected back to the child. Additionally, in many cultures, due to the pervasive dynamics of sexism, caregivers will often be more encouraging and accepting of early expressions of male grandiosity and more restrictive of such female expressiveness. This will adversely impact self-development with potential injury to self-esteem and ambitious strivings.

Another key function that caregivers provide is their availability as idealized selfobjects in which the child experiences the self as supported by an external source of strength, calm, and security. This function serves as the basis for self-regulatory, self-soothing and comforting, and self-empathic capacities to be internalized within the child's self-experience (Stolorow et al., 1987, p. 23). The experience of connection to a powerful, idealized other often provides a foundation for later mature ideals, goals, and guiding values (Kohut, 1977). These patterns of responsiveness and relatedness over time lay the groundwork for psychological self structure. When a parent is overwhelmed, inconsistent, anxious, and needy, s/he cannot fully provide a sense of comfort or security. When a child has not been treated with acceptance, respect, and compassion, s/he does not develop the capacity for self empathy.

Most of the time, parents have difficulty giving to their children what they, themselves, have never received or experienced. It may be difficult for parents to provide for the child's emotional needs when they are out of touch with themselves and have not received sufficient caretaking. In this instance, the child may be called upon to provide for the emotional and psychological (selfobject) needs of the parents. When this occurs, the child's own strivings for self-differentiation and self-demarcation may be thwarted by the parent who becomes threatened by the child's attempts to be her/his own person. The independent strivings of the child become burdened with guilt and conflict. The child may experience her/himself as destructive and dangerous. As the child experiences her/his attempts at self definition or differentiation as threatening to the parent, s/he may relinquish this process in favor of serving the parents' needs. This may cause an impairment in self-boundary formation (Stolorow et al., 1987, pp. 91-93). The child may experience confusion as to where her/his unique identity emerges and differs from her/his adherence to parental demands and expectancies. In these families, the formation and expression of the child's true self is associated with parental disapproval and rejection. The child may feel forced to choose between valuing and caring for her/himself and attending to the parents' needs and expectations.

Parental responsiveness to the child's needs and affects will depend on the subculture's notions and styles of childrearing regarding valuation of affect and need expression. Additionally, it will involve idiosyncratic factors within the experience of the caregivers such as the availability and adequacy of their own parents and extended family, their own developmental assets and limitations, and the amount of stress and dysfunction experienced presently and intergenerationally. Further, there are vast cultural differences as to ways in which individual identity, autonomy, and self-differentiation are encouraged or discouraged to be congruent with social values and group needs (McGoldrick & Rohrbaugh, 1987; McGoldrick, Pearce & Giordano, 1982). Bradshaw (1988), for example, explores how issues of dependency within the Japanese culture differ greatly from American psychological valuation of individuality and autonomy.

When experiences of mirroring, idealizing, identification, empathetic responsiveness, and support for self-differentiation are lacking, development is impaired. This impairment can impact three areas of functioning: the positive or negative tone of one's self-image, the sense of temporal stability or continuous self-identity over time, and the sense of self-cohesion (Stolorow & Lachmann, 1980).

In families where the child's psychological and emotional development is thwarted by a depriving, judgmental, controlling, abusive, or rejecting caregiving environment, it is likely that these experiences will also be introjected in the form of internalized oppression. The effects of internalized oppression have a direct impact on the affective tonation of the self. Feelings of self-hatred, shame, and low self-esteem all have a negative affective tonation. The development of a false self, which is exemplified in the phenomenon of passing, can lead to a situation in which major aspects of the self are repressed, denigrated, and denied. This is particularly true when there is an internalized identification with the dominant culture expectancies to the disparagement of one's own cultural experience and identity. In this instance, the disconnection from feelings, memories, perceptions, language, and values can lead to a lack of continuity of self. When one is overly adaptive to the needs of others, as a strategy for survival under conditions of oppression, one can easily lose a sense of oneself.

In this case, one's sense of self is essentially tied to one's relationships which become integral to one's identity. When a relationship is lost or when one is forced to spend time alone, there may be profound feelings of emptiness. This loss of a sense of self may lead to various forms of compulsive and addictive behaviors to fill the void. Since there is no sense of a core self, there is a lack of continuous self-identity over time. One's sense of self will vary greatly depending on the social situation. This type of individual is especially vulnerable to social dynamics of exclusion and oppression.

Finally, the lack of self-cohesion is usually the result of early and severe developmental failures in which caregiving is extremely inconsistent or insufficient. This may be the result of early trauma, loss, or abandonment leading to a sense of disintegration or fragmentation. Occasionally, these developmental impairments only become evident when the person faces external crisis or internal trauma in adult life. At this juncture, the individual does not have adequate internal resources or sufficient psychological structures to sustain a cohesive sense of self-identity.

It is within the psychotherapy relationship that these psychological deficits and developmental derailments can be addressed and repaired. The therapist becomes a new resource in which selfobject functions can be internalized and utilized by the client for the renewal of the maturation process. Specifically, the therapist's consistent acceptance of the client's needs and affects and empathetic attunement to these states facilitates the developmental process of self-articulation and self-differentiation (Stolorow et al., 1987, p. 23). It is through the transference relationship that the idealizing and mirroring ties that were ruptured in the past can now be reinstituted for the maintenance and restoration of the self and for further psychological growth to occur (Stolorow et al., 1987, p. 115). When misattunements to the client's inner world occur without being detected, explored, and realigned, a sense of psychic isolation can occur. The client then experiences reinjury and the reenactment with earlier failed responsiveness. For it is the attitude of attunement that leads to an experience of a shared world. "Without affective attunement, one's activities are solitary, private, and idiosyncratic . . . the lack of shared experience may well create a sense of isolation and a belief that one's affective needs are generally unacceptable and shameful" (Stern, 1985, p. 35). It is essential that there is enough trust in the therapeutic alliance for these ruptures in empathy and attunement to be explored, connected with relevant material, when appropriate, and the transference bond restored, for the healing process to proceed. In fact, it is this very process that is essential for psychological growth, as the understanding and processing of these ruptures helps the client to integrate disruptive affective states "in the concomitant mending and expanding of the broken selfobject tie" (Stolorow et al., 1987, p. 104). This psychotherapeutic process is one source of renewed growth and development of psychological capacities.

The ways in which psychotherapy can be more effective need to be identified. What are the processes and relationships which facilitate psychological growth, the internalization of self-regulatory capacities, and the development of psychological structures? There needs to be more attention paid to the process of internalization of selfobject functions. We need to be able to identify the factors which either promote or hinder the client's ability to utilize the relationship in ways which facilitate self-regulation as opposed to regulation by the environment (Hartmann, 1939).

In what ways do the perceived similarity between client and therapist impact the client's ability to identify with the therapist and to internalize regulatory capacities through the idealizing transference? When social differences are great, does this impede the facility of the client to develop an alter-ego or twinship transference bond which can provide a sense of sameness or belonging? This type of transference refers to a feeling by the client that s/he is similar to the therapist, which may provide a sense of connection. When this sense of belonging is absent from the therapeutic alliance, how does this affect the client's capacity to internalize these selfobject functions? If this type of transference facilitates internalization, this would make a case for referring clients to therapists who were perceived as more similar to themselves along certain social-psychological dimensions. Alternatively, the idealizing transference with a therapist from the dominant culture, may serve to expand social distance and replicate the power dynamics of society at large. This may make the internalization of psychological capacities more problematic within certain therapy relationships.

Psychotherapy from a Self Psychology perspective is potentially effective with a wide range of clients from differing backgrounds. This is particularly relevant as it underlines the importance of understanding the subjective experience of the client within her/his own frame of reference, while paying attention to our own subjective input as therapists. Additionally, Kohut (1984) asserts that "there is not one kind of healthy self, there are many kinds" (p. 44). Gardiner (1987) recognizes the significance of this proclamation noting that "it should free self psychology from any narrow criteria of normality or health, including such culturally determined values as independence, exclusive heterosexuality, or traditionally 'masculine' or 'feminine' personalities" (p. 242). Obviously, this relativity with respect to definitions of health extends to varied cultures, as well. Theoretically, this approach to treatment shows great promise. Practically, there are some factors which need to be identified that restrict the therapist's ability to utilize empathetic modalities for the therapeutic benefit of the client.

PSYCHOTHERAPY PROCESS: IMPEDIMENTS TO TRUST AND EMPATHY

Almost any form of psychotherapy involves empathy and open communication for the therapy to be effective. A necessary component of this process is the client's willingness to self-disclose which is often a function of trust in this interpersonal context. Racism, classism, and other forms of discrimination affect the minority client's willingness to disclose in anticipation of misattunement and misunderstanding of others. Ridley (1984) speaks to the construction defined by Triandis (1976) as eco-system distrust, in which "most elements in an individual's environment are perceived as potentially harmful" (p. 1235). This phenomenon leads to general mistrust and suspiciousness, a sense of needing to be vigilant and cautious in an effort to prevent reinjury and potential trouble. This construct is similar to the notion of healthy cultural paranoia, which validates abundant reasons for minority persons to be wary and mistrustful in interaction with members of the dominant culture. The repetitive experiences of oppression and insensitivity make the minority person perceive a wide range of environmental and interpersonal factors as stressful (Myers & King, 1983).

These factors obviously impact unfavorably in therapy. They make open self-expression and intimate self-disclosure more problematic for the minority client, especially in relation to a therapist from a dominant cultural background. Studies indicate that self-disclosure is enhanced when there is a high degree of perceived similarity between discloser and the therapist. According to Vontress (1971)

> People disclose themselves when they are fairly sure that the target person (the person to whom they are disclosing) will evaluate their disclosures and react to them as they, them-

selves, do. It is easy to see why racial differences become crucial barriers to disclosure. . . . (p. 10)

Even when the therapist's experience is substantially different from the client, self-disclosure will be facilitated when the therapist demonstrates an ability for accurate attunement and responsiveness to the client. This sense of interpersonal distance can be reduced when the therapist communicates a multi-level understanding of the client's objective and subjective experience. The role of the therapist's self-disclosure is complicated. It will vary greatly depending on the treatment modality, transference relationship, level of the client's psychological impairment, and the therapeutic style of the therapist. When self-disclosing statements by the therapist are appropriate, authenticity and conveyance of emotional resonance are essential ingredients for the communication to be potentially therapeutic.

To understand the dynamics of disclosure within therapy, Ridley (1984) borrows the conceptualization of the Johari window from Luft (1969), in which knowledge of self and other combine to form four possibilities. When what is known to the self is similar to what is known to others, this is called the open self. When what is known to the self is not known to others, this is called the private self. What is unknown to the self and known to others, is called the blind self. Finally, what is unknown to each is called the undiscovered or subconscious self.

For the therapist to be of use to provide a safe emotional environment so that effective treatment can occur, the client must be willing to disclose more of the private self to be seen and known. The therapist, through the process of empathetic inquiry and emotional attunement, contributes to the knowledge of the blind self; that is, brings to light ways in which the client is perceived by others and made aware of largely unconscious processes.

It is within the domain of the undiscovered self that analytic work is most suited. Through this unfolding of the client's inner world, facilitated through the attuned responsiveness of the therapist, the transference relationship can be utilized in the service of psychological growth. As mentioned previously, this developmental work can occur as the client feels progressively seen or understood or when misattunements and misunderstandings are detected, explored, and realigned. Through this process, with enough initial trust to sustain such ruptures, the broken selfobject tie to the therapist is restored and disruptive emotional states can begin to be integrated. Thus the understanding and processing of these interpersonal miscues and derailments can lay the foundation for further development. When there is a lack of trust and the therapeutic alliance is tentative or inadequate, or the misattunement is severe and/or of tremendous injury to the client, these ruptures may be too large to bridge and the therapist may be unable to reinstate the selfobject tie. In these instances, the therapy may end abruptly or the level of distrust may be too great to allow productive work to continue. When the client is inaccurately perceived and the resultant feedback misses the mark, the blind and private selves are reinforced. This is especially true when there is no recognition of the misattunement nor effort to address and repair the broken connection. These dynamics make it virtually impossible for the subconscious self to unfold and renewed growth to occur.

These factors create a therapeutic paradox (Ridley, 1984) which has often been interpreted as the client's resistance to treatment. The situation is one in which the client's vulnerability and risk-taking behavior may be met with insensitivity and miscomprehension on the part of the therapist. For the client, the ensuing situation is one in which insult is added to injury. Not only is the client deprived of therapeutic treatment, but blamed for the problem, as well. For therapy to be effective, self-disclosure on the part of the client is essential. With this disclosure, comes vulnerability to experiences of disappointment in not being seen or understood, and additionally, to the reenactment of prejudice, derision, and oppression.

COUNTERTRANSFERENCE AND DIVERSITY

The notion of countertransference has different formulations depending on one's theoretical orientation. For purposes of this discussion, countertransference will refer to the ways in which the subjective perception of the therapist and her/his affective reactions within the therapy context are influenced by past experiences and relationships. These responses are not directly related to the current psychotherapy relationship with a particular client, but may be triggered by components of her/his experience with this client.

As previously acknowledged, prejudicial beliefs, stereotypic responses, ethnocentrism, and internalized oppression and domination may interfere profoundly with the therapist's ability to respond to this unique individual from the perspective of the client's own experience. Thomas (1962) notes that the client's unconscious and conscious reactions to a therapist's "culturally determined, derogatory, stereotyped attitudes toward the patient in terms of the latter's sex, race, religion, or socio-economic status" (p. 895) can often be interpreted by the therapist as transference material. He warns that these client responses must be viewed in light of the therapist's attitudes to determine whether the client's reactions are not, in fact, appropriate responses to the therapist's unhealthy beliefs and behaviors. "In such instances, where the patient's apparently disturbed responses are actually appropriate and realistic, they can well be characterized as pseudo-transference reactions" (p. 894-5).

The therapist's countertransference responses that may arise as a result of the aforementioned factors include the following potential pitfalls. The therapist may feel inadequate due to her/his recognized lack of attunement and miscomprehension of the client's experience. S/he may be fearful of the client due to her/his preconceived stereotyping, and thus, use the client to project her/his own unacceptable impulses, characteristics, or affects onto the client (Bloch, 1968). S/he may be patronizing and foster dependency within the relationship due to an unconscious need to maintain the power dynamics of internalized domination, resulting from her/his own power needs (Jones & Seagull, 1977).

Another pitfall occurs when the therapist oversimplifies and attributes all of the patient's problems to issues of discrimination. Developmental deficits and the existence of character disorders, other psychopathology (Ridley, 1984), or other sources of stress may be overlooked. Another countertransferential response is denying or minimizing the impact of these differences on the client and the therapy relationship. This also colludes with the denial of the pervasive and pernicious effects of oppression. In reference to interracial relationships where the therapist is white and the patient is a person of color, Greene (1985) states that

> Colorblindness here may represent the therapist's resistance to confronting the meaning of the color difference. Therapists cannot help a patient confront and develop strategies for dealing with reality if they engage in defensive flight and avoidance of an anxiety-provoking issue. (p. 392)

Related to this dynamic is the tendency for the therapist to experience a pseudo-identification with the client in which the therapist is overly sympathetic in an effort to avoid any realistic confrontation with the client (Kupers, 1981). This serves both to avoid real issues within the therapy relationship as well as to communicate to the client information about the therapist's anxiety. The client may then feel compelled to take care of the therapist by skirting such issues, as well as other topics that might elevate the therapist's anxiety. This most definitely creates an unsafe environment for the client's own needs and affects.

The therapist may be overzealous and overinvolved with the client for reasons of alleviating her/his own guilt. This creates an element of false empathy; one that serves the narcissistic needs of the therapist, rather than true concern for the client (Jones & Seagull, 1977, p. 851). This can potentially serve to reenact earlier experiences of the parentified child who learned early in life to play a parental role to "caregivers" or echo experiences in which the child was used for the parent's own narcissistic needs. Guilt over one's privilege or prejudice can motivate the therapist to act in ways that are ingratiating and overly concerned with appearing politically correct. This can serve to undermine the client's expression of anger and keep the client at a distance. This stance denies the possibility of internalized domination and the reenactment of discrimination being operative in the therapy context. Racism and other forms of discrimination are seen as being "out there in the world," rather than potentially active in the current relationship.

Countertransference responses need to be consciously attended to by clinicians. It is the therapist's responsibility to get consultation when potentially anti-therapeutic issues arise. The therapist needs to acquire the information necessary to work effectively with a particular client. The clinician may need to attend workshops, seek special consultation, and do readings in order to educate her/himself fully with regard to her/his client population. S/he needs to explore her/his own experiences related to feelings of being different, invisible, discriminated against, or being a member of a hated target group. We, as therapists, need to have a sense of our own cultural identity and, at times, serve as role models for this kind of exploration.

We must also be respectful of those clients who do not choose to explore their ethnicity or social differences within their relationship to us. It may not feel safe for them to engage in this process and we may not be the person of choice with whom to embark on this area of self discovery. Boundaries and limitations need to be respected and appropriate referrals need to be made available.

CONCLUSIONS

Each therapist needs to explore her/his own attitudes and experiences in dealing with people from differing classes, races, and cultures. How are her/his experiences parallel or divergent from others whose differences may be less visible or may have qualitatively different experiences of dehumanization? To deal effectively with a wide range of clients, we need to have a developed socio-political analysis of the distribution of resources and power in this society. We need to acknowledge the existence of institutionalized forms of oppression and discrimination that are built into the fabric of this society and reflected within its social relations.

When socio-cultural differences are visible, it is important to address them directly. This needs to be done with great sensitivity and in a way that acknowledges the potential vulnerability of such disclosure. Questions as to how these differences may be perceived as affecting the therapy relationship need to be addressed. When these differences may be less visible or the client demonstrates some denial or an investment in "passing," the impact of these differences needs to be approached with care and with an understanding of the defensive functions they might serve. We need to be aware and respectful of the client's defenses and their survival value. We need to assess the degree to which they are operative and necessary for continued survival, coping, and functioning in a stressful environment. To the extent that experiences of oppression and violence have been overwhelming, we need to be able to bolster the client's defenses and honor the emotional boundaries beyond which experiences of self-fragmentation or impairments in self-organization may occur. We need to assess each client in terms of her/his current life circumstance, the level of social support, the developmental assets, and her/his structural capacity to handle intense affects, memories, and confrontations.

As psychotherapists, we must be able to assess levels of psychological functioning and developmental deficits. Our work needs to be approached from the level of client need and interventions geared therapeutically at the level that is required. At times, this may require acting in a variety of roles, including advocate or problem-solver. We need to continually view the client within her/his own subjective world, while viewing her/his problems and strengths within their cultural context. We need to be able to facilitate an understanding of the myriad sources of social, personal, and developmental problems, as well as to illuminate paths to change and growth.

Within the boundaries of proper therapeutic roles, the therapist must be able to be in touch with her/himself and be available for a healing relationship that is ultimately respectful, caring, and accepting of the client. We need to be especially sensitive to the unraveling of the nature and source of the client's pain and problems and be engaged in a process which promotes self-development and self-healing. This is an essential component of empowering the client and facilitating the incorporation of her/his own healing capacities.

Healing through relationship and relatedness is ultimately a feminist perspective. This curative process is one that needs to be undertaken with respect and honor for each other's humanity and uniqueness. When we are fully present with another human being and in our own self, we are able to create an environment that is both encouraging and affirming of the other's emerging selfhood. As we affirm our common needs for love, acceptance, validation, efficacy, and understanding, we are able to delight in the unique experience and expression of another. It is through this exchange that the spark of aliveness is fanned in the transformation toward growth, health, self-acceptance, and inner peace.

REFERENCES

American Psychiatric Association (1987). *Diagnostic and statistical manual of mental disorders-revised.* (3rd ed.). Washington, DC: Author.

Atwood, George & Stolorow, Robert, D. (1984). *Structures of subjectivity: Explorations in psychoanalytic phenomenology.* Hillsdale, NJ: The Analytic Press.

Bloch, J. (1968). The white social worker and the negro client in psychotherapy. *Social Work,* 13(2), 36-42.

Bradshaw, Carla (1988, May). *Japanese psychology: What can Eastern thought contribute to feminist theory and therapy?* Paper presented at AFTI, Seattle (in this volume).

Chesler, Phyllis (1971). *Women and madness.* New York: Doubleday & Co.

Friere, Paulo (1968). *Pedagogy of the oppressed.* New York: Seabury Press.

Giordano, Joseph (1973). Ethnicity and mental health: Research and recommendations. Institute on Pluralism and Group Identity, New York.

Glazer, Nathan & Moynihan, Daniel P. (1963). *Beyond the melting pot.* Cambridge, MA: M.I.T. Press.

Gardiner, Judith Kegan (1987). Kohut's self psychology as feminist theory. In Polly Young-Eisendrath & James A. Hall (Eds.), *The Book of the Self: Person, Pretext and Process* (pp. 225-248). New York: New York University Press.

Gilligan, Carol (1982). *In a different voice: Psychological theory and women's development.* Cambridge, MA: Harvard University Press.

Greene, Beverly A. (1985). Considerations in the treatment of black patients by white therapists. *Psychotherapy,* 22(2), 389-393.

Hartmann, Heinz (1939). *Ego psychology and the problem of adaptation.* New York: International Universities Press.

Hertzberg, Joan F. & Eschbach, Anthony, T. (1982). Social class and therapy: The dynamics of exclusion. *Issues in Radical Therapy,* X,2 6-11.

Jones, Alison & Seagull, Arthur (1977). Dimensions of the relationship between black client and white therapist. *American Psychologist,* 32(10), 850-855.

Joseph, Gloria (1981). Black mothers and daughters and their roles and functions in American society. In Gloria Joseph & Jill Lewis (Eds.), *Common Differences: Conflicts in Black and White Feminist Perspectives* (pp. 75-126). Garden City, NY: Anchor Press, Doubleday.

Kohut, Heinz (1959). Introspection, empathy and psychoanalysis. *Journal of the American Psychoanalytic Assoc.,* 3. 105-119.

Kohut, Heinz (1977). *The restoration of the self.* New York: International Universities Press.

Kohut, Heinz (1984). *How does analysis cure?* Chicago: University of Chicago Press.

Kupers, Terry (1981). *Public therapy: The practice of psychotherapy in the public mental health clinic.* New York: Macmillan Press.

Lipsky, Suzanne (1977). Internalized oppression. *Black Re-Emergence, 2,* 5-10.

Luft, Joseph (1968). *Of human interaction.* Palo Alto: Mayfield Press.

Mahler, Margaret, Pine, Fred & Bergman, Anne (1975). *The psychological birth of the infant: Symbiosis and individuation.* New York: Basic Books.

McGolderick, Monica, Pearce, John, K. & Giordano, Joseph (Eds.) (1982). *Ethnicity and family therapy.* New York: Guilford Press.

McGolderick, Monica & Rohrbaugh, Michael (1987). Researching ethnic family stereotypes. *Family Process, 26,* 89-99.

Meyers, H. & King, L. (1983). Mental health issues in the development of the black American child. In Gloria J. Powell (Ed.), *The Psychosocial Development of Minority Group Children.* New York: Brunner/Mazel.

Miller, Alice (1981). *Prisoners of childhood.* New York: Basic Books.

Miller, Alice (1983). *For your own good: Hidden cruelty in childrearing and the roots of violence.* New York: Farrar, Straus & Giroux.

Miller, Jean Baker (1976). *Toward a new psychology of women.* Boston: Beacon Press.

Moffie, H. Steven (1983). Socio-cultural guidelines for clinicians in multicultural settings. *Psychiatric Quarterly, 55,* 47-54.

Myers, Linda (1986). A therapeutic model for transcending oppression: A black feminist perspective. *Women & Therapy, 5*(4), 39-49.

Peoples, Karen (1988, February). *The trauma of incest: Threats to the consolidation of the female self.* Paper presented at the A.P.A., Division 39, San Francisco.

Pheterson, Gail (1986). Alliances between women: Overcoming internalized oppression and internalized domination. *Signs, 12*(1), 146-160.

Phillips, Leslie (1968). A sociological view of psychopathology. In P. Condon & David Rosenhan (Eds.), *Foundations of Abnormal Psychology.* New York: Holt, Rinehart & Winston.

Reich, Wilhelm (1966). *Sex-pol essays 1929-1934.* (Anna Bostock, Tom Dubose & Lee Baxandall, Trans.). New York: Vintage Press.

Ridley, Charles R. (1984). Clinical treatment of the non-disclosing black client: A therapeutic paradox. *American Psychologist, 39*(11), 1234-1244.

Stern, Daniel (1984). Affect attunement. In J. Call, E. Galenson & R. Tyson (Eds.), *Frontiers in Infant Psychiatry* (pp. 3-14). New York: Basic Books.

Stolorow, Robert & Lachmann, Frank (1980). *Psychoanalysis and development arrest: Therapy & treatment.* New York: International Universities Press.

Stolorow, Robert, Brandchaft, Bernard & Atwood, George (1987). *Psychoana-*

lytic treatment: An intersubjective approach. Hillsdale, NJ: The Analytic Press.

Suchman, Edward (1964). Sociomedical variations among ethnic groups. *American Journal of Sociology, LXX,* 328-329.

Surrey, Janet (1985). The self in relation: A theory of women's development. *Work in Progress, 84,2,* Wellesley: Stone Center Working Papers Series.

Thomas, Alexander (1962). Pseudo-transference reactions due to cultural stereotyping. *American Journal of Orthopsychiatry, 5,* 894-900.

Triandis, Harry Charalambos (Ed.) (1976). *Variation in black and white perceptions of the social environment.* Urbana: University of Illinois Press.

Vontress, Clemmont E. (1971). Racial differences: Impediments to rapport. *Journal of Counseling Psychology, 18,* 7-13.

Diversifying Feminist Theory and Practice: Broadening the Concept of Victimization

Lynne Bravo Rosewater, PhD

SUMMARY. Expanding the existing concept of victimization as a basis for all forms of prejudice is one means of expanding the base of feminist therapy. Such an expansion moves feminist therapy theory and practice away from a white middle class consumer base to a more racially and culturally diverse base. It is critical, however, that a broad concept of victimization not be used as a means of denying the uniqueness of individual experience. The therapist needs to both respect and value clients' different racial and cultural values and help the client find resolution in a manner consistent with those values.

INTRODUCTION

Feminist therapy has historically been seen as a white middle class enterprise. White middle class women therapists have seen white middle class women clients. Though women of color clearly are both providers and consumers of feminist psychological ser-

Lynne Bravo Rosewater is a licensed psychologist in private practice in Cleveland, OH. She is White, Jewish, married (23 years) and the mother of two young adults. She focuses on reframing roles for women and men in her work with individuals, couples, families and groups. Dr. Rosewater is one of the founding members and past chairperson of the Feminist Therapy Institute. As a national expert on both domestic violence and the Minnesota Multiphasic Personality Inventory (MMPI) profile for battered women, Dr. Rosewater prepares personality assessments for use in court with battered women who have killed their batterers. She is the author of *Changing Through Therapy*, co-editor of *Handbook of Feminist Therapy: Women's Issues in Psychotherapy*, and author of numerous chapters on feminist therapy and test interpretation.

Correspondence may be addressed to the author at: 23360 Chagrin Blvd., Suite 202, Beachwood, OH 44122.

299

vices, there is little in the feminist therapy literature that addresses issues that are particularly relevant to women of color (Belle, 1984). There have been some special issues of the *Psychology of Women Quarterly* which have consisted of articles about treatment/ mental health issues with women of color clients, specifically Black women (Muray & Scott, 1982) and Hispanic women (Russo & Amato, 1987).

While feminist therapy literature has not focused on the issues of cultural diversity, there is some existing feminist therapy theory that provides the basis to move toward building a more inclusive notion of feminist therapy. This existing theory consists of our understanding of the victimization process from a feminist therapy perspective. This article will address and discuss the concept of diversifying feminist theory and practice by broadening the concept of victimization.

UNIVERSALITY/UNIQUENESS

Victimization is a universal process; there is a commonality to suffering. Yet there is also a uniqueness to each individual's victimization experience. The intent of this chapter is to expand on the notion of victimization as a means of helping further the task of feminist theory building to be more multi-cultural and anti-racist. Focusing on similarities cannot, and should not, be used to deny differences. As feminist therapists we can empathize with our clients' experience of oppression, as we have all known oppression of some kind. But having experienced oppression does not mean that what or how we have suffered is interchangeable with another's experience. To deny uniqueness would be but another means of victimizing.

One example of the universality/uniqueness of victimization can be seen by the work I have done with battered women. My research to determine whether an MMPI profile (Minnesota Multiphasic Personality Inventory) existed for battered women was based on the test results of 118 battered women, all but 12 in currently abusive situations. These women, 58 White, 54 Black and 4 Hispanic, ranged in age from 17-53 (Rosewater, 1988). I expected to find some racial differences on the validity and clinical scales, as other research has indicated exists (Erdberg, 1970). However, my research found none of the expected differences for those scales (F, K, 4 and 8). In my research sample, the experience of being battered was a more powerful variable than race. On the other hand, what I experience with the individual battered women with whom I work is that race may effect the quality of services available to battered women. For instance, one Black woman whom I evaluated for her trial in which she was charged with aggravated murder felt that her color had been a significant variable in denying her the help she needed. Because she was dark-skinned, she did not show bruises as readily. While the police came numerous times to her home, they discounted the amount of violence she was experiencing.

MULTICULTURAL DIVERSITY
AND THE FEMINIST THERAPY INSTITUTE

From its inception the Feminist Therapy Institute (FTI) has been a place to share the growing edge of feminist therapy. It has never lacked excitement, controversy, or stimulation, but, until 1988, it has lacked women of color. In a book that grew out of the first Advanced Feminist Therapy Institute in Vail, Colorado in 1962 this absence was noted:

> Missing, however, is a presentation on the application of feminist therapy with minority women. Unfortunately such a presentation was absent from the Vail conference reflecting the ambivalence within the minority women's community toward embracing a feminist philosophy that may not reflect their concerns adequately. It is hoped that subsequent conferences and volumes will make greater effort to obtain a full exploration of these issues and to present relevant written material. (Rosewater & Walker, 1985, p. xxi)

Noticing the absence of women of color and understanding that absence are not the same thing. Many of the original hypotheses generated by white women in FTI about this absence reflected our own internalized racism and classism. Perhaps there were not advanced feminist therapists who were women of color because they were just finishing professional training, e.g., women of color could not be as advanced as white women. Perhaps women of color could not afford to come (e.g., all women of color, even those who are advanced therapists, are poor). Maybe what we needed to do was to get more women of color on the steering committee (the governing body of FTI) and let them tell us what we should do! At the time these seemed merely hypotheses, but in retrospect they are clearly racist ones.

I struggled for quite a while with not understanding the connection between trying to develop advanced feminist theory and having a multi-cultural feminist therapy institute. I knew I supported both things, but I could not see the interrelationship. Developing advanced feminist theory, at that time, seemed to be an intellectual pursuit. This intellectual exercise was based on the notion that the "personal is political" (Gilbert, 1980) and on a pursuit of social, political and economic equality for both women and men (Rawlings & Carter, 1977). My focus, however, was more on gender than race, more on theory building than politics. While I saw this as a political as well as an intellectual pursuit, somehow the political pursuit seemed to belong outside the Institute and the intellectual pursuit within the Institute. I supported the goals of being multi-cultural and anti-racist, but did not see how they applied to the advanced theory formulation towards which FTI was working. It is more than coincidence that my ability to conceptualize differently came *after* an anti-racism workshop that I attended, led by Ricky Sherover Marcuse for the FTI Steering Committee in 1987. By then we white women at least understood that being multi-cultural and anti-racist was not something women of color could do for us. The suggestion for this workshop came from our Task Force on Cultural Diversity who felt that the best place to start on creating a more inclusive institute was to start working on ourselves. The Steering Committee decided to have as part of its agenda an anti-racism workshop whose purpose was to raise our awareness (as white women) about anti-racism from an experiential rather than a didactic mode. In retrospect I realize that my ability to break-through the barrier between "intellectual" and "political" happened because the workshop was experiential. Forced to deal with powerful feelings, I moved from intellectual to emotional. In that process I was able to reframe my thinking.

One exercise in this experiential workshop was to have us deal with our own prejudice about ourselves. Apprehensive, I struggled to address my own internalized anti-Semitism. First we each had to list the stereotyped qualities we did not like about our own group (that was not too difficult, because I was comfortable with my bias). Then we had to see how those qualities had helped our people survive (that was much harder, because it made me have to reframe my thinking). That exercise made a profound difference in my feelings about my Jewishness; it also made me more sensitive to reframing the concept of bias in a way that allowed me to understand it as a victimizing process. Although at the same time being aware that the victimization I may feel as a Jew may make me more sensitive to the victimization of others, it does not make my victimization experience interchangeable with anyone else's.

Understanding behavior as a survival tool is a familiar framework for me. As an expert on domestic violence, especially battered women who kill, I am keenly aware of the process of victimization. Battered women are often blamed for the abuse, being labeled as masochistic (or self-defeating) (Walker, 1984; Rosewater, 1987, 1985). The behavior that allows them to stay alive is seen as pathological; their strength is perceived as weakness. Ironically it is the belief that the violence *is their fault* that keeps battered women in abusive relationships (Walker, 1979; Rosewater, 1985). Blaming the victim is not new (Ryan, 1976); it is, in fact, the basis of all discrimination. Seeing this connection allowed me to make my conceptual leap.

VICTIMIZATION AND FEMINIST THERAPY

Existing feminist therapy theory lays a groundwork for my clinical practice. Based on a presumption of health rather than illness, feminist therapy sees an individual's behavior as a function of being oppressed rather than confused or sick (Rosewater, 1984). Thus, feminist therapy does not embrace a medical model but rather fosters an educative, positive model of human behavior. Therapy is not aimed at adjustment, as defined by some authoritative therapist. It becomes an ongoing process of facilitating change, as that change is defined by the client (Rosewater, 1989). Further the focus of change is not merely on changing clients' behavior but also on changing societal standards (Rosewater, in press b). The recognition of the need to change societal standards is what makes feminist therapy unique, as it moves towards holding society accountable for oppression and its consequences rather than on blaming the individual who is overtly symptomatic. Such a focus highlights the role of oppression in creating stress in individuals' lives. In my clinical practice I routinely try to help sensitize clients to the victimization process in their own lives, i.e., not blaming them for oppression over which they have no control. At the same time, I try to help them realize where they do have control and to be in touch with their own personal power. This movement between understanding cultural powerlessness (i.e., that which is caused by oppression from the culture) and activating personal powerfulness is what makes feminist therapy practice so exciting.

Helping clients understand the consequences of oppression is based on helping them understand their own version of learned helplessness — how and why they are pessimistic about being able to change their circumstances when all the efforts they have made have been in vain. This concept is one that expands existing feminist theory to a more multi-cultural and anti-racist foundation. The broadening of this existing feminist theory in my own practice beyond issues of gender and violence is illustrated by the following example. One Black, 42-year-old woman client told me one day about her disillusionment with her parents. As a young girl her family left Chicago, where she had been raised, to visit relatives in the South. Traveling by car the family found that they were not permitted to use the restrooms in gas stations and were forced to use the side of the road to relieve themselves. Furthermore, they could not eat in most restaurants and had to carry food in the car. My client, now a doctoral student in psychology finishing her dissertation, was angry with her parents for passively enduring such treatment. She was enraged with her favorite aunt who dragged her from a local drugstore after my client had tried to sit at the soda fountain and order an ice cream cone, only to be told she "wasn't allowed to sit there.'' Her parents backed her aunt. After hearing this story I remarked that my client's rage seemed misdirected; she was angry with her parents and aunt for ''not taking care of her,'' when in fact compliance may have been the only way they felt they were able to ensure her safety. Further, I pointed out that her relative's actions were the result of longtime oppression that historically has included threats to personal safety for assuming equal rights. Helping her identify her parents' victimization process helped her to reframe her anger and to see her parents as protective rather than cowardly.

In therapy, clients sometimes deal with being victimized by the representatives of the mental health system from which they sought help. The gay man who came to see me after his former therapist told him that his ambivalence about his homosexuality meant that he really wanted, or ought to be, heterosexual was another example of how a victim is revictimized. To blame him for his ambivalence rather than recognizing the reality of such feeling given that being homosexual meant his civil liberties would be abridged, that his teaching job was at risk and that he faced a greater threat of physical violence (i.e., gay bashing) was blatant victim blaming. People of color who have ambivalence about their skin tones are reflecting their ambivalence about living in a racist society rather than acknowledging that they are ashamed of being inferior. An anti-racist, multi-cultural feminist therapy views sexual identity and skin tone as similar things; something with which one is born. This feminist view acknowledges ambivalence about being a minority individual as an appropriate reaction to culturally sanctioned bigotry.

It is easy to see the former therapist described above as being a victimizer, but harder to see ourselves in that role. Since my area of expertise is violence against women I had occasion to prepare a psychological report about whether a young woman was suffering from Rape Trauma Syndrome. This woman was suing her former place of business, where she was raped, for damages. While I saw myself as an advocate for this woman, she saw me as yet another victimizer who had power to confirm or not the very real and traumatic experience that she felt needed no further validation. Giving support for a client to rage at the oppressor, when we are the oppressor, is not an easy task, but a necessary one. Victimization is often accomplished by denying the reality of the other person's perceptions. My client's perceptions were relevant and appropriate and needed to be acknowledged.

As these clinical examples illustrate, understanding oppression as a cause of emotional distress, as feminist therapy does, goes beyond labeling sexism as unacceptable. Sexism, like racism, ageism, classism, heterosexism, or any form of oppression is a victimization process that blames the victim for his/her problem. Such a victimization process is based on inaccurate stereotypes that perpetuate inequality. Feminist therapy aims to create equal opportunity for women and men to gain personal, political institutional, and economic power (Rawlings & Carter, 1977). What is *unstated* is that equal opportunity is necessary for women and men of all colors, classes, ages and sexual identities. This explicit expansion beyond gender makes the focus of feminist therapy the wider process of victimization and moves feminist therapy (both theory and practice) to a broader focus, away from a white middle class theoretical and consumer base. Addressing the inadequacies of stereotypes and the tendency to victim-blame creates a framework that is based on feminist theory but with far greater application for feminist therapy.

FEMINIST THEORY AS DRIVEN BY PRACTICE

Feminist therapy theory is unique in that it is as often derived from practice as practice is derived from theory. Lerman (1986) describes this phenomena in her discussions about the development of a feminist theory of personality. Feminist therapy can be seen as the "cutting edge" of how a therapy can be viewed. The fact that theory develops from practice as well as practice developing from theory is one way of keeping theory evolutional rather than static. Thus theory is refined by practice and practice is refined by theory. For example, one framework for feminist therapy theory is that it is based on an egalitarian relationship (Rawlings & Carter, 1977). Douglas (1985) showed that power is *not* equal between client and therapist, thus showing that egalitarian did not mean that client and therapist shared equal power. Brown (1985) expanded on that notion saying that part of the ethical requirements of feminist therapy is that the therapist use her power and privilege in the client's behalf. These two papers led me to re-examine how the notion of an egalitarian relationship was practiced in my therapy office, leading me to define an egalitarian relationship as one that is equal in respect, not power (Rosewater, 1984).

I often find my discussions of presentations at FTI conferences with clients (see following) are a way of helping me in my evolution of feminist therapy theory. It was through such discussions that I was able to identify that much of what I do in my clinical practice is an integration of feminist therapy and anti-racism work. For example, helping my Black client concretize her experience as learned helplessness and that such an experience was a by-product of a specific victimization process labeled racism is an example of such integration. Thus, like the proverbial light bulb going off, I have realized that what I do in my therapy office is putting into practice what I have not yet fully articulated as feminist theory (it became articulated as a *result* of a therapy session, not the other way around).

In our attempts to make feminist therapy more culturally diverse, the practice of feminist therapy may be the inspiration for the development of feminist therapy theory. While we have clearly focused on the need to have FTI be comprised of more culturally diverse feminist therapists, we also have a wealth of information that is supplied to us by the culturally diverse clientele with whom we work. Thus, practice cross pollinates theory; the ideas can and should flow both ways. We need to exercise caution, however, in this process not to confuse issues of self and other.

Self versus Other

Understanding otherness means acknowledging the delicate balance between the universality of oppression and the uniqueness of the individual's experience. *While a feminist therapist can empathize with her client's experience of oppression, she cannot assume her experience of being oppressed is — or should be — interchangeable with what her client has felt.* For example I might understand the process of oppression from having experienced anti-Semitism, but I cannot assume that how I have experienced oppression is the same as a Black woman responding to racism.

Women of color clients need to have their ethnic and cultural values and beliefs acknowledged (Boyd, 1988). Kanuha (1988) and Boyd (1988) both suggest that as feminist therapists we need at times to become students and learn from women of color what their world is like. Further, as Boyd (1988) warns, we must examine our own ethnocentric bias that ethnic and cultural groups should aspire to the Western cultural standards of sameness.

This learning process, therapist as student, is one of the values I have found listening to presentations at the Advanced Feminist Therapy Institute conferences. One presenter, Jan Faulkner, is a collector of racist art. As a Black woman she feels that such a collection is a dramatic way of viewing racism historically as well as currently. In 1987, Faulkner's presentation was a slide show about her collection of racist artifacts. From this presentation I learned that racist expressions (or sayings that came from racist caricatures) could be adapted by oppressed people to be used in loving or endearing ways. Two that Jan shared in the course of her presentation were good friends being "as tight as the Golddust Twins" (The Golddust twins were a racist caricature on a cleanser product) and expressing concern for someone by saying "Don't just sit there looking like alligator bait" (a reference to young Black children being thrown into water to attract alligators during the slavery period). After the conference I shared some of my experiences with a Black woman client, originally from a poor rural sharecropper family in the South, and currently a professional woman. She also had some fond memories of those sayings. This discussion led us to a rich and insightful discussion of some of the trauma of her childhood.

Understanding "otherness" — in this case, what is considered racist when applied by a dominant group to a cultural/ethnic group is not necessarily considered racist when transformed by that group — is a key component of feminist therapy. The client, not the therapist, is the expert about her feelings and perceptions (Rosewater, 1984). The therapist is there, however, to help sort through those feelings, to help the client understand the origins of those feelings and their potentially negative consequences. For instance internalized self-hatred or negative self-image is common with women of color (Boyd, 1988) and lesbians (Kanuha, 1988), as it is among many women. Respecting the client's feelings and perceptions does not mean there is no need to change those feelings, but again the decision on whether or not to change rests with the client rather than with the therapist.

Feminist therapy has fallen short in providing research to help foster this understanding of otherness. Research on white middle-class females describes their sense of otherness in relationship to white men and is an improvement on using white middle class males to universalize all psychological development, but as Brown (1988) so eloquently argues, this is inadequate. As she points out, when we talk about women's experience, we must be clear *which* women we are talking about. How researchers ask questions about women's experience, and critically in what language they ask women about their experiences, has a profound impact on what information they receive (Ho, 1988; Protacio-Marcelino, 1988). Denying the uniqueness of native language is another piece of the victimization process.

CONCLUSION

Feminist therapy theory has long been based on the notion that oppression is damaging to emotional health. Sexism is clearly one form of oppression, but it is not the only type. As feminist therapists we need to be sensitive to all types of victimization, to the damage such victimization causes, and to the ethical imperative to work towards its elimination. Feminist therapy theory without being both multi-cultural and anti-racist cannot accomplish this immense task. Historically in feminist therapy, theory has driven practice and practice has driven theory. This process allows for evolution of theoretical beliefs and keeps feminist therapy theory from becoming static. As this article has described, in the efforts to create a broader, more inclusive theoretical base, we have a lot to learn from our clinical practice, particularly the work done towards identifying the process of victimization.

At the same time that understanding victimization can be a tool to expand feminist therapy in a more multi-cultural direction, it is critical to value the uniqueness each individual brings to therapy. Our task as feminist therapists is to understand our clients in terms of their milieu, not our own. We must respect different language, culture, customs and values. As therapists we are both teacher and student. As long as we can remain learners, available to and receptive to the rich differences our clients present, we can move on with the challenge to make feminist therapy truly representative of all people.

REFERENCES

Belle, Deborah (1984). Inequality and mental health: Low Income and minority women. In Lenore E. Walker (Ed.), *Women and mental health policy* (pp. 135-150). Beverly Hills: Sage.

Boyd, Julia A. (1988, May). *Ethnic and cultural diversity – Keys to power.* A paper presented at the annual Advanced Feminist Therapy Institute, Seattle.

Brown, Laura S. (1988, May). *The meaning of a multicultural perspective for theory-building in feminist therapy.* A paper presented at the annual Advanced Feminist Therapy Institute, Seattle.

Brown, Laura S. (1985). Ethics and business practice in feminist practice. In Lynne Bravo Rosewater & Lenore E. A. Walker (Eds.), *Handbook of feminist therapy* (pp. 297-304). New York: Springer.

Douglas, Mary Ann (1985). The role of power in feminist therapy: A reformulation. In Lynne Bravo Rosewater & Lenore E. A. Walker (Eds.), *Handbook of feminist therapy* (pp. 241-249). New York: Springer.

Erdberg, S. P. (1970). MMPI differences associated with sex, race, and residence in a southern sample. (Doctoral Dissertation, University of Alabama, 1969). *Dissertation Abstracts International*, (University Microfilms No. 340 5236B).

Gilbert, Lucia A. (1980). Feminist therapy. In Annette Brodsky & Rachael Hare-Mustin (Eds.), *Woman and psychotherapy* (pp. 245- 265). New York: Guilford Press.

Ho, Christine K. (1988, May). *Dealing with Asian domestic violence: A multicultural perspective in counseling.* A paper presented at the annual Advanced Feminist Therapy Institute, Seattle.

Kahuna, Val K. (1988, May). *Compounding the triple jeopardy: Women of color in violent relationship.* A paper presented at the annual Advanced Feminist Therapy Institute, Seattle.

Lerman, Hannah (1986). *A mote in Freud's eye.* New York: Springer.

Muray, Saundra Rice & Scott, Patricia Bell (Eds.) (1982). A Special Issue on Black Women. *Psychology of Women Quarterly*, *6* (3).

Protacio-Marcelino, Elizabeth (1988, May). *Towards understanding the psychology of the Filipino.* A paper presented at the annual Advanced Feminist Therapy Institute, Seattle.

Rawlings, Edna I. & Carter, Diane K. (Eds.) (1977). *Psychotherapy for women: Treatment towards equality.* Springfield, IL: C Thomas.

Rosewater, Lynne Bravo (1989). Feminist therapies with women. In Mary Ann

Douglas & Lenore E. A. Walker (Eds.), *Feminist psychotherapies: Integrations of therapeutic and feminist systems*. Norwood, NJ: Ablex.

Rosewater, Lynne Bravo (in press b). Public Advocacy. In Hannah Lerman & Natalie Porter (Eds.), *Ethics in psychotherapy: Feminist Perspectives*. New York: Springer.

Rosewater, Lynne Bravo (1988). Battered or schizophrenic? Psychological tests can't tell. In Kersti Yllo & Michelle Bograd (Eds.), *Feminist perspectives on wife abuse* (pp. 200- 216). New York: Sage.

Rosewater, Lynne Bravo (1987). A critical analysis of the proposed self-defeating personality disorder. *Journal of Personality Disorders, 1* (2), 190-195.

Rosewater, Lynne Bravo (1985). Schizophrenic, borderline or battered? In Lynne Bravo Rosewater & Lenore E. A. Walker (Eds.), *Handbook of feminist therapy: Women's issues in psychotherapy*. (pp. 215-225). New York: Springer.

Rosewater, Lynne Bravo & Walker, Lenore E. A. (Eds.), *Handbook of Feminist Therapy: Women's issues in psychotherapy*. New York: Springer.

Rosewater, Lynne Bravo (1984). Feminist therapy: Implications for practitioners. In Lenore E. Walker (Ed.), *Women and mental health policy* (pp. 343-358). Beverly Hills: Sage.

Russo, Nancy & Amato, Hortensia (Eds.). (1987). Hispanic women and mental health (Special Issue). *Psychology of Women Quarterly, 11*(4).

Ryan, William (1976). *Blaming the victim.* New York: Vintage Books.

Walker, Lenore E. A. (1987). Inadequacies of masochistic personality disorders for women. *Journal of Personality Disorders, 1* (2), 178-182.

Walker, Lenore E. (1984). *The battered woman syndrome.* New York: Springer.

White Feminist Therapists
and Anti-Racism

Elizabeth J. Rave, PhD

SUMMARY. The tenacity of White racism is analyzed and a model for active anti-racism is presented. The daily, on-going effects of White Privilege are also explored, including their impact on a White feminist therapist's work with her clients. Recognizing that an individual's personal anti-racism is never completed, the author discusses the necessity of individual feminist involvement in cognitive and affective domains in exploring Cultural Literacy and White Privilege. The importance of both external and internal motivators are also emphasized and suggestions given for developing external motivators when necessary. Applications of external motivators for anti-racism in therapy and community involvement, the personal and the political, are discussed.

How does a White feminist therapist keep anti-racism work as a priority? Why is it so difficult for a White woman, especially a White feminist, even in an academic setting, and particularly a White feminist therapist to maintain an on-going commitment to anti-racism? What factors contribute to maintaining that priority and what factors work against that priority? Most importantly, when a White feminist works in basically a White institution or

Elizabeth J. Rave, Professor of Professional Psychology and Women's Studies, is the granddaughter of Western European immigrants and the daughter of parents from different religious backgrounds. She was raised in a small Midwestern rural community and spent much of her youth involved in church activities. When she was 10, she started working in the corn fields, graduated to the canning factory in high school, and in the process learned all people were not Catholic or Lutheran. Involvement in the Civil Rights, anti-war, and feminist movements during the '60s and living for a time in Latin America during the '70s heightened her appreciation of diversity. She continues to learn about the impact of gender, ethnicity, and class on human interaction and potential.

Correspondence may be addressed to the author at: The University of Northern Colorado, Greeley, CO 80630.

works basically with White clients, how can that White feminist maintain and develop her anti-racism? Stated another way, how does one nurture respect for cultural diversity in a somewhat homogeneous setting? This article wrestles with these questions and presents suggestions for feminist therapists to deal with the effects of White Privilege both on themselves as therapists and on their clients.

Racism begins with the belief that human beings can be divided into racial groups and have distinctive characteristics, biologically determined and attributable to each racial group. Additionally, racism includes the concept that one race is superior to other races and, therefore, should have more power. By implication, then, anti-racism infers a belief in one race, the human race, and a recognition that no ethnic heritage is superior to another. Ethnic differences are discovered, respected, and valued. White Privilege refers to the automatic access bestowed on Whites in the United States, simply as a result of their skin color and their living in an historically racist society. Because feminists believe in the equality of all peoples, women who identify themselves as feminists imply they are anti-racists whether or not they are in actuality. For White feminists, being anti-racist also means understanding the effects of White Privilege on us, how we may be contributing to White Privilege ourselves, and how we can act against racism.

To deal with the issue of maintaining an ongoing commitment to anti-racism, it may be helpful to think of individual motivation along a dimension of external-internal factors plotted on a continuum. The higher the number of external motivators to reinforce anti-racism work, the fewer internal motivators needed to continue with it. Stated another way, external support(s) at all levels — national, regional, state, and local — contribute to and reinforce internal motivation to develop anti-racism.

EXTERNAL AND INTERNAL REINFORCEMENT

For example, during the '60s and early '70s, there were many external motivators in the environment for participation in anti-racist activities. Not only did the momentum of the '60s carry each feminist forward but each "successful" activity reinforced the idea that more could be accomplished. Just as "success breeds success," success also motivates working toward further success. Courses in psychology of prejudice, psychology of women, Black studies, Chicano studies, and related courses flourished. Development of these courses meant that feminists could learn from the rapidly expanding resources available in the area of cultural diversity. Written and visual materials were developed and many individuals were involved in anti-racist activities, some on campuses, some in local communities, and some in the larger communities. It was as if each had internalized and were acting on the feminist principle, "The personal is political," and responded accordingly.

During much of that era (1968-1980) Nixon and his administration were in power. His policy of "benign neglect" became an external motivator. Because he was so obviously "tricky" to those who disliked him and disagreed with him, he and his policies had the effect of unifying those working toward a more equitable society. Activists knew who and what the "enemy" was even though there was frequent and loud disagreement about strategies for accomplishing goals.

Then the '80s and Reagan hit. In some ways, many of the '60s activists employed in White institutions ran for cover or at least tried to find a "safe" umbrella for self-protection. It was comparatively easy to stand up and be counted during the earlier era when there was a support system for doing so, when gains — no matter how minimal — were visible, and the risk to individual livelihood was relatively minimal. But with Reagan came a rapid reestablishing of priorities, not only at the national level, but throughout the "system." What may have been most immobilizing was seeing hard-won "gains" erased with the stroke of the executive pen, such as in the areas of family planning and in governmental "openness" to its citizens. Additionally, Reagan is not a man with a permanent five o'clock shadow or a perpetually perspiring upper lip. He looks like what he is, an aging movie idol, someone who's hard to personally dislike. In other words, he did not unify opponents to his policies; he was not an external motivator. Reagan also had the knack for dissipating criticism by appearing well-intentioned. As a result, if charged with being insensitive to the needs of this country's minority citizens, he pointed to the time he wrote out a personal check for a minority person under temporary dire stress without ever dealing with or understanding institutionalized racism. Reagan personifies individualism run amuck. Individual charitable acts were positively reinforced through recognition, while activities to change oppressive conditions for groups of people were discouraged, e.g., lack of research monies to investigate societal or environmental factors. Funding guidelines directed researchers to look at or for individual characteristics which contributed to an individual's difficulties.

Reagan and his advisors did seem to understand the importance of using institutions to reestablish priorities under the guise of getting "government off the backs of individual citizens." Of course, even this concept is differentially applied according to whose interests are being served, the wealthy or the poor. As priorities shifted even more from human needs to "defense/security" needs at the national level, education at all levels became a target for national, regional, and local spokespeople, mainly male, to explain all of society's "ills" and how best to correct them. Bloom's book, *The Closing of the American Mind* (1987), is just one illustration of this phenomena. Bloom attributes what he sees as a decline in higher education to the activism of the '60s, particularly that of minority and women students who agitated for more relevant and diverse curriculum.

In higher education, and probably in most White patriarchal institutions, one result of this retrenchment was for governing bodies to bring in new administrators to refocus, streamline, and redirect universities. Declining enrollments on campuses, as well as declining resources, contributed to the urgency of restructuring. However, because those two forces merged at about the same time historically, decisions were made rapidly and generally from the top down. Reinforced by the supposedly national conservative climate, most decisions involved returning to "traditional" values. As any feminist knows, "traditional" equals "patriarchal." Not only were programs, frequently innovative programs, eliminated and faculty, including the supposedly safe tenured and full professor level faculty "dehired," but priorities for remaining faculty were changed. Research became, for all practical purposes, the only way a faculty member could get raises or promotion. Community service became unfashionable and unrewarded professionally. The definition of acceptable research also became more limited: laboratory settings and strict empiricism were considered the only valid research models. In other words, the institutional setting became antagonistic to direct activism at all levels and supported traditionally defined "research" as the only legitimate avenue for professional advancement.

One immediate effect of these influences on higher education is demonstrated in the professional literature. A literature search indicated that the number of listings dealing with racism or prejudice increased dramatically through the late '60s, '70s, and early '80s but dropped off just as dramatically by 1983. Focusing the literature search on Whites revealed that between 1967 and early 1988, there were only 19 listings with the identifiers of "White racism" or "anti-racism." The majority included identifiers in the abstract, not the title, and all but one was published in the '70s. External forces have taken their toll on developing knowledge as well. One can only speculate what our society would be like for all its members if research and theory-building in anti-racism had been encouraged during the last several years.

Most feminists have not been overtly racist in the '80s. Feminist professors still include issues of cultural diversity in lectures and coursework. Feminist therapists and supervisors still raise those issues when appropriate with a client or in therapy supervision with a student. Some feminists still participate in activities that impact institutions. However, for a variety of reasons the activity level has lessened. *My belief is that relative inaction has helped perpetuate racism*; when personal energy is focused more on surviving professionally, less energy is available for developing anti-racism work. The issue then is how to keep anti-racism in the forefront of a feminist's personal agenda when there is little support or reinforcement for doing so, when the external motivators are not readily available. Put another way, how does a feminist keep focused on "the political is personal."

There are some indications of a revitalized concern among feminists for dealing with anti-racism. Several recent conferences, including those of the Association for Women in Psychology, National Women's Studies Association, and the Feminist Therapy

Institute, have addressed racism. The Women Against Racism Committee at the University of Iowa Women's Resource and Action Center has sponsored a national conference and grass roots organizations, such as the National Coalition Against Sexual Assault and the National Coalition Against Domestic Violence, continued to keep anti-racism work on their agendas. Katz's (1978) book, *White Awareness: Handbook for Anti-Racism Training*, stands as a model for working with Whites in group settings. Ganley (1987) has outlined strategies for making education programs anti-racist and Brown (1987) has addressed issues in supervision of graduate students of color. In other words, the environmental, external supports for anti-racism work are again being encouraged within the feminist community.

DIMENSIONS OF ACTIVE ANTI-RACISM

Overall, there seem to be two dimensions in being actively anti-racist and the two are irrevocably intertwined and interconnected. They cannot be separated. If a feminist works in only one dimension, she can never make much progress in her own anti-racism because the two dimensions build on each other, encourage each other, and reinforce each other. One dimension of being anti-racist involves becoming culturally literate, learning about the diversity within and between cultures and developing respect and understanding for cultural differences. The other dimension involves learning how White Privilege affects us as individuals and how it affects our work, our beliefs, our values, our actions, and our therapy. Neither dimension is ever totally accomplished, totally completed. Each dimension needs continual nourishment and development to grow and expand. Obviously, some environmental climates are more conducive to growth than others; in some environments anti-racism thrives; in others the individual feminist has to consciously determine what is necessary to encourage anti-racism.

There is another qualitative difference between the two dimensions of developing anti-racism. Becoming culturally literate is a more "intellectual" process. It may arouse emotions at times as one identifies misunderstandings of the past but generally as a feminist learns about another culture, she is using cognitive skills. For example, I can read about Native Americans and increase my understanding of their cultures; I may feel pain from realizing the part my lack of knowledge played and plays in their lives. I may watch films or go to lectures on the same topic. I may contribute money to cause, write letters regarding institutional injustices and attempt to impact institutional changes, or become active in any number of ways as a result of my increased cultural literacy. All of these activities are important and may be emotionally involving but I can still do them from a personal emotional distance.

However, when I work with a client or supervisee who is a Native American, I must bring my cultural literacy into the process. I also need to be aware of my White Privilege, a potentially more difficult factor to "tease out" and confront. As the Feminist Therapy Ethical Code (Feminist Therapy Institute, 1987) states,

> A feminist therapist evaluates her ongoing interactions with her clientele for any evidence of the therapist's biases or discriminatory attitudes and practice. The feminist therapist accepts responsibility for taking action to confront and change any interfering or oppressing biases she has.

The responsibility for developing cultural literacy and understanding the impact of White Privilege is not the client's but rather the therapist's or supervisor's.

Rather than using the client to educate self about her/his culture, the therapist has a responsibility to learn from other sources, such as literature or a culturally literate consultant. If for some reason there is a lack of available alternative resources and the therapist has to rely on the client to increase her knowledge, it is the therapist's responsibility to clarify what is happening so that both are aware. Once the therapist's ignorance is out in the open, a side effect for the client may be an affirmation of her/his perceptions (Brown, 1987). In *extreme* situations, where the therapist's cultural illiteracy is pervasive, where there are *no* other resources or alternative feminist therapists, and the client needs to spend considerable time and energy facilitating the therapist's learning, the therapist may consider exploring methods of compensating the client for the remedial education s/he has facilitated. For example, the therapist might sug-

gest additional time or sessions without additional fees or at a reduced fee. The most facilitative way would involve the need and
methods of compensation being agreed upon before the cultural literacy "lesson(s)" had occurred. The ethical dilemma of role confusion must be addressed. As the Preamble to the Feminist Therapy
Ethical Code (Feminist Therapy Institute, 1987) states, "When ethical guidelines are in conflict, the feminist therapist is accountable
for how she prioritizes her choices."

The other dimension of anti-racism, learning how one is affected
by White Privilege, is a more difficult process and ultimately, I
think, a more emotional one for a White to confront. It is certainly
possible for a White feminist to intellectually understand how
White Privilege functions and to deal with it cognitively. Interestingly, one of the dynamics that *helps* Whites understand may be the
same dynamic that *inhibits* our understanding of White Privilege.
By being in the minority, White feminists may experience the limitations and negative consequences of one or more others' privileges. As a result, almost all White feminists understand Male Privilege; some White feminists understand Class Privilege; some
White feminists understand Heterosexual Privilege; some White
feminists understand Religious Privilege; some White feminists understand Married Privilege; some White feminists understand
Youth Privilege; etc., etc., etc. The very dynamic that facilitates
our identification as an "outsider" may be a barrier to seeing ourselves as the "insider." After all, when we have experienced being
non-privileged, how can we possibly be contributing to remaining
privileges? We can partially identify and empathize with women of
color because of our own experiences with the "isms" that have
oppressed or limited us. What is excruciatingly difficult for many
White feminists to comprehend is how we might be the perpetra-
tors, the enforcers, the reinforcers of White Privilege. It seems to
me that to begin to understand my part in the process I have to be
willing to understand and identify with the oppressors. I not only
resist identifying as an oppressor; I fight against doing so. The
whole process is extremely painful. It is so easy to avoid the pain;
all I have to do is look around and I rapidly discover another White
who is not as far along in anti-racist work as I am. With a sigh of
relief I can emotionally walk away from myself.

As an illustration of the difficulty Whites have dealing with this topic on a personal basis, I assign a group task in workshops or classes focused on prejudice and racism. The majority of students have been White upperdivision and graduate students. After considerable emphasis on theory of prejudice and racism and toward the end of the course, I assign a small group task of responding to the topic, "what I like/appreciate/value about being White." If there are students of color in the class, they are assigned the task of discussing what they assume Whites will say about the topic. The first reaction is silence. The next typical reaction is anger directed at me for assigning such a stupid, inappropriate, difficult, etc., topic. Once we all get past that reaction, the groups typically discuss what they *do not* like about being White. The reasons usually center around being blamed for the ills of society, feeling responsible for actions of other Whites they do not really think they were responsible for, never having personally oppressed anyone but still being accused of it, etc. When the groups finally begin to address the topic, the reasons they give all relate to White Privilege, especially access. It is extremely difficult to consider alleviating the ill effects of something that is still reinforcing on a personal basis. The value of sharing Privilege and extending it to others is a more tentative, vague, and global motivator.

Another factor contributing to the tenacity of White Privilege is that most Whites learned it by experiencing it. These learnings just "were." They were not explained or even pointed out; they were part of the air breathed. The Privilege, the assumed superiority, was internalized without questioning. An analogy may be made with the way most males internalize their assumed superiority.

Recognizing that the majority of their analyzed research was with White, middle class subjects, Maccoby and Jacklin (1974) reported an "unanticipated theme . . . boys seem to have more intense socialization experiences than girls . . . receive more punishment, but probably also more praise and encouragement" (p. 348). Additionally, these gender socialization experiences begin at a much earlier age for boys. They tend to experience the punishment for "inappropriate" gender behavior even before reaching school age and before they have developed the cognitive skills to understand. If a boy acts "like a girl" by age three, the odds are he receives negative messages from his external world. Because he does not have the cognitive skills to understand he is being criticized for "girl-like" behavior, he probably internalizes the message that "girls" themselves are negative.

In contrast, females, particularly White, middle class females, are allowed more latitude in the early years. When they approach puberty, when the significant others in their lives have ideas about female gender-appropriate behaviors, when peer acceptance is a primary motivating force, and when societal messages continuously model a limited view of "femaleness," the messages about what is appropriate and inappropriate gender behavior are spelled out strongly. Because the female child is more cognitively developed, she may question the restrictions put on her. She may resist and have few or incomprehensible explanations given to her. The point is that hers is less apt to be a stimulus-response type of learning than the boy's.

How do these gender learnings at different developmental stages affect female-male relationships, especially as they relate to Male Privilege? I hypothesize that it is more difficult to realize you are doing something if you learned it at a developmental stage when you did not cognitively realize you were learning to do it! Such a hypothesis helps me understand why so many men I know who are decent, well-intentioned, anti-sexist men have such difficulty generalizing from one sexist incident to another. At times in my frustration at once again discussing with an important man in my life what feels like exactly the same issue in a slightly different context, I have been known to irrationally charge him and all males with a genetic defect that contributes to male inability to generalize! However, I really do know that early learning is particularly tenacious, especially when that learning is habituated by reinforcing privilege. I also know that he needs an outsider, usually a female, to remind him, to nudge him, to educate him, until he finally "gets it right." In the best scenario, anti-sexist males connect with each other and serve as "educators" to each other.

In a similar manner, just as males learn negative ideas about females and learn Male Privilege at an early cognitive developmental stage, Whites learn Privilege and negative ideas about people of color at an early age. The negative messages are not always verbalized; instead the negative messages may be learned by omission — by Whites' lack of experiences, exposure, and/or discussion. The end result, however, probably is the same, an internalized sense of White Privilege. I have to wonder how many people of color have questioned whether I and other Whites have a genetic defect affecting our ability to generalize from one experience to another? And I wonder how many people of color have tired of "educating" us?

The Census Bureau reports that people of color are a minority in this country. If Whites had to rely solely on Blacks, for example, to educate them about anti-racism, each Black would have to educate 10 Whites, assuming equitable geographical distribution and that each Black would want to take on such a task. Even adding in other US minority groups leaves a disproportionate balance. In other words, to move anti-racism forward, Whites have to determine ways to facilitate each other's anti-racist development and not rely on or wait for people of color to work with us.

PERSONAL ANTI-RACISM ACTIVITY

Activity on both the external and internal dimension as well as both the cognitive and affective domains are necessary. Each group, feminist or not, needs at least two members committed to anti-racism to monitor each other. For example, in the early '70s I was part of the feminist group that established and developed the local Sexual Assault Team. In the mid-'70s I was part of the feminist group that established and developed the local program and shelter for battered women. In both cases, we agreed that we wanted to be anti-racist but we went ahead and established the programs as all-White groups. We said that "any" woman could use the services and some women of color did. But White women set the agenda and then "invited" women of color to join and participate. We advertised for bi-lingual volunteers and staff after we were established. The services were desperately needed but our blind spot, our White Privilege, interfered with our understanding how exclusive we were being.

In contrast, I recently attended a beginning meeting to develop a local women's resource center. All participants were White women. I took the position that women of color should be involved in establishing the agenda or we risked developing a racist rather than an anti-racist service. One other woman agreed. As others verbally agreed but behaviorally responded differently, she and I were both able to keep anti-racism in the foreground. I also think we were able to do so in a caring, basically non-threatening manner. What I personally learned from that experience is that I need another White woman to affirm my ideas, give me feedback regarding anti-racism, and keep me focused.

When I think about the application of anti-racism in feminist therapy, I realize that I am most cognizant of the necessity for such awareness when I am working with clients or supervisees who are culturally different. One of the legacies of the '60s is a multitude of resources regarding Cultural Literacy. Additionally, I can hire a consultant to monitor culturally illiterate or racist attitudes that I or the client may be expressing and that may be interfering with our professional work together.

What is infinitely more difficult for me is recognizing how my White Privilege may be affecting my work with Whites. A White client who is overtly racist is comparatively easy to deal with on this issue. That person makes her/his racism an agenda "item" by bringing it up. The more difficult clients to work with in terms of anti-racism are those Whites who have experienced a lifetime of White Privilege and who operate from assumptions and values reflective of that Privilege. Without realizing it, I may inadvertently reinforce racist values and attitudes by not being aware of them because they mesh with mine or they are reflective of an area I have not yet explored or discovered.

A way to deal with this dilemma may develop from an experience I had traveling alone in Latin America. Traveling alone gives one an opportunity to observe, particularly as an outsider. One day in a restaurant I noticed neighboring customers were served pie; not only was each piece served in what seemed like a "helter-skelter" manner but the diners ate the pie from the position it was set before them. The pie was not placed nor eaten with the point facing the customer; it was just eaten! As a result of my observations, I began an informal field study of pie serving and eating customs. Although Latin Americans are fairly loose about their "pie-eating behavior,"

North Americans are really rigid. I noticed that when a waiter/waitress served a piece of pie without the point facing the customer, the North American customer turned the plate so s/he could begin eating the pie from the point, rather than the crust end. I have even tried to get servers to intentionally set the plate down with the pie point to the side; most of them will not do it. Somehow, in some way, the majority of US citizens have internalized and habituated a "proper" way to eat a piece of pie. And most of us learned it *without* discussion.

How does the pie-eating analogy relate to therapy with White clients? The only reason I noticed the different pie-eating behavior is that I was an outsider. Yet is has never occurred to me before that I may need to work with an anti-racist consultant when I am involved with a White client. Someone from the "outside" may be in a better position to see if my White Privilege is reinforcing White Privilege with the client. Because such a consultant may not necessarily be another feminist therapist, it then becomes necessary for me to evaluate my work with the client so that I balance all perspectives carefully. It seems extremely important to monitor my behavior to insure that I appropriately include anti-racism work with White clients as well as culturally different clients.

In summary, anti-racism cannot be developed either solely cognitively or affectually. Instead, each individual's anti-racism moves forward through both domains with the emotional aspect in the foreground at some stages and the cognitive aspects in the foreground at other stages. The recent anti-racist focus of several national feminist organizations is a positive sign. An individual's anti-racist work is never completed and feminist therapists who have been around for awhile can benefit from review and revitalization. Feminist therapists who are comparatively new to the field not only have the benefit of recent knowledge but can learn from the past and recognize early that anti-racism is a life-long learning process. The external and internal dimensions also interplay and interweave. When an external motivator is not readily available, a feminist therapist needs to actively search one out, whether that means increasing her Cultural Literacy or understanding more fully the impact of White Privilege on her daily life.

REFERENCES

Bloom, Arthur (1987). *The closing of the American mind*. New York: Simon and Schuster.

Brown, Laura S. (1987, May). *Training issues for white feminist therapists working with women of color*. Paper presented at the meeting of the Advanced Feminist Therapy Institute, Woodstock, IL.

Feminist Therapy Institute (1987). *Feminist therapy ethical code*. Denver, CO.

Ganley, Anne (1987, May). *Feminism: A commitment to being anti-racist*. Paper presented at the meeting of the Advanced Feminist Therapy Institute, Woodstock, IL.

Katz, Judith (1978). *White awareness: Handbook for anti-racism training*. Norman, OK: University of Oklahoma Press.

Maccoby, Eleanor E. and Jacklin, Carol N. (1974). *The psychology of sex differences*. Stanford, CA: Stanford University Press.

Turning the Things That Divide Us into Strengths That Unite Us

Rachel Josefowitz Siegel, MSW

SUMMARY. This paper focuses on the interaction of my anti-racist work with my personal experience of sexism, ageism, and anti-Semitism, and how it informs and is informed by the theory and practice of feminist therapy. Using myself as an example, I draw attention to some aspects of the process of building bridges across the chasms that divide us, looking at the internal and external forces that would keep us divided and at the goals that motivate us toward mutual and collective empowerment.

The things that divide us can define us and help us claim ourselves; they can also be used against us, as ways of keeping us separate from each other and powerless. Only by writing and talking of our differences can we begin to bridge them (Conlon, da Silva, & Wilson, 1985, pp.11-12).

Rachel Josefowitz Siegel is a clinical social worker in private practice in Ithaca, NY. Born in Berlin in 1924, of Lithuanian Jewish parents, she immigrated to the U.S. in 1939. English is her third language. She has spent a year in Israel and has been a feminist activist in the Jewish community. She has written on stereotypes of Jewish women, on overcoming homophobia, and most recently on midlife and on old women. She is co-editor of *Women Changing Therapy* (The Haworth Press 1983, Harrington Park Press 1985).

Author note: "My thinking on diversity is informed by Adrienne Rich, Evelyn Torton Beck, Kris Miller, Ann Brous, and our learning experiences at previous AFTIs, especially Ricky Sherover Marcuse's workshop and presentations by Anne Ganley, Clare Holzman, Nan Jervey, Jan Faulkner, Jeanne Adleman and Kitch Childs. Thanks to Nina Miller, Ba Stopha, and Kathy Lilley for their sensitive and critical feedback."

Correspondence may be addressed to the author at: 108 West Buffalo Street, Ithaca, NY 14850.

At the Feminist Therapy Institute, we have been talking of our diversity since our first meeting in 1982, yet in 1988 we are still in the beginning stages of building bridges across the things that divide and separate us. My remarks in this paper are very personal. I hope that my words will touch some chords in you, be they of commonality or of difference. I imagine that some of the feelings and processes I describe in myself are shared by you, and that some are not. I know that we cannot generalize from our uniquely individual experiences, yet we can spin threads of understanding and empathy between us. My pain may touch your pain, my anger may reverberate with your anger, my fear may bring up your fear, my joy may release your joy.

In this article, I will focus on how my anti-racist work interacts with my personal experience of sexism, ageism, and anti-Semitism, and how it informs and is informed by the theory and practice of feminist therapy. Using myself as an example, I offer the following assumptions: (1) I can be more open to the agony caused by racism, poverty, and other oppressions when I also attend to the wounds caused me by anti-Semitism, sexism, and ageism; (2) my need to acknowledge and take responsibility for the privileges of my class, color, and heterosexual status grows out of the absence of security and status that I suffered as a Jewish refugee-immigrant adolescent, and in my present old age; (3) the pain of our diverse experiences is not interchangeable nor hierarchical, yet each of us must attend to all of it, whether we do it sequentially, in harmony, or in counterpoint; (4) we can be strengthened individually and collectively when we see, feel, and try to heal each other's oppressions with equal respect and compassion; (5) deep within us we feel the polarized forces toward unity on the one hand, and toward division on the other; our yearning to be united in a mutually supportive and empowering sisterhood lives alongside our deeply ingrained patterns of separations along such lines as class, color, sexual preference, ethnic origins, and many others.

Our early learning to stay divided from each other is constantly reinforced by society's institutions, assumptions, and expectations. Unlearning the patterns that divide us takes repeated and constant efforts, pain, and time; the process of reaching to unite us gives us strength, power, and joy. Though I have separated these assumptions in order to name them, they do not operate in separate spheres; combined and overlapping, they form the underlying perspective of my thinking.

As I approach the task of bridging across the things that divide us, I am filled with anxiety and ambivalence. My current feminist ideology contradicts the patriarchal taboos of my childhood. When I dare to cross the lines that keep us from uniting, I feel the internal and external fear of paternal, familial, and tribal rejection, I hear the horrified voices of my childhood: "How can you do this to your family? How can you do it to your people?" These early memories are like a screen that filters all new information. I am filled with the fear of Jewish annihilation. On one level I know that my fear does not fit my present reality, yet I also know, on another level, that virulent and overt anti-Semitism is on the rise in the United States (Anti Defamation League 1987), along with overt racism and anti-gay violence. Since the Holocaust, I carry an awareness that the unthinkable can happen, that the impossible is possible; I am frightened by the potential for a political progression toward institutionalized discrimination that could eventually include the annihilation of "undesirables."

When I look at how, why, and when I stay within the boundaries that separate us, I feel the shame of uncovering the intricate and hidden web of my own oppressive biases. I fear criticism and rejection from the sisterhood. I dare not expose my limitations, the non-responses, the long stretches of unawareness and inaction that keep me divided from my sisters.

I fear that you, another woman who has been oppressed, will not respond with enough empathy to the accounts of my own oppression, because you, like me, suffer similarly ambivalent feelings. I fear that I or you or both of us will be found unequal to the task that we have set ourselves. Though I trust our commitment to the process of building bridges of caring and understanding, I am embarassed by my own shortcomings and afraid of yours.

When I began to write this article, I felt a surge of anger and resentment, I felt tearful, confused and weary. These feelings are rooted in my earliest memories, and triggered by focusing on the oppression of "otherness." It is difficult to start; caution and hesitation often get in my way, especially when I feel that I am working in isolation. I am encouraged by the feminist concept of sisterhood and by my knowledge of the collective experience of consciousness-raising. It helps to have one or more allies; it helps to know other women who have taken such risks and continue to do so, and that some of us have done this within the Feminist Therapy Institute. It also helps to get in touch with the joy of moving in the direction of our individual and collective strength and power, our ability to change the status quo.

As a child, when I felt oppressed and isolated, I learned to protect myself behind a wall of apparently passive docility, made up of fear, anger, mistrust and avoidance. Within the family and in my broader environment, my pain was usually trivialized or ignored. As an adult in midlife, through my exposure to lesbian literature, and to the early feminist literature on battered women and on sexual abuse and harassment, I learned to recognize and to counteract the victim-blaming denials and trivializations imposed by dominant individuals and institutions. In feminist therapy groups, within the safety of woman-created environments, I learned to talk and to listen to the particular oppression of individual women and to the over-all oppression of women as a subordinate class. As a feminist therapist, I have come to notice and to appreciate the relief that comes out of naming the particular oppression, and the healing that occurs when the client feels validated and understood. This learning has become generalized to other situations and to understanding and validating my own experience more promptly and confidently. By helping others heal, I have gained the courage to speak of my oppression and to set aside the "lies, secrets, and silences" (Rich, 1979) that helped me survive as an alien, an immigrant, a woman, an old woman, and always a Jew. Through my own healing, I am now better able to both tolerate and set aside the pain of remembering.

My earliest memory of "otherness" was that of being Jewish. I was born in Berlin, in a family who had recently fled from post-revolutionary Russia and poverty stricken Lithuania. I have been both privileged and oppressed all my life. I was spared my family's earlier deprivations and persecutions, hunger, illness, and random bloodshed; yet I was repeatedly uprooted from one country to another, changing schools and languages without any appreciation or consideration for the trauma of each displacement.

My childish complaints were dismissed or ridiculed in a family so threatened by much more powerful external forces. Our status as barely tolerated alien Jews was a much more conscious and important worry. Our presence as Eastern Jews in pre-Hitler Germany was permitted only because of my family's wealth. We moved to Switzerland when I was six, here again our residence permits were temporary and could be revoked at the government's whim. When we arrived in New York in 1939, we discovered that some apartments and hotels were "restricted," these doors were closed to Jews. I also learned to pass: to speak, dress, act American, and to fake it if I did not know the songs or understand the jokes. American-born Jews were on the whole as disinterested as non-Jews in our histories, our multi-lingual culture, and the pain of our displacement.

My childhood was permeated with the sense of being barely tolerated or unwanted and at risk as a Jew, and privileged as a member of a rich family. Poorer Jewish families were subjected to infinitely more severe persecutions.

My early experiences of unrecognized "otherness" and "unwantedness," within a frame of wealth and privilege, have been multiplied throughout my life by ongoing incidents of being invisible and unwelcome as a woman, a Jewish woman, and now an older woman or a mother-figure, while enjoying the comfort of being white, middle-class, heterosexual, and educated. While I am supersensitive to "otherness" and feel a kinship of oppression with members of other oppressed groups, I also feel the weight of my own privilege and the fear of being resented or "put in my place," of having my own wounds minimized and criticized as unimportant and self-centered.

When I focus on reaching across the barriers that divide us, I want first to shout: "But what about me? What about my wounds?" I wonder to what degree each of us feels: "What about me?" when we begin to reach towards each other. *To what extent does your pain get in the way as mine does?* I know that if I want to overcome my own biases and to build bridges with others who are oppressed, I need to continue healing my own wounds by making visible that which was not seen as oppressive when I was a child, and that which is not seen as oppressive now in my old age. The ancient words of the Jewish sage Hillel still speak to me: "If I am not for myself, who will be for me? And if I am only for myself, what am I? And if not now, when?'' (cf. Hertz,1948)

When I hear your pain, I learn something new about naming my pain; when you hear my pain, it becomes less intense and I can hear you better. When we hear each other in this way, I feel less fear of you as the stranger, the non-Jew, the "goy," and I feel less guilt and shame as the oppressor, the rich, white, educated, heterosexual. Hearing each other can cut through the heavy curtain of fear, guilt and shame that would keep us immobilized and divided from each other.

When I fight against your oppression, I learn about fighting against my oppression; when I fight for myself and my people, I become more available to fight for you and your people. This may not happen simultaneously, for there will be times when I need to be totally focused and selective, just as you do. When we can both be available to fight our own and each other's oppression, I can feel truly joyful and empowered. The process is like a spiral where the work of fighting your oppression is reinforced by tending to the scars of my oppression; where acting on your behalf can be more effective and wholehearted when I also act on my behalf; and where these processes are just as true in reverse order. We are both strengthened by weaving threads of understanding and validation between us.

When I realize that I have been inattentive to the ways in which I contribute to your oppression, I feel a deep sense of inadequacy, combined with the full weight of my privileged status. I feel angry at you and at myself for uncovering my insensitivities. I also feel angry and wish to withdraw from you when you have been unaware of how you have contributed to my oppression, or when you persist in denying my pain. The barriers go up. This shame and this anger get in our way and would keep us divided. When we learn to forgive ourselves and each other our past errors, the positive work of valuing each other can go on. The effort to move from anger to empathy is painful and difficult; when it does happen, the rewards are joyful and invigorating.

The source of your pain is neither equal nor identical to the source of my pain; we have different histories and different sets of responses. Neither you nor I can judge the intensity of each other's suffering, nor can we evaluate it on a scale of legitimacy.

Adrienne Rich (1982) and Evelyn Thorton Beck (1983, 1984) first made me aware of the inextricable interactions of all biases and oppressions, and of the absolute necessity to understand and counteract the mutually reinforcing aspects of all exclusionary and oppressive practices and attitudes. In day-to-day implementation, this means an alertness to my own biases and a willingness to take on "your issues" as "my own." It also means that when I am working on "my issues" within this framework of mutuality, my work will be of ultimate benefit to you as well. Eventually, as we gain confidence in working toward our combined goals, we may be able to wholeheartedly perceive "your issues" and "my issues" as "our issues." At present it would be unrealistic to pretend that we have reached this level of understanding and empathy between us. Hard as it is to put these concepts into words, it is harder yet to put them in action. Elly Bulkin, Minnie Bruce Pratt, and Barbara Smith (1984) give an excellent account of the difficulties and complexities of working together on anti-Semitism and racism, as well as specific and useful strategies for coalition building.

Although I am intellectually convinced that racism is as damaging to me as are the oppressions that have been more directly aimed at me, I am also aware that I do not feel the harm as urgently or genuinely as I do "my own issues." I have shared significant responsibility for naming and implementing the multi-cultural and anti-racist efforts within the Feminist Therapy Institute, yet my motivation in this area feels more intellectual than personal. My anti-racist work sometimes requires a conscious and deliberate effort, and I feel less secure, less competent, and less spontaneous than in my work against sexism, heterosexism, ageism and anti-Semitism. I am beginning to look at the fears, hesitations and procrastinations with which I approach the work against racism. *When I want to work on "your issues," I am afraid of how you will perceive my efforts. I feel like a stranger who does not know the norms, the body-language, the boundaries of your space. Will you welcome my efforts or will you shame me, reject me, mistrust me? Will you hold my whiteness against me? Will I know when to hang in there long enough to get beyond your natural mistrust of me, and will I know when to back off because I have inadvertently invaded your space? Will I be able to tolerate and to learn from your criticism without falling into useless anger, without blaming myself or rejecting you? Will my well-meant efforts provoke your anger or add to your pain? The territory we need to explore between us feels fraught with dangers. How can I get past these hurdles without abusing your energy or feeling abused by you?* The image of "this bridge called my back" (Moraga & Anzaldua, 1981) has been useful to me on either side of every effort to overcome the oppressions, exclusions and inequities of our society.

Feeling the pain and fighting against oppression is not the same as recognizing the roots of my responses to diversity. As a child, I absorbed a lot of the misinformation about "inferior" and "superior" races that was so viciously applied at the time. I felt a sense of kinship with other members of non-Aryan races. While I lived the arrogance of wealth and of whiteness, I learned that I was White but not White enough. I also learned that "other than White" was not a good thing to be. It was, after all, an accident of fate that kept me from being exterminated as the member of an "inferior" race.

I mislearned very early that separations and divisions between people of different colors were the norm and should be maintained. When I came to live in New York, new to the ways of this country, I was not sure whether the Black doorman in our apartment building would allow a Black visitor to ride the elevator. Fifty years ago, seeing an inter-racial couple on the street would have been as disturbing to me as seeing a gay or lesbian couple holding hands. Today, while I rejoice at the slowly emerging acceptance of diversity in our society, I am annoyed when I find faint traces of as yet unexamined left-over misinformation in me, and I am angry when I see these biases in other people. Unlearning the early messages that not only divide, but subjugate and demean us, is a slow and ongoing process that requires constant openness to self-correction. We must fight the internal as well as the external oppression. This requires the mutual support and appreciation for our efforts that we can give each other, since we need to counteract the old and the new misinformation that permeates our environment.

The racist and classist messages I absorbed as a child are mixed up with negative experiences of my own "otherness." I feel both mutuality and diversity in relating to women of other backgrounds or life styles than my own. I have been quick to recognize the marginal position of women of color, since it resonates with my own marginality as a Jewish immigrant. I have been slower to appreciate diversities of class and status in the world.

I have been more open to the richness of your culture and the particularities of your oppression and otherness when these aproximate my own in some significant fashion. Thus, the horrors of pogroms and religious inquisitions are better known to me than the horrors of slavery; the "otherness" of uprootedness and forced migrations is more familiar to me than the "otherness" of immobility and generations of poverty; the experiences of a middle class Chinese American immigrant woman, or the bilingual struggles of a Hispanic woman feel closer to my own than the experiences of a rural poor White woman who has never left home and knows no language other than her own, or of a Black woman who grew up in an urban ghetto. *Within my range of empathic responses to your "otherness," it would be too easy for me to assume commonality just because a particular aspect of your experience is familiar to me, or to assume difference just because I do not yet know enough about you.*

The task of building bridges of understanding, compassion and support between us is most challenging when your people and my people are embattled with each other. *How can I sort out my priorities? How can I trust you to sort out yours? Will we be able to respect each other's fears or to understand each other's oppression? Will we be able to trust each other enough to begin the work that we need to do with each other? Will the armed power that our people use against each other prevent us from building the bridges we need to build?* These are tough questions, perhaps together we can look for some answers.

My efforts to know and to enjoy the diversity and richness of your culture and your community have caused me to be more effective in defending my right to look and to act like myself. I feel supported by feminist ideology and the women's movement in deviating from the artificial norms imposed on women, the white male-pleasing standards of blond, blue-eyed youth, thinness, genteel bearing, soft voice, and constant smile. I can be a loud, proud, fat, old Jewish woman and feel good about myself because of the work I have done defending your right to be the woman of whatever color, size, sexual preference, age, ethnic or personal style that you are or wish to be. I can be closer to you, laugh more, be more of a rebel, think better, act more decisively and be more real because of the strengths that unite us in the diversity of our sisterhood. Our "otherness" can be a source of pleasure and mutual enrichment when it is not being used against us.

REFERENCES

A D L (1987). Audit of anti-semitic incidents; Audit summary. Anti-Defamation League of B'nai B'rith, 823 United Nations Plaza, New York, NY 10017.

Beck, Evelyn Torton (1983). Unity in diversity. In Elaine R. Ognibene (Ed.), *Women in the Eighties: Strategies for Solidarity*; proceedings of New York State Women's Studies Conference, (pp.10-33). Sienna College, Loudonville, NY.

Beck, Evelyn Torton (1984). *Between invisibility and overvisibility: The politics of anti-Semitism in the women's movement and beyond.* Presentation sponsored by Hillel and Women's Studies Program, Cornell University, Ithaca, NY.

Bulkin, Elly, Pratt, Minnie Bruce, & Smith, Barbara (1984). *Yours in struggle: Three feminist perspectives on anti-semitism and racism.* Brooklyn, NY: Long Haul Press.

Conlon, Faith, da Silva, Rachel, & Wilson, Barbara (1985). *The things that divide us: Stories by women.* Seattle, WA: Seal Press.

Hertz, Joseph H. (Ed) (1948). *The authorized daily prayer book.*(rev. ed) p. 625. New York: Bloch Publishing.

Moraga, Cherrie & Anzaldua, Gloria (1981). *This bridge called my back: Writings by radical women of color.* Watertown, MA: Persephone Press.

Rich, Adrienne (1979). *On lies, secrets, and silence.* New York: W.W.Norton.

Rich, Adrienne (1982,) *What do we mean when we say we?* Unpublished workshop sponsored by Cornell Women's Studies, Ithaca, NY.